ALL ROADS LEAD TO SERFDOM

Confronting Liberalism's Fatal Flaw

Thomas Aubrey

BRISTOL
UNIVERSITY
PRESS

First published in Great Britain in 2022 by

Bristol University Press
University of Bristol
1–9 Old Park Hill
Bristol
BS2 8BB
UK
t: +44 (0)117 374 6645
e: bup-info@bristol.ac.uk

Details of international sales and distribution partners are available at bristoluniversitypress.co.uk

British Library Cataloguing in Publication Data
A catalogue record for this book is available from the British Library

ISBN 978-1-5292-2528-0 hardcover
ISBN 978-1-5292-2530-3 ePub
ISBN 978-1-5292-2531-0 ePdf

Cover design: Hayes Design and Advertising
Front cover image: Vintage film plate of asphalt road with crack on it © Freepik
Bristol University Press use environmentally responsible print partners.
Printed in Great Britain by CPI Group (UK) Ltd, Croydon, CR0 4YY

Contents

List of Figures and Tables

Figures

Tables

Preface

This book has been long in the making. Its origins go back to 1995, when as a postgraduate student, I became interested in the critique of utilitarianism and welfare economics in relation to housing policy. My interest in this theme was rekindled in 2013 when I become more directly involved in the public policy debate through Policy Network and the Centre for Progressive Capitalism.

In late 2015 I decided, perhaps somewhat foolishly, to write a book exploring post-Mill developments within liberalism in an attempt to find a more robust liberal intellectual foundation for a public policy framework. As a Germanophile, the path to post-Weimar German liberal thought and ordoliberalism was a logical one. This subsequently led to a much more extended project to sketch out how the underlying ordoliberal principle of power dispersion might be applied to public policy. Whether such a project is credible remains to be seen, although I would hope that it at least encourages liberals to make more of an effort to explain why freedom and equality are still ideas of fundamental importance.

Such a book so long in the making has naturally been the product of numerous conversations, debates, arguments, support and advice over some 25 years. In particular I would like to thank the following people for their generosity, including: Philip Allott, Werner Bonefeld, Vit Bubak, Willem Buiter, David Carruthers, Tobias Caspary, Tony Curzon Price, Meghnad Desai, Patrick Diamond, Nicholas Falk, Charles Goodhart, Lawrence Hamilton, Con Keating, Eric Lonergan, Carl Mossfeldt, John Muellbauer, Christian Odendahl, Ines Parsonson, Emmanuel Saez, David Sainsbury, George Selgin, Michael Seydel, Barbora Stepankova, Viktor Vanberg, Frank Vibert, Winrich Voss and Adelbert Winkler. I would also like to thank the OECD data team who were extremely helpful in responding to my data queries. In addition I would like to thank Thomas Piketty and Edwin Black for permission to use their data as well as Refinitiv LSEG and the Conference Board. I would also like to thank Michael Kenny, without whose encouragement I would have given up long ago. Finally, I would like to thank my family: Yanina, Thea and Ethan for all their support and for putting up with me spending far too long at my computer.

1

Introduction

Crisis of liberalism

Liberalism, the ideology of liberal democracies, is founded on the principles of freedom and equality. The freedom of individuals to pursue their own interest as long as it avoids harm to others, with everyone considered equal members of that society, has been a very powerful idea in legitimating liberal societies.

Since the demise of the potential Soviet threat to the liberal order, the idea that each person is treated equally in terms of access to legal and political rights has been progressively questioned. Furthermore, the ability of individuals to pursue their idea of freedom appears to be increasingly constrained by birth. Instead of the triumph of liberalism, liberal democracies since the end of the Cold War have presided over a growth in the concentration of power which has resulted in societies becoming increasingly divided. The coronavirus pandemic has highlighted just how entrenched these inequalities have become.

This rising dissatisfaction with liberal democracy has been accompanied by an industry of books and articles claiming that liberalism is in decline. The fact that electorates believe liberal democracies are merely serving to entrench specific interests suggests these criticisms are largely valid.[1]

The philosopher David Hume writing in a pre-industrial commercial society argued that concentrations of wealth and power would negatively affect society, discouraging all industry (Hume, 1994: 228). In the 19th century, the French writer Alexis de Tocqueville warned that out of an industrial society a new aristocracy of the wealthy would emerge, thereby undermining the idea of equality (Tocqueville, 2003: 645). Concentrations of wealth and power through time, therefore, pose a grave threat to liberal values.

One effect of electorates beginning to lose interest in the liberal ideology that underpins liberal democracies is that political parties that promote particular interests such as the nation are becoming increasingly popular.

To a large extent, there is no difference replacing the entrenched interests that have developed under liberal systems with more explicit interests. The main concern is that illiberal political parties attempt to use the will of the people to override the rules and institutions that have maintained liberal democracies with a focus on mythmaking to sustain their legitimacy.

This harks back to the days of Thucydides in ancient Greece where democracies had to lie to be believed (Duan, 2018: 144). However, such mythmaking is anathema to a liberal order and highlights the precarious nature of freedom and equality. Hence, when an American president refuses to accept the results of a presidential election or a British prime minister denies the creation of an internal customs border created by an international treaty which he negotiated – and crucially both leaders are supported by large sections of the population – liberals should be gravely concerned.

These long-standing concerns of democracies were raised by James Madison. Madison thought that pure democracies 'have ever been spectacles of turbulence and contention; have ever been found incompatible with personal security or the rights of property; and have in general been as short in their lives as they have been violent in their deaths' (The Federalist, 2001: 91).

If the ideology of liberalism and its principles of freedom and equality are to have a future, its supporters need to do a better job of articulating its benefits, and crucially identify how support for such an ideology might be reinvigorated.

The function of ideologies is to guide practical political conduct (Freeden, 2008: 6). In conjunction with an ideology, public policy needs to be supported by a set of procedural rules enabling a society to realize those principles upon which it is based. Since utilitarianism fused with liberalism in the early 19th century, the goal of public policy has generally been to maximize societal utility as a way of attaining its two founding principles. While there has generally been an agreement about the basic values of a liberal society, there remains a fundamental disagreement on how these values might be best realized.

This disagreement can be thought of as a dispute between the effectiveness of the market in maximizing societal utility and whether the state has the capacity and knowledge to improve on market outcomes. These two sets of procedural rules have tended to be categorized as either classical or social liberalisms, with both sides claiming to be 'heirs of the one true liberalism' (Bell, 2014).[2]

Historically, neither set of procedural rules has been able to sustain a liberal order which can be observed due to the tendency of liberal democracies to oscillate between these two forms. Hayek thought that social liberalism would result in a road to serfdom arguing that centralized control of an economy inevitably results in the coercion of individuals and the abandonment of freedom. These ideas gained credence following the breakdown of the post-1945 social liberal approach during the 1970s. However, the re-proselytizing of the market in the 1980s has led to a concentration of power impacting the freedom of individuals as well as their legal and political status. Both versions of liberalism it appears culminate in a road to serfdom.

Liberals have responded to these challenges by moving away from traditional utilitarian benchmarks such as gross domestic product (GDP) per capita towards broader measures of social and economic activity. Following the publication of the Fitoussi Report, the Organization for Economic Cooperation and Development (OECD) developed a Better Life Index combining a mixture of quality-of-life measures and material conditions to assess well-being as a potential alternative to income. The challenge for using well-being as an objective function is that it may be subject to change, and be distinct for different groups of people. Furthermore, it is unclear how one might systematically prioritize between policies.

Both classical and social liberalisms have generally sought to resolve conflicting claims or policies by maintaining a utilitarian approach to public policy which has been institutionalized through the development of welfare economics. Public policy economists have consequently formed a pragmatic and utilitarian approach to maximizing welfare in order to assess how best to allocate resources (Coyle, 2020). Hence, when policymakers attempt to resolve a specific issue, the default position is not to try and draw up policies that flow directly from the notions of freedom and equality, but instead to superimpose a utilitarian framework on the problem. This approach serves to highlight the practicality of utilitarianism and largely explains why it has become so dominant across liberal democracies using quantitative techniques such as cost–benefit analysis.

Although utilitarianism might be practical from a public policy perspective, it does not necessarily lead to the realization of freedom and equality. Amartya Sen argued that it ignores the initial allocation of goods; hence, the outcome of voluntary exchanges only reflects the initial allocation. And although redistribution has been seen as a tool by social liberalism to resolve this issue, such an approach often fails to address the underlying problem that caused the unequal initial allocation. Moreover, the persistence of unequal initial allocations can undermine the ability of citizens to feel they have equality of access in terms of how the polity should be governed, as well as the power to act based on their preferred choices.

By attempting to maximize total societal utility or welfare based on a set of initial conditions, utilitarianism has indirectly served to entrench vested interests, thereby undermining liberalism which is rooted in the concept of natural equality. Larry Siedentop has argued that 'the fundamental or root concept of liberalism is equality, and its commitment to liberty springs from that' (Ryan, 1979: 153). Siedentop goes further noting that reducing liberalism to a crude form of utilitarianism or satisfying preferences have undermined liberalism. By focusing on the 'second word of the core liberal value "equal liberty" at the expense of the first word ... they sacrifice the emphasis on reciprocity ... which gives liberalism its lasting moral value' (Siedentop, 2015: 363).

During the 1930s when liberalism last came under attack, a new form of liberalism began to emerge that disregarded utilitarianism and instead harked back to the underlying principles of freedom and equality. Supporters of this new approach included Walter Lippmann, Frank Knight and Henry Simons in the United States (US), but it was in Germany that these ideas were set out in greater detail. This non-utilitarian form of liberalism has been termed 'ordoliberalism' based on the work of four key thinkers, including Alexander Rüstow and Wilhelm Röpke who went into exile in the 1930s, and Franz Böhm and Walter Eucken who remained at the University of Freiburg.

One of the central tenets of this approach was that public and private power ought to be continually dispersed, thereby enabling greater equality in initial conditions prior to voluntary exchange. The ordoliberals thought classical liberalism only led to concentrations of power which resulted in a breakdown of society and the need for the state to reassert itself. They were also critical that the state might be able to solve economic and social challenges through an increase in compulsory organization due to the complexity of human affairs and the limited capacity of officials.

Rather than creating a set of procedural rules for public policy to maximize utility, the ordoliberals argued that the concentration of public and private power could be hindered by altering the legislative rules of the game across different fields of public policy. Such rules would enable the market to function more effectively given that power relations were 'normalized' prior to exchange. The ordoliberals thought this approach was more in keeping with the underlying principles of freedom and equality. This followed on from the proto-liberal thinker John Locke who thought that in a free society, no one should have more power and jurisdiction than another (Locke, 1993: 263). To achieve this, economic agents must be prevented from accumulating power over others, which by definition restricts freedom.

This ordoliberal tradition ought to be seen as an alternative strand of liberal thought and not, as is often assumed, merely a German version of contemporary neoliberal thought. This assumption may have arisen given that much of the work of Böhm, Rüstow and Eucken remains untranslated into English; the translation of many of Röpke's books into English was the exception. While the ordoliberal movement can be considered a broad church of ideas (Dyson, 2021), a common thread that linked Rüstow and Röpke in exile with Böhm and Eucken who remained in Freiburg, was the focus on the dispersion of power thereby improving fairer initial allocations or *Startgerechtigkeit* prior to voluntary exchange. If people do not believe that conditions prior to trading are fair, they are less likely to maintain support for liberal ideology.

During the post-war reconstruction of West Germany, the principle of dispersing public and private power was pervasive during the political and economic debates. While these ideas did have some influence on the development of political economy in West Germany, they were not as ubiquitous as the economics minister, Ludwig Erhard, subsequently argued. Indeed, ordoliberal policies were often ultimately rejected in many areas of policy due to the strength of vested interests.

Contemporary investigations of this alternative strand of liberalism have tended to focus on its place in intellectual history rather than as a potential vehicle to address public policy challenges. This maybe because the ordoliberal movement made little attempt to develop a quantitative framework that could measure the dispersion of public and private power. Hence, any assessment of the success of policies to amend rules to disperse power was too subjective and linked to the personal preferences of the proposer. This makes it much harder for policymakers to help prioritize between competing claims and to demonstrate fairness.

This book proposes to use the maxim of dispersing public and private power to improve the justice of initial conditions priory to voluntary exchange as the basis for an alternative liberal public policy programme. Based on the policy framework developed by Eucken, policy rules would be drawn up across five key areas; all of which must be directed towards the dispersion of public and private power. This includes three continuous fields of policy where power dispersal must be constantly manufactured by governments across labour markets, product markets and the state itself. These pillars must be supported by two foundational policy fields where policy is more binary in nature, including private property rights and ensuring agents are liable for their actions, as well as the stabilization of the currency. Policies in these fields must also be drawn up in such a way that they disperse public and private power.

To facilitate the development of rules to disperse power, a set of quantitative measures is developed to provide a potential alternative to the current utilitarian welfarist approach. These measures also provide some insight as to which OECD countries demonstrate a greater dispersal of power, indicating which societies are more in keeping with the principles of freedom and equality.

If liberal democracies are to thrive once more, then electorates must be convinced they can become vehicles enabling citizens to realize freedom and equality, rather than simply a rules-based system of entrenched interests. To what extent an ordoliberal approach to public policy provides an attractive enough alternative to utilitarianism remains to be seen. Although the intention of this book is to engage with both classical and social liberals on whether an ethical foundation of a liberal society based on improving initial allocations prior to voluntary exchange is worth further exploration, it is crucial that liberals re-engage once more with the core ideas of freedom and equality. Ideas that have inspired individuals throughout history; ideas that have been fought for time and again; and ideas that can once more be the driving force of political and economic discourse in liberal democracies.

Structure of the book

Chapter 2 focuses on the development of utilitarianism and its influence on public policy for both forms of liberalism. The approach to maximizing welfare has been supported by the institutionalization of welfare economics which remains a key plank of contemporary public policy. Despite this highly practical approach, there is increasing evidence that utilitarianism has instead impeded the spread of freedom and equality. While criticism from the likes of Rawls, Buchanan and Sen have highlighted many of the flaws in utilitarianism, the maximization of societal utility still remains the foundation of public policy in liberal democracies to resolve competing claims.

Chapters 3 and 4 explore the alternative liberal agenda that developed in the US and Germany during the 1930s which focused on the dispersal of public and private power to improve the fairness of initial allocations prior to voluntary exchange. This body of thought was sceptical of the market, constant state intervention and a utilitarian calculus. The ordoliberals also argued that economics alone was not sufficient to legitimate a polity. There had to be something more to life, which they thought should be based on community living with strong links to the natural world. During the foundation of West Germany many of these ideas were debated, and some did become influential in the political economy of West Germany. By the end of the 1950s, however, the movement had begun to decline, although Michel Foucault did revive interest in this strand of liberalism in the late 1970s.

Following on from Eucken's qualitative framework for public policy, an attempt is made to explore the implications of this approach and how one might disperse power across the five core policy fields. Chapters 5–9 of the book address each policy area in turn, providing an alternative lens for public policy professionals to assess current policy challenges.

This includes monetary policy where the traditional ordoliberal policy of stabilizing the price level to stabilize the currency is questioned, as there is evidence that it benefits certain segments of society at the expense of others. This demonstrates the importance of constantly reviewing the rules of the game and to propose alternative rules that are more in keeping with the underlying ethical framework such as targeting nominal wages.

Corporate governance remained another key area for ordoliberal policy discourse which required the directors of firms to be held liable for their actions. The failure to hold directors to account merely results in concentrations of power. The existence of private natural monopolies and intellectual property such as patents also increases concentrations of power. Hence, new rules of the game ought to be constructed to avoid such concentrations through improved corporate governance frameworks, socializing private natural monopolies and placing limits on the use of patents to support greater freedom and equality.

The decentralization of public power remained a key component of an ordoliberal framework, where communities are the foundation for social and economic development that also take account of the natural environment. Hence, there ought to be a balance of power between humanity and the biosphere as well. While individuals and their families were expected to contract directly for welfare services via contributory insurance schemes to avoid the erosion of the private sphere by the state, there was an expectation for the state to step in where insurance contracts were impracticable and provide a universal safety net. This resembles how welfare states have developed in parts of Northern Europe that emphasize both the contributory principle and universal benefits to maintain a reasonable standard of living. This community foundation was also to serve as the basis for closer economic interaction with like-minded states. This highlights the need to not only devolve power but also to consider how communities can cooperate voluntarily through supranational organizations such as the European Union (EU). A continuous measure of power dispersal is proposed to facilitate the debate on how an ordoliberal policy in this field might be constructed and measured.

Finally, it is essential that power is dispersed across labour and product markets. This requires power relations between labour and capital to be balanced, which in turn depends on continuous training to maintain that balance. The European Commission's policy of flexicurity resembles how one might proceed based on this ethical framework in order to deal with the challenges facing workers across developed economies. Product markets must be enforced by rigorous performance competition rules that prevent the abuse of power while encouraging innovation. Such ideas have been influential in the development of competition law within Germany as well as the EU, which differ from the anti-trust approach taken in the US based on consumer welfare.

In addition, free trade between like-minded countries was to be supported to reduce the power of domestic firms, hence such agreements must take account of power imbalances between countries. This is particularly important with regards to the challenges facing the multilateral trading system today where China has been able to maintain unequal conditions prior to trade through state subsidies. Continuous measures are also suggested to help facilitate further discussion for both product and labour markets.

The book concludes with some reflections on the challenges of public policy and how such an alternative framework might be implemented more widely to reinvigorate support for a liberal order. The empirical analysis based on the quantitative benchmarks indicates that the Nordic countries have been the most successful in dispersing public and private power across the OECD. There is not any evidence though that Nordic countries have deliberately pursued an ideology to disperse public and private power. However, historically most of the Nordic countries were not faced with the huge inequalities of landownership that were created by the feudal system. Hence, the starting point for voluntary exchange was already more equal. Moreover, women experienced a greater degree of gender equality partly due to labour shortages at the end of the 19th century which encouraged them to join the workforce. Furthermore, the reforms to the Nordic welfare model in the 1970s largely devolved policy responses for expediency purposes, while remaining open to globalization. This is not to suggest that public policy in other OECD countries should follow the Nordic model, but rather that that Nordic model follows the maxim of power dispersal more closely than other developed countries.

Ideas are central to both politics and policy. But for ideas to be of use from a public policy perspective they need to have a clear ethical foundation to help prioritize between competing claims. This is why utilitarianism has been so successful as it removes arbitrary decision-making. Unfortunately for liberalism it has resulted in the increasing destruction of freedom and equality and until an alternative foundation is in place, the outlook for liberalism is clouded. The ideas of freedom and equality still resonate in many parts of the globe, but it is up to liberals to work out how they can be revived. This book is an attempt to reinvigorate this debate.

The Liberal Order and its Utilitarian Foundation

The rise of utilitarianism and its influence on public policy

Trafalgar Square lies at the heart of London. Besides its illustrious location, sandwiched between the National Gallery and Whitehall, it has often provided space for the British electorate to make their views heard when they are in conflict with government. In 1887, Trafalgar Square hosted a demonstration against policy towards Ireland organized by the Social Democratic Federation and the Irish National League. The demonstration turned violent and has subsequently become known as Bloody Sunday. Tragically for British–Irish relations this was not to be the last Bloody Sunday. Over a hundred years later in 1990, the All-Britain Anti-Poll Tax Federation called for a demonstration in Trafalgar Square against the community charge, which was a flat tax on the electorate. By the evening the demonstration had developed into a full-blown riot with running battles between police and protestors. Such is the potential outcome of a clash in ideology.

This chapter explores the development of utilitarianism and its influence on contemporary public policy for both forms of liberalism. This utilitarian approach to public policy has been reinforced by the rise of welfare economics providing additional quantitative tools to help drive policy decisions. Despite criticism that utilitarianism is an illiberal political philosophy, this system largely remains intact due to its practicality for policymakers. While public policy professionals have started to measure different aspects of social and economic activity, these approaches have not yet developed an effective method of resolving conflicting claims.

Ideology is central to political discourse which helps us to understand and interpret the social and political world in which we live. As noted by Freeden, this justifies whether the political arrangements that affect society should either be altered or maintained (Syrjämäki, 2012). Liberal ideology is founded on the principles of freedom and equality, and since the 19th century these ideas have largely been represented by utilitarianism in terms of the aims of public policy. The doctrine of utilitarianism, which emerged from the writings of Jeremy Bentham in the late 18th century, is related to practical choices and actions which seek to maximize the happiness or pleasure of the greatest number of a society.

Central to Bentham's principle of utility was the extent to which the consequences of every action taken by an individual or government tended to augment or diminish happiness. Bentham thought the value of pleasure or pain could be measured based on its intensity, duration, certainty and remoteness as well as purity of feeling and the number of people affected. By summing up 'all the values of all the pleasures on the one side, and those of all the pains on the other … the balance, if it be on the side of pleasure, will give the good tendency of the act upon the whole' (Bentham, 1838: Vol I, 140). Thus the so-called felicific calculus was born; a system of public policy that attempted to quantify the potential benefits of policy outcomes. Utilitarianism is therefore judged by the consequential acts of policies on the assumption that they increase societal utility.

Bentham's principle of utility marked a shift away from Adam Smith's society of free individuals founded on the virtues of prudence, justice and beneficence. Smith thought these virtues had a tendency to produce only the most agreeable effects and were further tethered by self-command which engenders a sense of propriety with regard to the sentiments of the supposed impartial spectator. Smith reinforced his position against pleasure as an ethical construct noting that 'without the restraint which this principle imposes, every passion would, upon most occasions, rush headlong, if I may say so, to its own gratification' (Smith, 1982: 266) According to Smith, we approve of an action (approbation) not because we find it useful to society but because we judge it to be right (Schliesser, 2018: 86).

Bentham's calculation engine took the ethical foundations of a commercial society in a firmly different direction, one which was more self-centred and individualistic. Bentham thought virtue was less important, arguing instead that the balance of human actions which drives the highest utility is the most important factor in determining improved moral outcomes. He argued against beneficence, noting that 'if every man were disposed to sacrifice his own enjoyments to the enjoyments of others, it is obvious the whole sum of enjoyment would be diminished, nay, destroyed. The result would not be the general happiness, but the general misery' (Bentham, 1838: Vol I, 52)

Bentham's originality in the development of a method of public policy came at a time when the demand for government to do something about rising social and economic issues stemming from industrialization began to surface. Indeed, he was perhaps the first thinker to provide such a detailed exposition of how a societal end goal could be measured, and hopefully improved upon. Although the specificity of the calculus remained somewhat elusive, it did provide a framework for policymakers when thinking about how to 'improve and solve' for a specific issue. According to the jurist A.V. Dicey, Bentham's ideas were hugely influential on legislation between 1825 and 1870 (Dicey, 2008). One example of this was the 1868 Pharmacy Act which required drugs to be sold in containers with the seller's name and address. This closely followed J.S. Mill's recommendation that there ought to be some form of recording of poison transactions to limit deliberate harm to individuals (Mill, 1985: Ch V). Another early attempt to use this framework for public policy was developed by the French engineer Jules Dupuit, who in 1844 attempted to assess the utility to society of a footbridge (Dupuit, 1952). This can be thought of as a precursor to cost–benefit analysis that has dominated public policy since the post-war era.

Crucially for utilitarianism, Bentham's felicific calculus became central to the new subject of economics. William Stanley Jevons made it clear that his objective was to treat the economy following Bentham as, 'a Calculus of Pleasure and Pain' and hence the 'object of Economics is to maximise happiness by purchasing pleasure ... at the lowest cost of pain' (Jevons, 1888: 38) For Jevons, arriving at a satisfactory theory of exchange was central to the maximization of utility as the exchange of commodities proceeds until each party has obtained the maximum benefit from the acquired quantities. The process of exchange also results in the tendency of the economic system to move towards equilibrium which maximizes societal utility or welfare. This idea has since become one of the central tenets of neoclassical economic theory.

The theory of maximizing welfare is based on the two fundamental theorems of welfare economics. The first fundamental welfare theorem argues that markets will tend towards a competitive equilibrium given certain conditions such as rational expectations and perfect competition with a set of prices where aggregate supply will equal aggregate demand. Hence, the market is able to coordinate the different objectives of individuals, thereby maximizing welfare (Arrow & Debreu, 1954). The second welfare theorem was developed to enable units of account to be transferred to satisfy equity concerns followed by the decentralized functioning of competitive markets to take care of efficiency. As Arrow argued, 'thems that have, get' (Duffie & Sonnenschein, 1989), indicating power relations prior to exchange favour wealthier households.

These two welfare theorems whose objectives are to maximize total societal welfare or utility largely reflect the public policy debate that has been central to the oscillation of social and classical liberalisms. The first welfare theorem has become the go-to principle for classical liberals while the second theorem has been used by social liberals arguing for greater redistribution.

Classical liberals such as Herbert Spencer thought that the welfare of society could be improved through greater mutual dependence enabling greater individuation where, 'every man has freedom to do all that he wills provided he infringes not the equal freedom of any other man' (Spencer, 1851: 67). To counteract this, social liberalism sought to use the ideas of improving societal welfare to promote their ideas of redistribution. Utility provided the motivation to reform, which was understood as a rationalized remedying of social ills resulting in social reform being perceived as central to liberty. Furthermore, Bentham's ideas had increasingly seen the role of the state as an agent of change, which dovetailed with the social liberal view of the interventionist state (Freeden, 1978: 13–15).

While the debate between social and classical liberalism tends to focus on their differences, it is worth reflecting that both are still forms of liberalism and still have much in common with each other. Both versions of liberalism can be understood as an alternative set of procedural rules that attempt to maximize total societal utility, whether it be via market outcomes or through state-driven redistribution. These procedural rules can also be thought of as the basis for a theory of justice enabling competing claims to freedom and equality to be resolved with social liberalism focused on distributive justice and classical liberalism through commutative justice. The principle of distributive justice focuses on how things like goods should be distributed among a group of people, whereas commutative justice focuses on how individuals should be treated (for example, in a transaction) so that each person receives what is due to them.

Milton Friedman thought the debate was not about differences in basic values but more about the level of the prediction of the economic consequences of pursuing certain actions. For Friedman, policy remains 'utilitarian in terms of its ability to deliver improvements to the anonymous public' (Barry, 1988). The end state of maximizing utility ought therefore to be seen as a pragmatic and practical way of helping to support public policy decisions within a set of procedural rules.

The utilitarian goal of improving total societal utility in liberal democracies has also been institutionalized within public policy through the development of welfare economics. Since the post-war period, cost–benefit analysis has become entrenched within public policy guidelines,[1] which contain important links to the theoretical literature on welfare economics (Boadway, 1974; Pearce, 1985). Welfare economics remains ubiquitous in terms of thinking about how it might be possible to improve societal welfare which can also be understood as societal well-being or utility. Thus, public policy economists have largely formed a pragmatic and 'more or less utilitarian, approach to social welfare in their empirical work' (Coyle, 2020: 41). Hence, it has been argued that welfare economics continues to provide 'the basis for judging the achievements of markets and policy makers in allocating resources' (Besley, 2002).

The post-1945 approach to public policy was heavily influenced by the ideas of social liberalism that emerged in the late 19th century. These ideas arose from the squalid working conditions of industrial society with its stark levels of inequality and hence tended to focus on the role of the state to improve working conditions. In 1909, John Hobson argued in his Peoples Charter for the government to have the power to tax and redistribute and take increasing responsibility for social functions (Hobson, 1974).

These ideas also developed in the US through Herbert Croly who urged the use of Hamiltonian big government to restore liberty. This was to be achieved by the federal government nationalizing large corporations and having union representatives run these businesses alongside management. He argued this corporatist framework was the future and that the Sherman Act should be repealed which discriminated against them. Croly thought that the 'existing concentration of wealth and financial power in the hands of a few irresponsible men is the inevitable outcome of the chaotic individualism of our political and economic organization, while at the same time it is inimical to democracy because it tends to erect political abuses and social inequalities' (Croly, 1912: 14).

The main thrust of social liberalism was that the state could facilitate an improvement in overall utility, and hence realize greater freedom and equality for individuals. While this model worked well for the post-war era, by the 1970s it had begun to break down. Liberal democracies were struggling to contain inflation, firms were losing their competitiveness and attempts by the state to intervene did not necessarily improve outcomes. This was notably the case for President Johnson's war on poverty in the 1960s, which appears to have increased rather than decreased inequality (Dunning, 2017).

Throughout the post-war period a group of thinkers who advocated a revival of classical liberalism and its focus on market outcomes attacked social liberalism on two specific fronts. Milton Friedman argued that continuous federal expansionary policy to maintain full employment introduced an inflationary bias (Friedman, 1962). The effect of this expansionary policy increases the bargaining power of labour which not only drives up inflation but also erodes profits and reduces investment. The second was the extent to which governments could successfully implement policy to improve outcomes for society. In 1945 Friedrich Hayek published 'The Use of Knowledge in Society', arguing that the main challenge of attempting to construct a rational economic order was the problem of the utilization of knowledge not given to anyone in its totality (Hayek, 1945).

Hayek noted that all economic activity is a function of planning which requires those who do the planning to assimilate information from multiple sources. Hence, the challenge of planners who might be in a tech start-up, large firm or government is to understand what is the best way of utilizing knowledge that is initially widely dispersed, and to what extent this knowledge is sufficiently understood once it is assimilated.

In addition to this inherent uncertainty, the consequences of a dynamic system renders this information out of date almost immediately. Sometimes only small changes need to be made, but other times a plan might need to be completely reconstructed. But to do this requires a planning culture to be highly responsive and continually adaptive. Hayek concludes that the people who are best able to adapt are those who are most familiar with the particular circumstances affected by change, rather than a centralized body that receives information. This means a form of decentralization is required, which is why Hayek placed such an emphasis on the price system which communicates subjective values enabling individuals to coordinate the parts of their plan.

Soon after Hayek published the article, another Austrian émigré, Peter Drucker, completed *The Concept of the Corporation* which argued that firms ought to function using a federal decentralized approach. Although the book was based on a two-year long study at General Motors (GM), GM management were unimpressed with his recommendations. However, Japanese carmakers became influenced by his ideas, which is one reason why firms like Toyota became world leaders through decentralized production. Drucker's central insight was that individuals and teams closer to production are best placed to solve issues and recommend improvements (Drucker, 1946).

As the economy floundered in the 1970s, liberal democracies began to shift away from the redistributive approach of social liberalism towards the market as espoused by the revival of classical liberalism, which has since been labelled as neoliberalism. This alternative view advocated that a globalized market would result in improved outcomes with a focus on freeing up entrepreneurial activity. According to one writer, neoliberalism can be thought of as a system where 'state interventions in markets … must be kept to a bare minimum because … the state cannot possibly possess enough information to second-guess market signals … and because powerful interest groups will inevitably distort and bias state interventions … for their own benefit' (Harvey, 2005: 2) Thus, the role of the state shifted to install and protect this institutional framework. Although it has been argued that neoliberalism is distinct to classical liberalism as it requires the state to create the market relations in the first place (Mirowski and Plehwe, 2009), both ideologies place their faith in the outcome of the market.

The challenge for contemporary neoliberalism as defined by Harvey, which can be understood as a version of classical liberalism that promotes market outcomes, is that it has led to increasing inequality and charges of elitism which jar with the underlying principles of liberty and equality. Data from the OECD indicate that the income share flowing to the middle classes across a majority of OECD countries has fallen since the 1990s, suggesting that the middle class is shrinking (OECD, 2019a). A large body of literature has developed laying the blame on an excessive faith in deregulated markets and globalization.[2]

This rising inequality has also challenged the principle whether there really are equal chances for all. If inequality is persistent through time, higher-income households can increase their purchasing power within the political system resulting in the creation of laws that are beneficial for specific groups. Indeed, there is a growing band of criticism that the rules of the game are biased in favour of elites, enabling them to maintain their concentration of both economic and political power.[3]

Furthermore, if lower-income households begin to feel that their voices are no longer being heard in the political debate, then the liberal idea of equality no longer holds. It has recently been argued that the increasing divide in many Western liberal democracies has created the notion that the 'we' of a polity no longer translates to the enlightenment idea that 'we are all in it together' (Emmott, 2017).

This shift has resulted in a burgeoning of publications on the decline of the West and the liberal order.[4] However, there has been far less focus on what might be done to reinvigorate liberalism and its foundational ideas of liberty and equality. Liberal magazines such as *The Economist* recognize there is a problem, but their attempts to reinforce the values of free markets and limited government have not led to any resurgence in support (The Economist, 2018a).

Indeed, electorates are instead increasingly demanding to take back control from global economic forces and are less enamoured of relying on the outcome of the market. One contemporary critique of the liberal order has caught the zeitgeist better than most arguing that 'today's widespread yearning for a strong leader, one with the will to take back popular control over liberalism's forms of bureaucratic government and globalised economy, comes after decades of liberal dismantling of cultural norms and political habits essential to self-governance' (Deneen, 2018: xiv).

As left and right populism begin to make inroads, liberalism appears to be floundering. Neither social nor classical liberalism has proven itself in the market for ideas. Indeed, both forms of liberalism have been attacked as being an escape from the complexity and dynamic of reality (Maier-Rigaud & Maier-Rigaud, 2001: 284) with neither economic growth nor economic redistribution resolving the predicament liberalism finds itself in. Oren Cass argues that while growth is necessary for a prosperous society it is not sufficient, particularly when the outcome of vanishing jobs results in households becoming dependent on handouts or told to leave towns that appear to be unsustainable (Cass, 2018: 29).

This perceived failure has created a vacuum within liberal thought. When the post-war social liberal consensus broke down, a set of ideas linked to classical liberalism were waiting in the wings to provide a framework for a new policy paradigm. Today, the alternatives on offer appear to be a return to an era of populism which tends to be discriminatory against certain groups and disdainful towards the rule of law, or big government where large sections of the economy are socialized and owned by the state.

The short-lived attempt by centre-left parties in Europe and the Americas in the 1990s and 2000s to correct some of the most egregious outcomes of the market was to largely leave the existing neoliberal economic system intact, while raising taxes for increased redistribution. However, this approach was not sustainable given the neoliberal system has not performed as well as its supporters promised, reducing the state's ability to redistribute. In the United Kingdom (UK), Lord Mandelson, one of the politicians most associated with the so-called Third Way under the Blair government, argued this experiment ought to be seen as a failure.[5]

While both versions of liberalism have struggled to maintain their legitimacy, it is plausible that the issue lies with the common end state as represented by the maximization of societal utility. Hence, the pursuit of Bentham's felicific calculus using the tools of welfare economics may instead be a greater obstacle to freedom and equality. Indeed, the lack of interest in confronting ethical issues related to inequitable distribution prior to voluntary exchange is of particular concern.

The problem with welfare economics

To avoid dealing with thorny ethical issues of unequal initial allocations, welfare economics instead focused on maximizing welfare along utilitarian lines once the initial allocations have been dealt out, as expounded by the Italian economist Vilfredo Pareto.

Lionel Robbins supported this approach, advocating that economists ought to disentangle economic analysis from its ethical foundations. He stated that 'economics deals with ascertainable facts; ethics with valuations and obligations. The two fields of enquiry are not on the same plane of discourse' (Robbins, 1932: 132). Robbins described the welfare of a society as being dependent on the utility of individual households in that society. He thought that a foundation of provisional utilitarianism was desirable as a first approximation in handling questions relating to the lives and actions of large masses of people (Robbins, 1938).

While the founders of neoclassical economics believed that perfect competition led to an optimum in exchange and production provided that the distribution of income was appropriate, the reality was that the initial distribution was not always appropriate. And as Samuelson pointed out, they did not believe that perfect competition would rectify the imbalance of the initial allocations. To avoid dealing with this issue, Samuelson and Bergson followed the Pareto principle where competition produces a maximum collective utility regardless of the distribution of income (Samuelson, 1947). Hence, a Pareto optimal outcome is one where resources cannot be reallocated to make an individual better off without making another individual worse off, thus implying resources have been allocated in the most efficient manner.

The outcome of Bergson and Samuelson's research was the development of the social welfare function, where the social welfare of a society (W) is a function of all the utilities of the constituent members that make up that society (U), taking into account all possible variables impacting individual welfare. This has since become the foundation of modern welfare economics. In addition, the new welfare economics developed by Hicks and Kaldor suggested it may be necessary to compensate those who lost out from any changes so that utility could be increased without making anyone else worse off.

Some economists thought this approach far too restrictive, which put an immense premium on the original distribution of income. James Meade tried to reposition the role of welfare economics to 'consider how a given redistribution of income could be achieved with a minimum sacrifice of economic efficiency', particularly given that practically every conceivable change of policy will in fact be to someone's detriment. Indeed, Meade states that if economists were to confine themselves to the consideration of policies which made no one worse off, they would have virtually no contribution to make (Meade, 1976: 31).

But Meade then proceeded to sidestep the ethical problem by arguing that policymakers must allot marginal utilities to the spendable money income of individuals and that economists should 'proceed on the basis that the choice is made' (Meade, 1976: 60). Thus, Meade appears to follow Robbins' mantra that economics should not be about ethics and instead proceed once the ethical judgements by politicians have been made.

Despite the rich intellectual foundation of welfare economics which has come to dominate public policy, neither of the two welfare theorems has been able to provide a robust framework approximating a freer and more equal society. As has been noted by Diane Coyle, 'markets and governments fail for similar reasons. Externalities mean prices give a misleading signal of social benefit and costs. The market does not internalise them ... but governments do not have the information needed' (Coyle, 2020: 291).

In a paper entitled 'The Strange Disappearance of Welfare Economics', Tony Atkinson criticized economists for not devoting time to investigating the values upon which their analyses are based. According to Atkinson, modern economic theory uses welfare economics to think about how an economy works based on the behaviour of identical households or representative agents. It is then assumed that changes in social welfare can be judged according to whether the representative household is better or worse off, using household income as a measurable parameter. This in turn implies whether society as a whole is better or worse off as a result of a particular policy (Atkinson, 2001). But households do not necessarily agree with each other to the extent that a policy will increase household utility. Furthermore, it is not always the case that a consumer's choices will result in higher utility. These frustrations with welfare economics are, however, not new. Indeed, a minority of economists have long argued that the underlying apparatus of welfare economics is useless and has little value for public policy purposes.

In his review of welfare economics published in 1950, Ian Little was particularly critical of Robbins. He thought that the conclusions of welfare economics are inevitably value judgements, and that it would be better to be explicit about these value judgements in an attempt to make them as widely accepted as possible. While people are not likely to dispute that a person with higher income is better off, they might dispute the fairness of taxing one to subsidize the other (Little, 1973: 65).

Little concludes that value judgements which might lead to an increase in economic welfare are purely a matter of opinion which is particularly obvious in the case of changes which affect income distribution (Little, 1973: 115). The result of this is that people who differ on the subject of distribution will seldom agree on the desirability of economic changes.

The South African economist Jan de Van Graaff criticized welfare economics for its lack of realism because it assumes that the desired distribution of wealth has already been attained. He was highly critical of lump sum redistributions, which he argued were impractical particularly when thought of as a continuous process. He also saw interpersonal comparisons of well-being as questions of ethics rather than questions of fact. If two people disagree on the contributions which various levels of individual well-being make to social well-being, it is extraordinarily hard to think of some objective test which would settle the matter to the satisfaction of both. The question is therefore an ethical one (Graaff, 1975: 167).

Graaff concludes that:

> The possibility of building an interesting theory then hinges on the possibility of obtaining a sufficient consilience of opinion on ethical matters to enable specific injunctions to be deduced. Now clearly there is some degree of consilience of opinion in any reasonably homogenous society ... but whether or not the common ground is sufficiently extensive for the purposes of welfare theory is another matter. ... I doubt if any two people really agree in detail on the best

way of securing full employment, no matter how many may agree that
it should be secured. ... It seems to me therefore that the possibility
of building a useful and interesting theory of welfare economics ... is
exceedingly small. (Graaff, 1975: 168)

Matters deteriorated further for welfare economics when Lancaster and
Lipsey argued that even if only one of the Paretian optimum conditions
cannot be fulfilled, an optimum situation can only be achieved by departing
from all the other Paretian conditions (Lipsey & Lancaster, 1956). Hence,
it is futile to attempt to move towards the objective knowing that not all
conditions are optimal, and therefore second-best outcomes or piecemeal
welfare economics may in fact result in worse outcomes. Lipsey noted that
in practical situations we just 'do not know the necessary and sufficient
conditions for achieving an economy-wide first best allocation of resources'
(Lipsey, 2007), thus rendering welfare economics mostly useless. Given
the complexity of the modern economy this outcome is in many respects
unsurprising given the requirement to be so precise about the effects of
specific policy interventions.

These criticisms indicate that the assumptions of welfare economics
that have attempted to justify a laissez-faire or redistributive outcomes
are without a solid foundation. Indeed, as the economist Mark Blaug has
argued, 'there is little advantage and much disadvantage in cluttering up
the conclusions of welfare economics by indiscriminately combining the
value judgements underlying the concept of Pareto-optimality with those
relating to the economic justice of different distributions of income' (Blaug,
1985: 608).

Despite more than a century of research on welfare economics, there
is a strong case to be made that it has been mostly unhelpful because it
has ignored ethics. As the monetary economist Ralph Hawtrey noted in
1925, economics cannot be dissociated from ethics (Hawtrey, 1925: 184).
The assumption that under certain conditions markets will tend towards a
competitive equilibrium is problematic given that these assumptions rarely
apply in the real world. Moreover, the process of lump sum redistributions
rarely resolves the underlying structural issue that required the lump sum
to be made in the first place. This might result in the development of an
underclass which is hard to equate with legitimating a liberal society where
individuals are supposed to be free and equal.

While it might be argued that welfare economics has failed in its attempt
to provide a sufficiently robust public policy framework for a liberal society,
this may be more related to the goal of utilitarianism itself that welfare
economics has been set up to support. Indeed, there has been much criticism
of utilitarianism as being an illiberal political philosophy. Hence, it is perhaps
not surprising that liberalism is currently struggling in the battle of ideas.

The post-war attack on utilitarianism

The 1970s Harvard debate between Rawls and Nozick attempted to recast the social versus classical liberalism debate using a Kantian universalist foundation rather than a utilitarian one. This followed on from the enlightenment view that it is possible to come to a rational agreement on how to organize society. Kant argued that an individual's will is the source of morality, but that a universal form of rationality enables individuals to distinguish between right and wrong (Kant, 1992).

Rawls criticized utilitarianism on the basis that due to the initial allocation, individuals were unable to experience a minimum level of welfare based on a notion of primary goods such as adequate food, clothing and shelter, which in turn negatively affected liberty and opportunity. His colleague and sparring partner, Robert Nozick, noted that the experience of utility was highly uneven which might result in 'utility monsters who get enormously greater gains in utility from any sacrifice of others than these others lose' (Nozick, 1974: 41). Nozick thought that if life were just about experiencing anything that a person desired and a machine were created for this purpose we would not use it.

This can also be understood as a criticism of happiness economics, which in recent years has attempted to return Bentham's felicific calculus to its original focus (Layard, 2005). If happiness really were the objective of society, then administering copious quantities of happiness-inducing drugs would be a logical proposal.[6] But freedom and equality do not necessarily dovetail with a continuous feeling of happiness. Indeed, the idea that the pursuit of happiness might undermine freedom is suitably captured by Nietzsche who quipped that, 'man does not desire happiness, only the Englishman does' (Berlin, 1972).

Rawls' second principle of justice required that social and economic inequalities ought to be arranged so that all citizens operate under conditions of fair equality of opportunity. In addition, such arrangements had to be of greatest benefit to the least advantaged member of society known as the difference principle. Rawls thought that as individuals would not know into which section of society they would be born in to, they would rationally choose to organize society in this way (Rawls, 1973).

One weakness in this argument is that people do not necessarily behave rationally (Kahneman, 2011). Hence, the original position is unlikely to be agreed upon universally. Rawls' work has also been criticized as being ahistorical which disregards the impact of the social organization (Freeden, 2008: 227–9). Rothstein goes further in his criticism, supporting Milton Fisk who noted that the 'entire idea of reasoning our way to general principles of justice on the basis of some universal rationalism and independently of the surrounding material world is a vain and hopeless enterprise' (Rothstein, 1998: 11).

Finally, Rawls pays little attention to the issues of how the state might be run, and how vested interests might divert policies away from the original position.

For Nozick, what mattered most were individual universal rights which the state was not entitled to interfere with, hence society should recognize that people ought to be entitled to develop and own their natural assets without any intervention. Nozick thought that the state ought to be as minimal as possible so it could not be highjacked by specific groups to further their own interests. Nozick's theory though tells us nothing about initial allocations, and hence is unhelpful for thinking through public policy challenges for a liberal society.

Despite both philosophers being firmly anti–utilitarian, their attempt to provide an alternative foundation to liberalism based on universal Kantian ethics has not been successful. The challenge of any rational-based approach is that it ignores the central importance of language, culture and feelings in humans. Johann Herder, one of Kant's students, argued that individuals belong to a particular culture with its own past and tradition. And each culture has its own inner spirit which individuals form a part of. His crusade against French universalism and rationality instead promoted the beauty and diversity of individual cultures.

This reaction to universalism was influenced by David Hume who thought that we cannot trust the fallacious deductions of our reason which are liable to error and mistake. Hume instead sought refuge in the ordinary wisdom of nature to secure an act of the mind through instinct or mechanical tendency (Hume, 1988). This placed Hume firmly in the realm of belief, thereby supporting the romantic reaction (Berlin, 1993).

But Herder's message was not one of conquest and superiority. He strongly criticized Europeans for setting themselves above the people of the other quarters of the globe in arts, science and cultivation (Herder, 2016: 206). Patriotism for Herder was the recognition that one's purpose is an intrinsic element in a larger pattern of a particular culture and network of relationships rather than a utilitarian calculus or an impulsive solidarity. Herder, though, was not a conservative and had little time for backward-looking ideology that has come to be associated with Edmund Burke. The spontaneity of a culture was the driving force of history enabling the triumph of the bold to move that culture to a higher level. Herder also had little time for the state authority and its institutions, which he thought constrained the future path of the free human (Berlin, 2006).

Hence, for romanticism, any attempt to impose a mechanistic order upon humanity was merely distorting reality, which provided an important caveat to societies that believed they had discovered a unified answer to resolving human affairs. As Berlin suggests in his lectures on romanticism, incompatibility and imperfection are central to humanity, hence any imposition of a universal order is likely to be ruinous, forcing people to compromise (Berlin, 1972). Romanticism had understood something more fundamental in the way humans functioned that rationalist enlightenment thinkers had just not thought to be relevant.

Given this universalist failure, it should not be surprising that utilitarianism remains the default ethical foundation for liberal societies. Another alternative theoretical development to counter utilitarianism is constitutional economics which is associated with the economist James Buchanan. Buchanan thought that it might be possible to develop a substitute to a welfare function; a function that was focused on individual choices rather than preferences. He focused on how the political process might be organized that respected the authority of individual citizens but permitted the political system to function. This followed Buchanan's views that people generally make decisions based on their own interests.

Buchanan argued that embedded interest groups will attempt to make the system work for themselves, hence historically determined institutions of legal order need not be those which are best and that such institutions can be reformed. Buchanan concludes that 'there seems to be no grounds for the faith that the natural forces at work in an economy will ensure a workably competitive order' (Buchanan, 1977: 59).

This leads Buchanan down the contractarian approach of Rawls. He argues that the social structure or rules of the game can be modified using a constitutionalist approach. This means that the general framework of rules is the target for reform rather than specific policies. But crucially for this to happen it requires all players to see such changes as fair. The contractarian approach therefore requires unanimity. Buchanan was influenced by the Swedish economist Knut Wicksell who stated in his 1896 essay that public funding proposals should be voted on by members of the political body, but that only those with unanimous backing should be passed.

However, unanimity becomes problematic from a practicable perspective. If there are differences in initial allocations which provide certain interest groups with greater market power, it is unlikely that those who benefit from market power would decide to relinquish their position. Constitutionalism therefore appears to have an inherent bias for those who have benefitted from initial allocations and have been able to influence the rule-making process to maintain the imbalance in market power. Although constitutionalism recognizes the in-built bias, its methodological approach prevents any realistic change to the system itself.

As Buchanan argues, current entitlements must be respected and those who lose out must be compensated (Buchanan, 1977: 138–40). Thus, the argument appears to revert to the dead end of New Welfare Economics where in the example of the corn law reforms, landowners should have been compensated. But the rationale for reforming the corn laws was to amend societal rules based on the fact that it was considered the right thing to do.

A closer reading of Wicksell indicates that the notion of unanimity was in fact rather different to Buchanan's interpretation. Wicksell's unanimity approach was predicated upon the issues of market power being resolved prior to voting. Wicksell rejected Pareto's first welfare theorem stating that perfect competition maximizing social welfare is unlikely given that perfect markets do not exist. As market outcomes largely depend on the initial allocations, the 'operation of the unanimity rule therefore required that inequities of distribution of income (and wealth, power, and access to government) be rectified prior to the imposition of the unanimity rule' (Johnson, 2008).

The idea of the levelling of market power is therefore central to Wicksell's framework. Despite the limitations of Buchanan's approach to political change, his point that the rules of the game can and ought to be altered to improve market outcomes by focusing on the initial distribution of pre-market endowments and capacities is an important shift.

Another and potentially more significant breakthrough in thinking about the ethical foundation of a liberal society was made by Amartya Sen who argued against the concept of utility and commodities or primary goods and replaced it with capabilities. At a philosophical level, the concept of capability as freedom appears to be more in keeping with the pre-Benthamite ideas of Adam Smith.

Sen, like many other critics of utilitarianism and modern welfare economics, emphasizes that Pareto optimality is indifferent to distributional considerations (Sen, 2017: 261). He also noted that the focus of welfare economics on providing mathematical exactness of the formulation of utility has proceeded with a 'remarkable inexactness of content' (Sen, 2014: 2).

Furthermore, the idea that an individual's preference ordering reflects their interests and welfare, while describing their actual choices and behaviour seems highly unlikely. On the one hand this requires a person to be rational, revealing no inconsistencies in choices, but if there are no distinctions between these different concepts then he thought the person must be a bit of a fool (Sen, 1999: 99). For Sen, the Pareto principle in traditional welfare economics does not seem to survive close scrutiny.

Another reason for Sen's shift away from welfare economics was that he thought it was illiberal. Not only did it override ideas of rights, but also it did not enable individuals to pursue their goals and hence freedom. This can be observed in his theorem *The Impossibility of a Paretian Liberal* where Mr Prude and Mr Lewd fight it out over a copy of *Lady Chatterley's Lover*. Mr Prude prefers that no one reads it, particularly Mr Lewd, while Mr Lewd prefers that both read it, and particularly Mr Prude. The upshot is that there is no choice that satisfies both a liberal outcome and the Pareto principle (Sen, 2017: 131–2).

Sen suggests that social preferences may not be the best approach in guaranteeing individual liberty, and that individual values should be developed that respect each other's personal choices. This leads Sen to propose a new approach to welfare in terms of basic capabilities. Sen didn't think that the problem of evaluation is made any simpler by proceeding in this direction raising the concerns around how one might index basic capability bundles (Sen, 1999: 368). But he thought it was better in 'capturing the totality of functionings ... that make life worthwhile and which are to be reflected in the person's well-being' (Sen, 2014: 45). In essence Sen moves away from the attempt to resolve interpersonal conflicts in the assessment of social states towards obtaining a common standard of well-being.

But the implementation of this capability approach was something that Sen did not appear to be as interested in. Following Sen, a number of theorists such as Martha Nussbaum have attempted to list out all the necessary capabilities that every individual requires. The challenge with this approach is that it becomes very hard to come to an agreement on which capabilities are the ones that ought to be the focus of public policy, and how they should be measured.

Sen appears to recognize the limits of this approach from a theoretical standpoint where 'the actual substance of this process of judgement will and must be determined in practice. It thus ought not be specified at the level of theory' (Hamilton, 2019: 18). This raises the question how one might achieve some form of decision-making based on individuals achieving their capabilities without interfering with the freedom part of liberalism? Sen suggests it is feasible to reach an outcome based on majority decisions by improving the scope and reach of public reasoning to establish and validate values (Sen, 2017: 408).

However, this optimistic argument that individuals will come to a collective majority agreement is not particularly well substantiated. How might this deliberative approach deal with the reality of initial allocations and the effect they have on power relations within a polity? Hamilton has suggested that Sen's view of deliberative democracy lacks any realism and is characterized by a lack of interest in assessing and criticizing existing power relations and the impact they have across economic and political institutions. Thus, Sen's outlook is more of an idealist project where certain stakeholders deliberate and discuss, 'but it may also be a world in which very little effectively gets done' (Hamilton, 2019: 120).

Despite the growing criticism of utilitarianism, Bentham's felicific calculus approximated using the tools of welfare economics remains ubiquitous mainly because of its practicality as an instrument of public policy. But this hasn't prevented policymakers from trying to improve on outcomes. Indeed, there remains a strong recognition that approach to policy needs to improve.

Changing parameters

Rodrik in his critique of hyper globalization argues that one might be able to agree on a number of 'common sense' principles to provide the foundation for a new economic system. Rodrik suggests that these 'common sense' principles would result in a saner globalization and one that is more legitimate (Rodrik, 2011: 236). This approach is largely founded on getting the right balance of policies between the state and market.

But a shift towards proposing lists of policies raises a number of questions including the practicality of agreeing to 'common sense' principles, given that what is common sense for classical liberals may not be the case for social liberals. Presumably what Rodrik means as a common-sense principle is one that would do a better job of maximizing welfare or utility, and hence can be seen as an attempt to reinvigorate the current utilitarian outlook. However, both strands of liberalism have used markets and the state to varying degrees to address public policy issues, hence it is not clear why this time things might be different. More recent suggestions on targeting inequality appear to be focused on trying to reinvigorate support for social liberalism through more redistribution (Blanchard & Tirole, 2021). But these policies do not address the issue of power relations which is one of the underlying causes of inequality, nor whether the government has sufficient knowledge to increase welfare. Furthermore, as the jurist H.L.A. Hart has argued, 'some liberties ... are too precious to be put at the mercy of numbers even if in favourable circumstances they may win out' (Ryan, 1979: 96).

Hence, this technocratic solution to find a trade-off between production efficiency and distributional fairness based on lists of policies, appears to be without much of hope of success in sustaining a liberal order. Following Sen's ideas on human capabilities, an alternative approach is to measure different aspects of public policy, thereby removing the monopoly of the traditional utilitarian benchmark of income or GDP per capita. In 1990, the United Nations Development Programme launched its Human Development Index as part of its Development Report which combines GDP growth with life expectancy and a number of educational measures. This was largely the brainchild of the economist and former Pakistani finance minister Mahbub ul Haq. This index has now been expanded to look at a whole series of other measures such as gender equality and environmental degradation across nearly 200 countries.

In 2008, President Sarkozy of France invited Joseph Stiglitz, Amartya Sen and Jean Paul Fitoussi to assess the limits of GDP as an indicator and to consider what other factors might be required to assess social progress. The report proposed that the way in which the economy is measured ought to take into account people's well-being. The recommendations suggested to focus on income and consumption rather than production, and to emphasize the household sector which can perform differently to national data. In addition, the report recommended that the distribution of income, consumption and wealth be considered, and to broaden measures to non-market activities. These include health, education, governance, political voice as well as environmental and sustainable factors.

One of the direct outputs of this report was the OECD Better Life Index that was initially published in 2011. This index combines a mixture of quality-of-life measures and material conditions to assess well-being, and was an input into the first national well-being budget instigated by New Zealand. The 2019 New Zealand budget referenced over 60 measures, although these were reduced to five priorities cutting across mental health, child poverty, addressing Maori inequalities as well as a focus on digital development and a low-emission economy.

Despite the rhetoric of the budget, it is not clear whether this signals a new approach to public policy beyond traditional redistribution and the desire to increase the rate of policy intervention in new areas. While redistribution will provide some respite for low-income groups, it doesn't necessarily address the concerns with regards to initial allocations and power relations. In addition, the desire to increase policy interventions into well-being also appears to ignore the fact that many policy recommendations are unlikely to work. Particularly as the objective of well-being may be subject to change and be distinct for different groups of people. Modern society is highly complex and diagnosing the underlying problem and proposing solutions that do not affect other variables is often outside the scope of our knowledge.

Crucially, if well-being is to replace Bentham's felicific calculus, it must be able to systematically prioritize between competing policies and neither the OECD index nor the New Zealand budget appears to have developed a systematic way to do this. For example, while mental health was prioritized in the New Zealand budget, the lack of resources for affordable housing and to address deficiencies in the education system (Aotearoa Report, 2019) may negatively affect the same mental health issues the budget has prioritized. In addition, while the budget recognizes the importance that everyone should benefit from growth, it is not clear what the impact of lower or negative growth might mean if well-being policies are prioritized instead.

Despite these challenging and mostly unanswered questions, organizations and national statistical offices continue to generate new metrics for public policy including measuring environmental factors, happiness, poverty, inequality or welfare benchmarks. One important point to note is that although GDP does not measure welfare directly, according to Coyle, it is highly correlated with things that definitely do affect our well-being, such as life expectancy and infant mortality (Coyle, 2014: 117). This may well be another reason why Bentham's felicific calculus based on income per capita has lasted so long.

While there is a broad recognition of the underlying challenges of utilitarianism and the ongoing legitimation of liberal societies, public policy is still trying to come to terms with what might be able to realistically take its place. The conflict between utilitarianism and the principles of liberty and equality suggest that a new moral foundation for liberalism is both desirable and necessary.

Despite these weaknesses, until an alternative system is in place, there is little value for public policymakers to discard the utilitarian system of welfare economics given that it provides them with a simple and systematic method to resolve conflicting policies and priorities.

One lesser-explored alternative is to instead reject the utilitarian framework with its focus on optimizing outcomes based on a set of initial conditions, and replace it with an end-state alternative. This is precisely what Rowley and Peacock suggested in their critique of welfare economics, proposing to use freedom as an end-state alternative for an alternative ethical framework. In their view the major threat to freedom stems from concentrations of political and economic power, which if sustained over lengthy time periods are a potential source of danger to liberalism. Hence, public policy should attempt to minimize the degree of coercion by individuals over others which is contrary to the positions proposed by Rawls and Buchanan (Rowley & Peacock, 1975: 90, 152, 157). Despite this interesting line of argument, there was little technical detail on how this might be achieved beyond using the Herfindahl index for competition policy and reducing the overbearing power of unions.

The idea of breaking up concentrations of power as a central tenet of an alternative liberal ideology initially developed in the US and Germany during the 1930s when liberalism last experienced a major crisis. The arguments focused on how concentrations of power had negatively impacted the fundamental ideas of freedom and equality. These ideas not only harked back to the writings of John Locke and Adam Smith, but were also anti-utilitarian and anti-rationalist in nature as they sought to take account of culture.

During the 1930s there was a dawning realization by these thinkers that neither classical nor social liberalism was able to sustain a polity based on freedom and equality. This led to the emergence of a new strand of thinking which at the time was labelled as both positive liberalism and neoliberalism.[7] Thus, the original ideas behind positive liberalism or neoliberalism were quite distinct to the ideas of classical and social liberalism. By the 1980s the term neoliberalism had become increasingly associated with the Washington Consensus of free markets, deregulation, tax cuts and privatization, which can be understood as a version of classical liberalism (Reinhoudt & Audier, 2018: 4). It is this version of liberalism that has been the subject of so much analysis and criticism.

The net result of the widespread criticism of the modern neoliberal system as a branch of classical liberalism is that the initial thinking behind positive liberal ideas from the 1930s has been largely ignored. But this tradition did develop a distinct set of ideas to both social and classical liberalism. While some headway was made in the US, it was mostly German liberalism that continued to develop this strand, which subsequently has been labelled as ordoliberalism.

While ordoliberalism has become something of a broad church sharing a number of ideas with neoliberalism (Dyson, 2021), one of its most distinctive and unique contributions to liberal thought is the view that the dispersal of public and private power was an alternative end-state. Crucially, an end state that could potentially resolve competing claims between freedom and equality resembling Locke's idea, where no one ought to have power over another. This strand of liberalism should not be seen as a middle way between markets and the state, but rather as a separate, independent framework. Hence, further exploration of this strand of liberalism may provide an alternative public policy framework to the current utilitarian outlook.

3

The Rise of Ordo

The Lippmann Colloquium and the Chicago attack on power

The Paris office of the International Institute of Intellectual Cooperation (IIIC) was inaugurated in the Montpensier wing of the Palais Royal in Paris in 1926. The IIIC was an advisory organization for the League of Nations which fostered international exchange between scientists, artists and intellectuals. The Palais Royal built by Cardinal Richelieu and noted for its splendour, hosted an event to discuss the failings of liberalism in 1938. This has subsequently come to be known as the Lippmann Colloquium.

The five-day meeting chaired by the French philosopher Louis Rougier was to discuss Walter Lippmann's new book *The Good Society*. Among the 26 attendees were Friedrich Hayek and Ludwig Von Mises from Austria along with Wilhelm Röpke and Alexander Rüstow from Germany – all of whom were now in exile.

The Lippmann Colloquium provides an insight into a potential alternative form of liberalism: a view that was sceptical of the market, constant state intervention and of a utilitarian calculus. This chapter explores the development of these ideas in the US, and in Germany where they developed further including a focus on the role of the community and the environment. Central to the German ordoliberal movement was to create rules that eliminated concentrations of power, thereby improving upon initial conditions prior to voluntary exchange.

The Good Society launched an attack on the collectivist shift in social liberalism. During the Great Depression, President Roosevelt had argued his interventions were necessary to save capitalism and democracy. This led to the National Industrial Recovery Act which created the Public Works Administration and also introduced price and wage fixing. In France, price controls had been introduced as part of the Matignon Agreements in an attempt to end strikes by increasing real wages in addition to a programme of nationalization. The British government towards the end of the 1930s began to pursue a policy of cartelization in an attempt to bring scale to industry in the belief this would drive up productivity.

Alongside his attack on social liberalism, Lippmann asked the question why classical liberalism had failed so spectacularly. He thought that classical liberalism was just not sustainable and would eventually lead society to react with a shift towards collectivism. He noted that the immediate response to any disorder or misery was to attempt to resolve the issue through more compulsory organization. 'The big businessmen argue that if they have their own way they will make the country prosperous; the fascists that they will make their people strong and glorious; the socialists that they will plan and provide for the welfare of all' (Lippmann, 1938: 331). According to all these groups, the ends justified the means.

Lippmann thought this approach to solving economic and social challenges was delusional given the infinite complexity of human affairs and the limited capacity of officials. Instead he urged policymakers to look at the underlying legal rights and duties of individuals to ascertain whether there was an existing bias in the system.

While Lippmann's attack on collectivism was unsurprisingly well received at the Colloquium, his argument against classical liberalism was not unanimously supported. Lippmann thought that classical liberalism was incapable of guiding public policy, and the idea that any aspect of the market economy is unregulated by law was a major error. Lippmann emphasized that it is not the case that under laissez-faire, markets are as good as they might be. These ideas were also raised by Karl Polanyi in *The Great Transformation* nearly a decade later who noted that all economic activity is governed by law.

Lippmann's summary of the crisis of liberalism was that citizens were 'asked to choose between the liberals who came to a dead stop ... on the right road up to wealth and freedom and justice, and the collectivists who are in furious movement but on a road that leads down to the abyss of tyranny, impoverishment, and general war' (Lippmann, 1938: 204). He thought that liberals' task was to carry on in the tradition of Adam Smith by criticizing the status quo and develop principles enabling institutions to adapt to the industrial revolution.

For Lippmann, such reforms had to strike at the various kinds of monopoly that led to maldistribution through unearned income. Lippmann stressed that any reform had to be corrected at the source by attacking monopoly and privilege.

> A mere levelling of incomes by taking from the rich and giving doles to the poor would defeat itself and would merely paralyze and impoverish the whole economy. The equalization must be effected by measures which promote the efficiency of the markets as regulators of the division

of labor; they must strike, therefore, not at the profits of successful competition but at the tolls of monopoly. (Lippmann, 1938: 227)

Using the example of private property rights, Lippmann noted that private land tenure which happens to prevail at one moment in a country is not the only possible system of land tenure. The landowner has no absolute rights to appropriate the monopoly rent of the land, but rather conditional rights. Critically, for the legitimacy of the liberal order unearned increments should be expropriated. Indeed, he thought if nothing were done to expropriate unearned increments then society would break down with the dispossessed and disinherited arousing the revolutionary impulse to abolish all their rights. 'It is not loyalty to the cause of private property to confirm the monopolists in their privileges. To do that is to prepare the extinction of private property either by general disorder and pillage or by the establishment of an administered collectivism' (Lippmann, 1938: 277).

Lippmann also attempted to tackle the legitimation issues that arise from the global expansion of trade. He thought that liberals had been too complacent in accepting the human costs of industrial progress when industries relocate halfway around the world (Lippmann, 1938: 223). Lippmann saw no reason why a free society should be indifferent to the human costs, suggesting that a tax could be levied that insured workers against their personal losses as a result of the progress of industry. If society as a whole is richer when an industry moves from a place where costs are high to one where they are lower, then some part of that increased wealth can be used to relieve the victims of progress, to re-educate them for new occupations, or to settle them in new places if they have to move.

The nature of the debate following Lippmann's speech clearly highlighted the emerging chasm between the classical or Manchester liberals (following William Cobden) headed by Von Mises and the larger group who saw a role for positive liberalism. The positive liberals argued that the market was not a spontaneous order but rather a function of a legal order, therefore the idea of removing obstacles made little sense. Hence, for Röpke and Rüstow the state needed to be strong and impartial to guarantee the efficient functioning of markets, the price mechanism and competition to prevent the state being highjacked by dominant interest groups. A legal order therefore needs to adapt as society changes (Reinhoudt & Audier, 2018: 31, 98–9).

The Colloquium attendees were mostly in agreement that the tendency towards economic concentration leads to arbitrary behaviours of the price mechanism. Moreover, the lack of intervention at the level of power relations meant that liberalism had become a philosophy of neglect, falling into passivity and refusing to proceed with social adaptation (Reinhoudt & Audier, 2018: 15). Mises, however, disagreed arguing that this was because of the state intervening in the first place.

The issue of identity and rationality was raised by Rougier who thought the enlightenment view of rational man within liberalism was flawed as passion causes man to follow illiberal movements. Röpke also emphasized the importance of social and spiritual integration indicating that Bentham's calculation engine could not suffice as a foundation of liberalism. Rüstow attacked utilitarianism arguing that 'the most important economic social task is to give to the economy such a form not that it provides to the greatest possible number of the men the highest possible income but a living situation that is as satisfying as possible' (Reinhoudt & Audier, 2018: 158).

The Lippmann Colloquium raised the possibility of liberalism forging a new path. A path that recognized the limitations of a rational society and accepted that those with power distorted the price mechanism to generate unearned income. This required the state to intervene at the source of monopoly and privilege, rather than focusing on redistribution.

This approach was a return to the ideas of Adam Smith and commutative justice, where the object was to create a society of equal individuals requiring less redistribution. Smith thought that justice was the most important of the virtues, which he defined as 'abstaining from what is anothers' (Smith, 1982: 273). Thomas Paine was also dismissive of distributive justice, which he thought would merely maintain an existing elitist system in place (Paine, 1894: Vol II, 205). Instead of maximizing utility, what mattered more was the equality of conditions prior to voluntary exchange. Indeed, Smith had argued that people will usually wish to live in a society in which other people are not grossly oppressed or deprived (Rothschild, 2002: 156).

These ideas had begun to be explored by Frank Knight and Henry Simons in Chicago in the early 1930s. Knight positively reviewed *The Good Society* (Knight, 1938), although he thought Lippmann had been insufficiently critical of laissez-faire, and far too optimistic on the success of intervention due to the complexity of the economic and social system (Burgin, 2012: 62).

Knight argued that although laissez-faire or complete economic freedom had been advocated by bright and idealistic people, it was essentially indefensible and rarely resulted in free competition (Knight, 1967; Knight, 1982). Indeed, Knight thought that the market fundamentalists were negatively impacting the cause of liberty by going to extremes. Knight was probably referring to Ludwig Von Mises, whose work he found 'slightly impatient and dogmatic and often simply contrary to fact' while his colleague Jacob Viner referred to Mises' later work as 'eccentric or crank economics' (Burgin, 2012: 33).

Unrestrained markets tend to create unsustainable inequalities in the distribution of power, hence Knight thought a social system that prioritized the market above all else would become imbalanced and prone to collapse (Burgin, 2012: 36, 118). Although Knight argued that economics could improve the lot of man, he was doubtful that it would be able to resolve social issues. He thought that the most potent agency of social control was an individual's sense of decency and the pressure of opinion, akin to Smith's ideas of virtue and approbation. But Knight accepted that as the market was not able to resolve social issues, there was a clear role for the state to step in. The challenge was that the complexity of the economy and its inherent uncertainty constrained the ability of the state to successfully implement policy. This was also why Knight did not believe there was a general tendency towards equilibrium (Knight, 1923; Emmett, 2009: 67).

Knight also noted that economists have been notoriously afflicted with a naively utilitarian, rationalistic and individualistic bias. (Knight, 1982: 305). This utilitarian doctrine according to Knight had a fatal defect in that it confused freedom and power, hence voluntary exchange as described by the two welfare theorems cannot maximize freedom. For Knight, 'Everything depends ... on what individuals bring to the exchange ... Historically viewed, the significance of the doctrine is to justify inequality, and the project is a failure' (Knight, 1929). Knight argued that utilitarianism merely provided a reason for the majority to dispossess and exploit the rest of society at their pleasure, hence the maximization of happiness overrides individual liberty.

For Knight, freedom to act requires the subject to be in possession of the requisite means of action, and that means power. Voluntary exchange per se cannot be the solution as it only reflects the original allocation and therefore sanctifies the status quo. Knight concludes that the equal right to use unequal power is not equality (Knight, 1982: 8, 87). In addition, Knight thought that liberty had to take precedent over any notion of efficiency which in the production of goods might require an increased concentration. But any such concentration of power violates the principle of equality of opportunity (Knight, 1923).

Tackling the issue of unequal power thus began to take centre stage for this new strand of liberal thinking with Knight concluding that:

> the amount and kind of economic power possessed by any person *now* depends largely on the amount and kind he possessed *last year*. For economic power is used not merely to produce satisfaction-yielding goods, but also through investment in capital or personal training to multiply itself. The important point is the powerful tendency for inequality to increase cumulatively, compounding at an enormous rate. For the more wealth or income-producing capacity one possesses the easier it is to invest not merely the same but an increasing fraction of the yield. (Knight, 1929)

The notion that liberty could be attained by a policy programme that attempted to equalize power relations prior to voluntary exchange began to be sketched out in 1934 by Henry Simons. Despite its title, *A Positive*

Programme for Laissez-Faire, the programme was firmly interventionist albeit in a specific way. Although Simons thought that the real enemies of liberty were those who advocated centralized planning, he accepted that both types of liberals, 'must agree on one vital point, namely that there is now imperative need for a sound, positive program of economic legislation' (Simons, 1934: 2).

Simons attempted to recast laissez-faire as the maintenance of an institutional framework within which the price mechanism and competition can function effectively. This required the state to take on a number of responsibilities including, 'the maintenance of competitive conditions in industry, the control of the currency ... the defence of the institution of property ... not to mention the many social-welfare activities' (Simons, 1934: 3). For Simons what mattered was the type of intervention, and he remained firmly opposed to political interference in relative prices which he thought was one of the great errors of economic policy. For Simons, political liberty could survive only within an effectively competitive economic system.

Simons famously stated that 'the great enemy of democracy is monopoly, in all its forms: gigantic corporations, trade associations and other agencies for price control, trade unions – or, in general, organization and concentration of power within functional classes. Effectively organized functional groups possess tremendous power for exploiting the community at large and even for sabotaging the system' (Simons, 1934: 4). Simons opposed all and any concentration of power.

Crucially, the concentration of power has a negative effect on justice as the distribution of power is at least as important as the distribution of economic goods or income. Hence, Simons argued that justice would be better served if well-intentioned reformers would reflect seriously on what their schemes imply with respect to the distribution of power. For Simons this meant that policy needed to focus on conditions prior to exchange rather than redistributing goods after the event. While this required a focus on commutative rather than distributive justice, Simons was critical of the laissez-faire view of commutative justice which simply took for granted an existing distribution of capital among persons, families, communities, regions and nations (Simons, 1948: 5).

Simons followed Smith's argument on commutative justice that government restrictions and monopolies interfere with exchange resulting in people not being able to claim what is rightfully theirs. Hence, for market participants to abstain from what is anothers, they cannot justly generate returns from monopoly profits. Smith also noted that the sovereign ought to provide society with the key building blocks of education and infrastructure which improve the equalization of initial allocations enabling improved outcomes through the process of exchange. This required a system of public finance to raise money from citizens which Smith made clear ought to be progressive.

'It is not very unreasonable that the rich should contribute to the public expense, not only in proportion to their revenue, but something more than in that proportion' (Smith, 1904: Vol II, 269). Simons following Smith thought that progressive taxation was an effective means of addressing unequal power relations by preventing the monopolization of wealth and income. Crucially, Simons argued that the drastic reduction of inequality through taxation is attainable without much loss of efficiency in the system, and without much impairing of the attractiveness of the economic game.

Simons thought that the equality of opportunity was an ideal that free societies should constantly pursue, even at the cost in terms of other ends. Freedom without power, like power without freedom, has no substance or meaning. The practical problem of freedom was therefore one of dispersing or redistributing power among organizations. This redistribution of power is central to tackling the issue of inequality which is overwhelmingly a problem of investment in human capacity, that is in health, education and skills, which can hardly be scratched by redistributions of wealth (Simons, 1948: 6–7).

Simons' policy prescriptions to improve commutative justice outcomes are radical, even by today's standards. Their premise was based on improving the conditions within which the individual can thrive. He advocated the elimination of private monopoly in all its forms using drastic measures to establish and maintain competitive conditions in industries where competition can function. For Simons effective competition was indispensable for the dispersion of power within industries and functional groups.

He thought that few gigantic corporations could be defended based on the argument that their present size is necessary for reasonable full exploitation of production economies. To this end he advocated for the Federal Trade Commission (FTC) to become the most powerful state organization to prevent corporations from exploiting monopoly power. 'If we dislike extreme inequality of power, it is appropriate to view with especial misgivings the extension of political (and monopoly) control over relative prices and incomes' (Simons, 1934: 12). This is why Simons thought collectivism was, 'a name for an extreme form of governmental centralization or power concentration' (Simons, 1948: 22). In essence, capitalist systems where large corporations dominate should be seen as collectivist.

In areas where competition could not be made to function effectively, Simons thought there ought to be a gradual transition to direct government ownership. Horizontal combinations should be prohibited; and vertical combinations should be permitted *only* so far as is clearly compatible with the maintenance *of* real competition.

While Simons and Knight are often thought of as being members of the Chicago School, their attitude to laissez-faire placed them in direct conflict with the post-war Chicago's school restatement of classical liberalism. Indeed, Knight, Viner and Simons were all accused of advocating collectivist ideas

(Burgin, 2012: 41). Coase noted that Simons' positive programme for laissez-faire was a highly interventionist pamphlet including the proposal to nationalize utilities. Furthermore, when Friedman reread the pamphlet later in his career he was astounded as he thought it had been strongly pro-free market in orientation. Delong sums up the post-war Chicago school's view of Simons who 'had some libertarian intuitions, but he also had many "interventionist" failings' (Delong, 1990).

The short-lived revival of the foundational ideas of freedom and equality during the 1930s did not develop further in the Anglo-Saxon world. Indeed, by the 1960s, it had largely been superseded by the Chicago's school restatement of classical liberalism. Hayek had initially been sympathetic towards this interventionist approach and in *The Road to Serfdom* largely restated Lippmann's attack on laissez-faire noting that the liberal argument is not to leave things as they are but, 'of making the best possible use of the forces of competition' (Hayek, 1994: 41). This requires the state to interfere in many areas to preserve competition such as limiting working hours or require certain sanitary arrangements. Hayek also thought that such a competitive system needs to be intelligently designed with a continuously adjusted legal framework (Hayek, 1994: 43, 45). However, Hayek subsequently rejected this approach in the latter part of his career (Kolev, 2010).

A recent book on the Mont Pelerin Society founded by Hayek in 1947 highlights the initial split between the classical liberals and the interventionist positive liberals that opposed power concentrations. This split resolved itself in 1960 when the positive liberals left claiming the Society had conflated private enterprise with individual liberty. The onset of the Cold War and the relative success of the Soviet Union appeared to have hardened the attitude of many liberals, thus the Mont Pelerin Society became increasingly identified with an anti-communist laissez-faire ideology (Burgin, 2012: 107, 150).

The publication of *The Constitution of Liberty* marked the beginning of Hayek's conversion away from his earlier ideas of positive interventionism. He argued that any attempt by society to deliberately build civilization stems from an erroneous intellectualism that regards human reason as something standing outside nature and possessed of knowledge and reasoning capacity independent of experience. Instead a spontaneous order described the development of freedom, which was the outcome of individual voluntarist actions (Hayek, 1960: 75). Hayek also hit back at Knight's criticism on the need for effective power arguing that confusing liberty with power inevitably leads to the identification of liberty with wealth, which merely results in liberty being used to support a redistribution of wealth.

By the 1970s, Hayek had shifted his focus to the nature of common law which he thought would naturally reflect the view of society through time. Hayek did not countenance that any bias could creep into the common law system as long as there was equality of general rules of law. He had previously set out that this was the only kind of equality conducive to liberty and the only equality which we can secure without destroying liberty (Hayek, 1960: 148).

Friedman's restatement of classical liberalism in 1962 argued that government assistance via tariffs, tax legislation and legislation with respect to labour disputes and the licensing of professions merely institutes monopoly power. He remained unconcerned about the inequality of income because he thought it was merely an outcome of individuals making the most of their initial equality. He also refuted the argument that inequalities arising from inherited wealth can be distinguished from those arising out of merit. As far as he was concerned all outcomes are a result of the individual's will. Friedman saw almost no positive role for the state arguing that the market could resolve all information and coordination issues. Indeed, he concluded that the government's lack of knowledge meant that private monopolies were better than a public monopoly or public regulation. From this view followed the idea that collusion and cartels didn't matter either as they were generally unstable and brief in duration (Friedman, 1962: 111).

This was supported by Aaron Director, Friedman's brother-in-law, who taught in the law school at the University of Chicago. Director opined that 'as with monopoly, the competitive forces would control corporations and ensure they approximated the ideal of competition'. This even applied to large corporations that gained their size via vertical or horizontal mergers. 'Since economic theory demonstrates that the presence of monopoly is much more often alleged than confirmed … less rather than more regulation ought to be prescribed' (Mirowski & Plehwe, 2009: 218, 220). This shift in thinking about monopoly and intervention was synthesized by Robert Bork in his book *The Anti-trust Paradox* published in 1978. The book argued that consumer welfare ought to be the main thrust of antitrust policy, which should not interfere with any firm of any size that was created by internal growth as the high probability is that any such interference will lead to a net loss in consumer welfare (Bork, 1993: 178, 405). Consumer welfare refers to the individual benefits derived from the consumption of goods and services based on individual preferences.[1]

Despite the withering of this new form of interventionist liberalism in the Anglo-Saxon world in the post-war period, these ideas developed in parallel in Germany in the 1930s.[2]

Against state planning, laissez–faire and utilitarianism

Freiburg University was one of the few places where liberalism was kept alive during the Third Reich by the economist Walter Eucken and the jurist Franz Böhm. Along with Alexander Rüstow and Wilhelm Röpke who both went in to exile in 1933, these four thinkers are most associated with the ordoliberal movement. Ordoliberalism is a broad church of ideas, although since the eurozone crisis it has tended to be labelled as a German ideology promoting austerity across eurozone countries so that they live within their means (Blyth, 2013: 143). But this is not an accurate reflection of the movement.

One of its important distinguishing features during its formative years was the focus on how one might alter power relations to improve the equality of initial conditions prior to voluntary exchange. In 1932, just as unemployment was hitting 30 per cent, a conference in Dresden was held entitled *Germany and the Global Crisis*. Most of the speakers emphasized the ongoing challenges of unemployment, deflation and investment, which to a certain extent were clouded by a sense of Marxian determinism. The global economy seemed to have reached a certain point from which it appeared almost impossible to extricate itself from. The speech by Alexander Rüstow took a rather different trajectory. Rather than focusing on economic variables, he spoke about the structure of the economy and society. Rüstow thought that the current crisis was largely caused by persistent intervention and subsidy by the public authorities (Boese, 1932: 62). Rüstow argued that the underlying structure of society needed to be altered rather than to pursue continuous intervention, which he thought was hopeless just like a screw without an end.

Rüstow stated that he was not against the market, but he made it clear that Manchester (classical) liberalism merely resulted in poverty. Of particular concern for Rüstow was a weak state, which he thought was merely prey for the most powerful groups in a pluralist society which was unable to withstand the onslaught of these vested interests (Boese, 1932: 66). Unless the state was strong enough to dissipate market power, spontaneously developed rules will merely reflect the will of those with market power and impair the political system (Labrousse & Weisz, 2001: 206).

Rüstow believed that the state needed to be above economics and vested interests. But for this to work it required the state to guarantee market freedom and fair competition, with rules of the game that work for everyone. A weak state merely enables the private concentration of power, which, through interest groups, threatens individual freedoms (Boese, 1932: 67).

The backdrop of the end of the Weimar Republic loomed large in Rüstow's thinking demonstrating the negative effect that this kind of pluralism was having on society. In many respects Rüstow's reflections on the state as prey by vested interests are increasingly relevant to the challenges faced by a number of advanced industrial societies today. Thomas Philippon in *The Great Reversal* provides a bleak assessment of the contemporary US economy in relation the effects of lobbying (Philippon, 2019). Recent evidence from the UK on the lack of a competitive tender process for more than £10 bn of personal protective equipment contracts (National Audit Office, 2020) has led to a growing criticism of cronyism with contracts being awarded to those connected to the ruling Conservative Party.

In 1933, Rüstow went into exile and took up a teaching position at the University of Istanbul, while continuing to develop an alternative to classical and social liberalism. These ideas in particular drew heavily on the work of Adam Smith. Indeed, the ordoliberals argued their ideas were the natural development of Smith's work. Their concept of *Ordnungspolitik* described how one might create the necessary conditions under which the invisible hand can do its work (Bonefeld, 2017: 70) thereby generating a positive outcome for society as a whole.

Smith's view that competition was a prerequisite to attain the common good, was central to the ordoliberals thinking as was the notion that self-evident moral issues constrained pure self-interest (Maier Rigaud & Maier Rigaud, 2001: 93). Rüstow thought the arguments of laissez-faire were based more on theological metaphysics than observation, (Rüstow, 2009: 183) as in the eyes of its supporters the market could do no wrong. This theological approach rejected every human intervention in the divine spontaneity of the free economy as sacrilege. But the dogma that all state intervention should be prohibited led to disastrous consequences and the onset of collectivism (Maier Rigaud & Maier Rigaud, 2001:112).

The notion that Smith's view of liberty was merely about the removal of restraints was also not the case. For example, Smith argued for compulsion when it came to education which can be understood as the need to improve power relations. 'For a very small expense the public can facilitate, can encourage and can even *impose* upon almost the whole body of the people the necessity of acquiring these most essential parts of education' (Smith, 1904: Vol II, 220). Furthermore, Smith thought that the public can require every man to undergo an examination to ensure he is fit for the workplace.

Rüstow believed that unbridled competition merely left workers and their families starving once there was no demand for their labour. This unsurprisingly led to a reaction by unions and firms to seek monopoly control to manage this insecurity (Rüstow, 1949: 116–17). But this tendency towards a more planned economy had implications for the nature of freedom itself, which Rüstow thought was fundamentally undemocratic. Hence, neither Manchester liberalism nor state planning could provide the framework for a free society within which individuals could develop and thrive.

These ideas were also developed by Rüstow's colleague and fellow exile from Nazi Germany, Wilhelm Röpke. Röpke followed Rüstow to Istanbul before moving to Switzerland which became influential on his thinking of what constituted a free society. Röpke in his landmark work, *The Social Crisis of Our Time*, argued against the libertarian fanatic, the apostle of equality and the utilitarian calculus – based on men's rational behaviour (Röpke,

1950: 49). For Röpke, all of these constructs were contrary to human nature and therefore were not sustainable.

Röpke noted that the remnants of the feudal system were responsible for differences in income, capital and power, which allowed a corresponding agglomeration of enterprises and factories paving the way for corporate capitalism distinguished by giant enterprises and monopolies. This in turn, he thought, had burdened the market economy 'with an unjust odium under which property won by honest work and faithful service also has to suffer' (Röpke, 1950: 116).

These feudal remnants could be seen in land holdings, monopoly concessions, subsidies and other unclean sources of great fortunes, where powerful forces prey on the state to ensure that the rules are written for their benefit. These sentiments are increasingly echoed today with economists arguing that the rules of the game are inherently biased towards those with power (Stiglitz, 2015). These sources also include those who have gotten their gains illegally. In the UK alone it is estimated that the proceeds of money laundering potentially runs into the hundreds of billions of pounds (Treasury Committee, 2019). For Röpke, the problem was that there was no ethical, legal and institutional framework corresponding to the principles of the market system to enforce and remove these systematic biases.

As a result, Röpke thought that all arguments in favour of monopoly must always be dismissed, particularly those using prices as a benchmark. Röpke gives the example that the monopolistic concentration of the press may make newspapers much cheaper; however, the cheapest of all would be the single paper of the totalitarian state. For Röpke, the list of sins of monopoly are wide ranging including:

> privileges, exploitation, rigidity of the market, the distortion of the economic process, the blocking of capital, the concentration of power, industrial feudalism, the restriction of supply and production, the creation of chronic unemployment, the rise in living costs and the widening of social differences, lack of economic discipline, the uncontrollable pressure on state and public opinion, the transformation of industry into an exclusive club which refuses to accept any new members. (Röpke, 1950: 229–30)

Röpke's approach was sharply in contrast to the utilitarian ideas of welfare economics that pervades antitrust thinking today such as the policies expounded by Bork where the consumer and low prices remain at the heart of decisions. Rather than focusing on the concept of utility, the ordoliberal emphasis was on the dispersion of power, which in turn caused them to focus on the underlying legal relations. This further suggests the closeness of links with Adam Smith whose theory of government was founded on jurisprudence (Smith, 1896).

The approach of linking economics with law gave the ordoliberal movement a somewhat more practical focus to complement the broader policy ideas emanating from the pens of Knight, Simons and Lippmann. This approach was particularly associated with the jurist Franz Böhm. Unlike Rüstow and Röpke, Böhm remained in Nazi Germany and had been a vocal critic of cartel behaviour during the Weimar Republic. His book published in 1933 on competition and monopoly power detailed his concerns based on his experience working in the Economics Ministry up until 1931. Böhm's approach was closely aligned with Smith's philosophy of the impartial spectator where an exchange economy is based on equitable rules (Mestmäcker in Böhm, 1933: 10) rather than a utilitarian outlook based on self-love.

In his essay on the freedom from cartels and freedom of competition, Böhm argued that a society must choose as a point of principle within law between the freedom of competition as opposed to the freedom to contract which may subvert the very nature of free competition (Böhm, 1958: 203). In essence, a liberal society must limit the freedom of individuals to pervert the course of the economy through growing market power. It is the nature of the free market price mechanism itself that creates freedom; hence, any attempt to undermine this mechanism subverts freedom.

Böhm argued that 'in the market economy ... it is possible to make a source of income out of cheating ... by deliberately abusing their private autonomy whether in the disreputable form of unfair competition, usury and fraud, or ... by forming cartels' (Peacock & Willgerodt, 1989b: 64). Böhm also noted that it was much more effective for interest groups to elevate cheating to a legislative or governmental programme. A classical liberal system, therefore, results in a tendency towards cartels and monopolistic behaviour as well as rising calls for redistribution due to the failure of commutative justice. Hence, when private power grows too large, the invisible hand does not create harmony (Peacock & Willgerodt, 1989a: 22).

The logic of this argument is that Hayek's spontaneous order also moves society on a road to serfdom because the private concentration of power destroys liberalism, encouraging populism, fascism and socialism. In essence, where private power is abused, the outcome is no longer in the public interest (Koslowski, 2000: 157). Freedom for the ordoliberals triumphs over efficiency. Such an approach clearly leaves very little room for welfare economics and utilitarianism with regards to the practice of public policy.

Böhm's concept of competition is where the individual and public interest align, which had to be achieved through the dissipation of power. This dissipation of market power also enables individuals to enter into voluntary exchange based on the idea of the equalization of legal rights. Hence, an ordoliberal system is one that enables the maximum fulfilment of individuals' spontaneous plans, which are constrained by the fact that individuals are not able to abuse private power (Böhm, 1950).

Furthermore, private market power not only reduces the freedom of the many in favour of domination by the few in an economic system, but it also penetrates and impairs the political system. Private market power is regarded as an evil not only because it cripples the price mechanism and its allocative potential, but also because it allows infringements of the liberty of others. In essence, the role of competition goes beyond economic importance; it also has the power to curb unequal power relations in society (Labrousse & Weisz, 2001: 208). Organized competition was not considered the ultimate end but rather a means to the solution of social problems (Megay, 1970).

To achieve this requires the state to come into conflict with those who have been able to increase their market power to restore freedom. But this can only be achieved by applying the theory of the market economy to policy areas rather than an approach that is based on managing the economy centrally. This requires the elimination of all privileges and hindrances to competition as it is only by focusing on these privileges and hindrances to competition that positions of power can be undermined. This in turn requires the legal system to function accordingly. For Böhm, no member of society must be restricted and none may have more powers than those vested with private autonomy. He further clarified that 'within society itself no power groups should be formed which would make it possible for others, individually or as groups, to be subjugated and exploited. The populace should be protected against this danger by the system of price competition' (Peacock & Willgerodt, 1989b: 58).

Hence, for Bohm, unregulated power is incompatible with a dominion-free social order. To attain freedom, therefore, requires individual laws to disperse power, thereby bringing an end to the concept of *Herrschaftsordnung* or the order of the dominion of elites over others (Böhm, 1933: 135, 137, 139). But it wasn't just private power that was of concern; Böhm had numerous reservations on the centralization of public power too.

While compulsion and the domination of centralized power might be required for war, Böhm was clear that it demoralized the human spirit and its corresponding communal structures. To enable freedom requires local communities to have the courage and inner strength to embrace decentralization which can purge the dangers to individual liberty. What mattered was to create a society of groups working together within the nation where:

> A central body maintained the authority to intervene using force, but to make use of this power only where vital interests are at stake …

In all other cases however, the rules should be relaxed wherever the innate strength of a bottom up approach is better suited to the tasks of social life than ministerial decree or the imposition of law. (Böhm, 1933: 158 – author translation)

Böhm's analysis on the relationship between law and economics was complemented by Eucken's attack on the neoclassical school of economics. Eucken noted that modern industrial economies were all quite different due to their unique institutional structures which affected the way an economy operated. Hence, the idea of modelling an economy was merely simplifying a highly complex system and therefore remote from economic reality.

This approach resulted in Eucken arguing that the problem of the structure of economic systems is not a quantitative one. Eucken thought that 'economic life does not consist of quantities, but of various kinds of purposive activities. An economist who thinks in quantities is said to be thinking "like a natural scientist", or "materialist", and to be failing to understand the historical aspect of economic life and that economics is a "moral" science' (Eucken, 1950: 295).

Eucken's insight along with his fellow ordoliberals was that the modern industrial world does not of itself produce an effective economic system but demands specific controlling constitutional principles as a foundation. This requires the price mechanism to be assessed as to whether it is being distorted, and if so, enforce rules to remove those distortions. With regards to competition, Eucken argued that distortions can be detected if a supplier or consumer generates a plan based on the effect of that distortion. Although the enforcement of competition remained a key ordoliberal principle, the development and enforcement of constitutional rules might be required to address a whole variety of issues including property rights, patents, monetary policy and international trade.

For Eucken, unregulated markets tend to restrict or eliminate competition which is the cause of instability of the system (Chaloupek, 2015). The social question is therefore not related to excessive competition but rather a lack of competition. Hence, Eucken's main target is to minimize power in politics and abolish it in the economy (Koslowski, 2000: 116, 249). Full competition is therefore not about efficiency but rather the absence of coercive power preventing one individual gaining an advantage due to the bias in the initial allocation.

Despite this focus on economics and the functioning of the price mechanism, the ordoliberals were highly sceptical that wealth alone was sufficient to legitimate a society. Of particular concern was how to revive a feeling of community that industrial society had torn away from humanity. This may have been the influence of German romanticism coming through, and perhaps like Isaiah Berlin, they thought that romanticism was much closer to what it was that moved human beings rather than any universal rational plan. The focus on taming power would appear to be an appropriate course of action, given the downside of romanticism is the unpredictable nature of the human will. Hence, by minimizing the power of each human will, a society might be spared the worst of an unpredictable will's potentially destructive power. This is why Simons thought the great enemy of democracy was monopoly in all its forms.

Massification, *Vitalpolitik* and proto-environmentalism

The ordoliberals did not view the market as contributing to social cohesion. As much as competition was considered to be an indispensable arrangement, it did not facilitate social integration (Zweynert, 2013). Industrialization had led to an increasing concentration of politics and economics that was undermining the social fabric, transforming society into an amorphous mass. Rüstow described this process as 'massification', which he thought was the worst and most common sickness of the times (Hunold, 1957: 215).

Rüstow thought that industrialization was the underlying cause of workers' deep unsatisfaction (Rüstow, 1949: 141). Industrialization broke down the community ties that had bound individuals together and was why many workers turned to socialism and fascism for salvation. These are the very same concerns raised by Deneen in his recent criticism of liberalism. To reverse the process of massification, there has to be a focus on decentralization. For Rüstow, this required local groups to have self-governing powers, rights and responsibilities (Hunold, 1957: 226).

This decentralization is also critical as Smith's ideas of approbation and the restraint of human appetite are less likely to function if local ties are broken. People are far more likely to restrain their excess and respond to the perception of others if they have a stake in that community. The idea that skin in the game is a central component of the legitimation of a free society has also been expounded by the author Nassim Taleb (Taleb, 2018).

Both Rüstow and Röpke believed the solution lay in the decentralization of life and work and the promotion of smaller production and settlement units, which would be created through policies that dispersed political power. For Rüstow this process was key, as economic growth on its own was insufficient to bond society together. There had to be a spiritual element to people's lives to counter policies of a materialist nature. This notion of decentralization is thus distinct to the classical liberal view of the state by thinkers such as Lord Acton who saw federalism as purely a way of limiting power.

This led Rüstow to develop the idea of *Vitalpolitik* which he thought was more important than economic performance. This notion of vitality or enhancing the quality of life was based on creating a life worth living, and if necessary, worth fighting for. But this required the revival of the idea of community, which was based on independence, self-reliance, family solidarity and an economy based on craftsmanship and small firms. The economy is there for the sake of man, not man for the sake of the economy (Maier-Rigaud & Maier-Rigaud, 2001: 143). These issues are beginning to surface in contemporary advanced economies with books such as *The Third Pillar* by Raghuram Rajan (Rajan, 2019), arguing that community is a central pillar of our economic and social structure, and yet it has been largely ignored.

For Rüstow, the process of demassification requires workers to be effectively 'de-proletarianized' so that they see benefit from working with the system rather than trying to overthrow it. The role of *Vitalpolitik* is to ensure that each individual is endowed with sufficient assets and property and has the tools to become self-reliant through the mechanism of entrepreneurship (Bonefeld, 2013a).

Röpke also cautioned that while competition was a necessary social arrangement, it wasn't a social gospel likely to make us enthusiastic. The free market economy, therefore, has to go hand in hand with *Vitalpolitik*, which provides something that is humanly positive (Röpke, 1950: 235). Like Rüstow, Röpke was afflicted by the notion of massification and the effect that industrialization had had on the spirituality of humanity.

> Like pure democracy, undiluted capitalism is intolerable ... Today we have achieved the realization to a great extent unknown to previous generations that men cannot bear without excessive harm to themselves and to society, the constant mental, nervous and moral tension which is forced upon them by an economic system dominated by supply and demand, market and technology, nor can they withstand the insecurity and instability of the living conditions which such a system entails. (Röpke, 1950: 119)

Another key component of *Vitalpolitik* was the importance of nature in living a good life. The ordo mantra of eliminating power concentrations was also applied by Röpke to maintain a balance between economic development and the natural world. This idea has increasing relevance today with regards to the destruction of the biosphere, and the increase in greenhouse gas levels.

For Röpke, massification had been accompanied by the mechanization of productive activity and crucially an estrangement from nature. *Vitalpolitik* instead required individuals to root their lives in nature within their community (Bonefeld, 2013b). Hence, decentralization plays a central role in facilitating a greater interaction between nature and the built environment in contrast to the massification and wasteland of giant cities. Röpke's proto-environmentalism was based on two strands including an attack on environmental destruction as well as the importance of nature for the soul or what he thought it meant to be human.

Röpke references the race between technology and population growth, noting that growth cannot go on indefinitely in relation to the earth's resources, an argument that the Club of Rome would take up in the 1970s. Röpke's argument is, however, not that resources would necessarily run out but that the net result of a continual expanding population projected to be 300 billion in 2300 would completely ravage the natural environment. Indeed, Röpke's attack on such environmental destruction already indicated a shift in power concentration towards humans and away from the stability of the biosphere. For Röpke it was central for humans to treat trees and beasts as equals rather than as materials or machines (Röpke, 1960: 84).

Röpke was, however, acutely aware of the benefits to humanity resulting from the economic revolution noting that 'nobody can seriously wish to put the clock back to the previous stage of development'. But he raised the extremely pertinent question whether humanity is aware of the 'high price that had to be paid for it and that we will continue to have to pay, and we are by no means still certain that the price is not too high' (Röpke, 1950: 47). Röpke concludes by striking at the heart of contemporary economic theory that we must be prepared to consider the point at which the price for the increase in productivity is no longer balanced by its material advantages. The implication is that the pursuit of growth per se therefore cannot be the goal of society.

The logic of Röpke's argument was that he remained committed to maintaining a balance of power between humanity and the environment within which humans live. 'We must be grateful to anyone who warns us that we cannot depart too far from nature without imperilling our spiritual health and our existence ... But if, on the other hand, a man throws himself too impulsively on nature's breast, he forgets that civilization implies liberation from nature' (Röpke, 1946: 111–12). Similar sustainability arguments were developed by James Lovelock in his Gaia thesis in the 1970s related to the need to balance human achievements and the natural environment (Lovelock, 1979).

Vitalpolitik was also central in the fight against all forms of collectivism, indicating that economic freedom alone was not sufficient. Röpke thought that the non-collectivist world would be able to deal with the dangers of collectivism successfully only 'when it knows how to deal in its own way with the problems of the proletariat, large-scale industrialization, monopolism, the multitudinous forms of exploitation and the mechanizing effects of capitalist mass civilization' (Röpke, 1950: 177). Work and life needed to have dignity and meaning.

This leads to the broader philosophical attack on welfare states with Rüstow arguing that the welfare state consolidates proletarianism rather than eliminates it. According to Rüstow, freedom from want undermines the real freedom of entrepreneurial decision-making and there is no such thing as freedom without risk (Bonefeld, 2017: 98). Despite this general hostility towards an all-encompassing welfare state which in his view eliminated self-reliance, independence and responsibility, there was a strong support for social policy as long as it was market conforming. One of the reasons to oppose a welfare state is that cash transfers did not facilitate the entrepreneurial life of *Vitalpolitik* and hence would not transform people's well-being (Siems & Schnyder, 2013).

Critically though, the ordoliberals did agree that there ought to be a safety net for everyone, although insurance arrangements ought to be private where possible. One other central component of their policy approach was to embed the idea of social policy within the economic structure. Their view was that the market was by nature social because it stimulated production. This in turn increased output and the demand of labour, and therefore incomes.

The dispersion of power to maintain a competitive economy in conjunction with a policy to reinvigorate community life and entrepreneurialism was central to the ordoliberal outlook. But the ordoliberals were generally negative about constant government intervention. That was precisely Rüstow's criticism of the 1930s. Instead the focus from a policy perspective ought to be on changing the legislative rules enabling the market to function more effectively.

A constitutional economy

At the heart of Rüstow's approach to public policy was the concept of *Startgerechtigkeit* which can be understood as the justice of initial or starting conditions prior to voluntary exchange. If the distribution of income is left to the outcome of an economic system characterized by competition and the market mechanism, then the demand for social justice must concentrate on the conditions prior to exchange or starting conditions – which extends in particular to wealth and education (Rüstow, 1949: 146).

For Rüstow, 'Starting inequality through the hereditary principle is the mechanism by which feudalism lives on the market economy, which turns it in to a plutocracy; dominance by the wealthy' (Rüstow, 1949: 152 – author translation). Education was the most important factor as its monopoly has led to the formation of plutocracies. Rüstow thought that it was critical that the educational advantage of the upper classes be completely removed (Rüstow, 1949: 147, 151). He also thought that the complete elimination of this educational monopoly was easier to achieve. Central to this idea was the policy that no one should be denied access to training for financial reasons. Such costs in the grand scheme of things are manageable and are crucial to meeting the demands of social justice.

In addition to this focus on educational equality, the implementation of a mechanism to prevent the accumulation of private power in the market was also central to the concept of *Startgerechtigkeit* to avoid excessive concentrations of wealth. If economic agents can increase their market power through means other than performance competition, then this will negatively affect the justice of starting conditions. This is why the ordoliberals remained so concerned by the feudal tendencies of market economies. For Rüstow, 'if the equality of starting points can be achieved to avoid the unjust hereditary inequality, then individuals are only able to gain or lose advantage through competition, which will significantly change ... the mood of the economy and the prevailing attitude towards life' (Rüstow, 1949: 150 – author translation).

Röpke took up this point in more detail noting that while some feudal practices had been eliminated, many continue to emerge due to the weakness of the state permitting the 'refeudalization' of the economy. These practices lead to unjust starting conditions resulting in unequal outcomes in terms of income and market power. Understanding the market as autonomous and natural must therefore be seen as a catastrophic mistake. This highlights the importance of having an ethical legal and institutional framework which corresponds to the principles of the market system that prevents concentrations of power (Röpke, 1950: 115–18). The attack on monopoly and market power is therefore central to the ordo concept of justice – one which is quite different to the contemporary view of neoliberalism. Hayek in his later years was quite sceptical of the idea of *Startgerechtigkeit*, suggesting that this would require the government to control every aspect of a person's life (Hayek, 2013: 247).

This view was not shared by Röpke who noted that the destruction of monopolies must be attacked accordingly by assessing the source of market power including tariffs, subsidies, privileges, patent laws and company laws. Without any equalization prior to voluntary exchange, people will distrust the system as it is unreasonable for individuals to compete without a fair starting point (Röpke, 1950: 234–5). This point was also taken up by Frank Knight, as well as by Stiglitz and Atkinson, on how to make outcomes more dependent on luck and hard work rather than any initial allocation (Atkinson & Stiglitz, 1980).

Rüstow also advocated policies with regards to the labour market and innovation to disperse unequal power relations. Although he argued against a minimum wage, Rüstow was in favour of the state stepping in if wages fell below certain levels in conjunction with compulsory insurance against unemployment. He also advocated a life-long vocational education system supported by a public not-for-profit employment service, including careers advice, pre-employment training, retraining and relocation assistance (Rüstow, 1949: 137). This approach is quite similar to the contemporary

Danish policy of flexicurity which integrates a flexible labour market with an element of financial security and employee training.

He promoted state research institutes to support small and medium sized enterprises (Rüstow, 1949: 135), thus implying that the application of science ought to be socialized, enabling small firms to gain equal access to new innovations. He also argued for corporate taxation to be progressively linked to business size in order to make large companies unviable (Hartwich, 2009). Rüstow also suggested there ought to be a general licensing of patents to encourage competition, as patents had become increasingly associated with attempts to hinder competition between large corporations (Rüstow, 1949: 135).

The ordoliberal antipathy towards big business is why Rüstow and his colleagues put so much emphasis on competition. Monopoly stops the market functioning, which in turn leads to the economy degenerating into a subsidized pluralist economy where interest groups take over the state for their own interest. (Maier-Rigaud & Maier-Rigaud, 2001: 121, 127). In the words of Bastiat, the state is a fiction where everyone tries to live from the costs of others. Rüstow therefore advocated that the state must police market freedom. Where competition was not possible in sectors such as railways and public utilities, then the monopoly structure had to be socialized (Rüstow, 1949: 134). This was very similar to Henry Simons' recommendations.

Free trade also played a major role in breaking down market power, which was different to the classical liberal framework which used free trade to attain a Pareto optimization and the maximization of total societal utility. Monopoly and protectionism had resulted in a brutal society with highly unequal starting points, and free trade could help in breaking down these barriers. Röpke, in particular, advocated this approach, but he was clear that free international trade had its limits.

Such economic integration requires a code of standards, values and principles in addition to a freely convertible and stable currency which assures material security for the claims arising from trade. Only when these prerequisites are fulfilled can international trade flourish. 'Economic integration – as far as its geographical extent and its intensity are concerned – always presupposes a corresponding non-economic "social" integration ... The economic integration cannot in the long run extend further than the social integration' (Röpke, 1959: 72–3). For Röpke, this was a cardinal law that governs the rise and fall of trade in the history of humanity.

These points are further emphasized by Röpke's argument that liberal countries engaging in trade with countries based on different values are liable to break down, causing harm to the liberal country. He was particularly vocal in his attack on East–West trade during the Cold War where Western firms were trading with the Soviet bloc.

This trade is highly dangerous and objectionable and is apt to strengthen the power which the free world, if it is not to delude itself, must recognize as its own worst enemy ... It is precisely the habit of respecting business interests which leads Western politicians to lend their ears to businessmen who profit from East–West trade and want to transpose into this political minefield the functions of business which are legitimate and proved in our own economic and social order. There are but few who stop to think whether in this case their business interests are not in conflict with overall political interests. (Röpke, 1960: 139–40)

Such arguments are beginning to surface today due to increasing trade frictions between liberal and authoritarian countries. This raises the question how sustainable the current international trading system is, and is one reason why the global trading system managed by the World Trade Organization (WTO) is under severe pressure. For Röpke, the danger of trade with authoritarian countries may have negative consequences for the future of a liberal order.

Rüstow also cautioned against an absolutist approach to free trade. Free trade was often described as trade between town and country writ-large, but free international trade requires recognition of the underlying ethical principles as a prerequisite. (Maier-Rigaud & Maier-Rigaud, 2001: 96–8). Without those ethics in place, international economic integration cannot be sustained.

The central component of ordoliberal public policy though was unsurprisingly related to competition. The ordoliberals saw competition in dynamic terms with the view that a general rise in real income was only possible when improvements in productivity are made. Indeed, without the opportunity for firms to make profits, higher investment would not be forthcoming, and without bringing forward sufficient investment under competitive conditions, full employment could not be attained (Chaloupek, 2015).

This implies imperfect monopolistic competition is more effective than perfect competition in raising living standards. This requires there to be no agreement between producers, with everyone having the opportunity to compete on the same terms and that there are several independent players in an industry to drive competition (Peacock & Willgerodt, 1989b: 162–3). This is particularly challenging given that managers and unions might come to an arrangement to protect the status quo in order to prevent increased competition as Croly had advocated.

For Röpke, this required legislation to prevent the formation of monopolies and financial concentration which took into account company law, patent law, bankruptcy law, antitrust laws as well as the strictest supervision of the market to safeguard fair play (Röpke, 1950: 179). In essence, for a free society to function there has to be a free market and genuine competition for private enterprise to compete under fair and equal conditions. This requires the state to constantly intervene which is justified *only* by whether it is able to maintain the functioning of the market (Peacock & Willgerodt, 1989a: 118).

Eucken labelled this approach to public policy as *Ordnungspolitik*, which can be understood as the adaptation and transfer of ideas from liberal political theory to the economy (Bonefeld, 2017: 70). By creating a set of constitutional rules, it enables the market to function which in turn provides the necessary legitimacy for the polity. The maintenance of the price mechanism under full competition is fundamental in steering this course. Hence, anything that interferes in the price mechanism can be considered as a hindrance. State intervention to create a functioning market therefore falls well within the role of government.

For Eucken, this approach resulted in two key principles. The first is that the state's policy should be aimed at dissolving economic power groups or limiting their functions. The second is that the economic activity of the state should be directed towards the organization of the economic order, not at the direction of the economic process (Eucken, 1959: 188–9).

This led Eucken to expound a framework of eight underlying principles for pursuing freedom which was quite different to the utilitarian approach supported by welfare economics. Eucken's framework was by far the most comprehensive policy programme expounded by any ordoliberal thinker in terms of how the theory might be implemented, and is worth highlighting in full (Eucken, 1959: 160–79).

Principle 1: The fundamental principle was against interference in the price mechanism generated by full competition. Hence, any distortion to the price mechanism had to be removed.

Principle 2: The primacy of monetary policy or currency stabilization was central to the functioning of the price system. This was of particular concern to Eucken given the experience of the Weimar Republic and was his attempt to prevent the money supply being manipulated by politicians.

Principle 3: Open markets were necessary to ensure private interest groups were unable to influence the price mechanism. This might require a reduction in tariffs and subsidies, antitrust policies, free trade and changes to patent law, such as requiring patent owners to license them for a fee.

Principle 4: Private property is required to maintain a competitive order as it incentivizes individuals to use the price system to steer their course in life.

Principle 5: Freedom of contract enables households and firms to drive their own plans and is required to maintain competition. This also requires there to be a power balance between employers and employees.

Principle 6: Liability is required to inject responsibility into the economic system so those who reap the benefit must also bear the losses, with every limitation of liability triggering a tendency towards centralization of the economy as it interferes with competition. Liability is also important for competition as it hampers affiliations with other firms and therefore can reduce private power concentrations.

Principle 7: Continuity of economic policy to ensure that investment levels are maintained, as less investment leads to less employment.

Principle 8: Interrelatedness of the underlying principles requires that all principles of the economic constitution need to be present for them to be function.

Eucken also made it clear that a set of social policies is integral to the underlying economic order. Social policy should therefore not be seen as an appendage to an economic argument but is rather central to the economic argument. This is quite different to the more recent developments in 'third way' thinking which took the market outcome as a given and then appended a social policy to reduce the negative effects of those outcomes.

For Eucken, an economy that adhered to these principles would naturally result in a superior social policy, where the efficiency of production supported all members of the community including workers, pensioners and other dependents. The approach to welfare was focused on the state providing individuals with sufficient assets to thrive in society, enabling individuals to set aside money for potential future risks through forms of insurance. However, the state was obliged to ensure that the risks which could not be managed individually were socialized and provided through a universal safety net. There was also support for a progressive income tax as long as it didn't impinge on investment.

The ordoliberals fundamentally disagreed with the laissez-faire system precisely because it resulted in poor outcomes in terms of commutative justice, which then created the demand for large-scale redistribution. Instead, they argued it was the obligation of the state to improve on outcomes by eliminating all private power concentrations and providing individuals with sufficient capabilities to live a life of vitality.

In 1948, the ordoliberals created their own journal *ORDO – Jahrbuch für die Ordnung von Wirtschaft und Gesellschaft*, which is still in print today. However, the movement lost its impetus after Eucken died in 1950. Röpke, who had railed against power concentrations in the 1930s, shifted his outlook siding with the anti-communist classical liberals and ended up supporting Apartheid South Africa from the 1960s (Slobodian, 2018). Furthermore, the distinctiveness of the need to intervene to disperse power faded, as ordoliberalism was often lumped together as part of the broader contemporary neoliberalism debate. This outlook was partly sustained by

Hayek becoming honorary president of the Walter Eucken Institut in 1970, a role that was subsequently awarded to Buchanan in 2003.

However, ordoliberalism did have some success in influencing public policy at the birth of the Federal Republic of Germany. The economics minister Ludwig Erhard was sympathetic to the ordoliberal ideology and appointed a number of ordoliberal advisors to help him develop policies which has subsequently been labelled as the *Soziale Marktwirtschaft* or the social market economy. The relative success of the West German economy and the stability of its society after one of the greatest social and economic upheavals in history is a strong reason to further investigate the foundation of West Germany. This in turn provides further insight into whether an alternative non-utilitarian liberal ideology might be viable.

4

The West German Experiment and the Decline of Ordo

Erhard and *Wirtschaftswunder*

The IG Farben building lies in the northern outskirts of the German city of Frankfurt. The site completed in 1930 became the corporate headquarters of the IG Farben conglomerate. Despite significant bomb damage to the surrounding area during the Second World War, the building remained largely intact and became the headquarters of the US occupation forces. The ousted IG Farben management team were on trial for war crimes at Nuremberg. Among other things, one of the subsidiaries of IG Farben had produced the gas Zyklon B which was used at a number of Nazi concentration camps to exterminate mostly Jews.

Despite this dark history, the boardroom at IG Farben has since become something of a landmark in the post-war revival of liberalism. At a meeting there in July 1948, Ludwig Erhard, the director of the economic council of Bizonia, and General Clay, the military governor of the American Zone, had been discussing Erhard's decision to abolish rationing, as well as removing wage and price controls. Such a dramatic shift in economic policy by Erhard in such a short space of time raised serious questions by the occupying powers.

Clay addressed the German official. "Herr Erhard, my advisers tell me that what you have done is a terrible mistake. What do you say to that?"

"Herr General," Erhard replied. "Pay no attention to them! My own advisers tell me the same thing" (Hartrich, 1980: 4).

Erhard went on to pitch his idea of the social market economy, an economic system that used markets but required the state to intervene to maintain the competitive functioning of those markets thereby generating fairer voluntary exchanges. Erhard had been influenced by the ordoliberal movement. Indeed, Walter Eucken and Franz Böhm were both members of Erhard's advisory council.

54

The foundation of West Germany is of interest due to its superior economic performance during the 1950s under Erhard's leadership, and because it is one of the intellectual sources of the ordoliberal policy debate. This chapter explores whether there was anything distinctly ordoliberal about this period, and the underlying reasons for West German economic success. This taps into the polarized debate between contemporary neoliberals who have asserted this success was due to Erhard's adherence to the market, and those in favour of a more redistributive outlook who argued it would have happened anyway due to post-war reconstruction. There is evidence that some institutional development in West Germany was influenced by ordoliberal ideas; however, by the end of the 1950s ordoliberalism was in decline. These ideas were subsequently revived by the French philosopher Michel Foucault in the late 1970s as a distinct strand of liberalism that potentially provides a new framework for the contemporary public policy debate.

Erhard was clear that the state had to play a central role in achieving a just society, and he thought it highly unrealistic that the functions of the state were likely to shrink given the complexity of modern society. However, he argued that everything possible should be done to limit the functions of government in order to prevent any abuse of power. Erhard's social market economy, therefore, sought to reduce the need for government intervention by making the market work effectively in the first place. He argued that the reshaping of the economic order had to reduce the inequality between the 'thin upper crust able to afford anything, and ... a broad lower stratum with insufficient purchasing power', which hampered development and created tensions across society (Erhard, 1958: 1). This required policy to tackle the inequalities that exist at the start of economic life in order to provide all citizens with the opportunity to thrive (Nicholls, 1994: 101).

These ideas had been explored in the Ahlener Programme of 1947 which was driven forward by Konrad Adenauer, who became the first chancellor of West Germany. The 1947 programme explored how to integrate a social framework into the economic system. Adenauer sought to distance the *Christlich Demokratische Union* (CDU) from a capitalist system based on profits and power and a socialist system of nationalization, towards one that served the spiritual and material needs of the people based on the *machtverteilendes Prinzip* or the principle of the distribution of power (Schwarz, 1995: 374). The programme sought to 'Strengthen the economic position and freedom of the individual by preventing the concentration of economic forces into the hands of individuals, societies, companies, private or public organizations through which economic or political freedom could be jeopardized' (Ahlener, 1947 – author translation).

These ideas, which are aligned with the ordo principle of the dispersal of public and private power, thus provided an important ideological foundation for the social market economy that was subsequently built into the foundations of the Federal Republic of Germany.

A stable currency that maintained its purchasing power was considered central to the new polity given the experience of the Weimar Republic. The challenge here was to prevent political manipulation of the currency resulting in the collapse of its value. Private property was also considered critical to the social market economy, incentivizing workers to become self-reliant thereby reducing the need for the state to intervene.

The ideas of individual responsibility were also baked into the social provisions that the state was to provide. Hence, rather than providing an all-encompassing welfare state, welfare provisions were proposed on an insurance basis, encouraging individuals and families to be responsible for their own future. However, where necessary, the state would step in to provide for those who were not covered, or where insurance was not practicable. The focus of social protection was primarily focused on supporting the most productive forces of society, rather than those in distress, although provision was still universal (Mau, 2001).

The West German state was also founded on the idea of the decentralization of power through its federal structure. The idea that power had to be dispersed so communities could take responsibility for their own future would not only prevent the abuse of power by central governments but also supported the ideas of *Vitalpolitik* with decisions being taken locally. This would also enable the ties of community to develop thereby improving the legitimation process.

Measures were introduced in the labour market to ensure that unions and management could work together which required a greater equalization of power between them. The idea of the equalization of capital and labour not only improved industrial relations, but also the notion that everyone had a stake in the economy.

Finally, the new state superimposed the price mechanism on West German society with enforcement procedures to ensure its effectiveness including an interventionist competition policy to prevent cartels forming and support for free trade. The price mechanism was considered central in providing information to households and firms, enabling them to make better decisions on investment, saving and consumption.

The importance of the price mechanism in ensuring equitable voluntary exchange meant that it had to be protected from the abuse by all stakeholders at all costs. This had been the key lesson from the Weimar Republic where, in the words of Rüstow, the state had been mere prey for private power concentrations to promote their exclusive interest.

At a superficial level, Erhard's programme appeared to be a triumph of ordoliberalism. The results of Erhard's social market economy have subsequently led to analyses and assessments on an industrial scale, largely

Table 4.1: Comparative economic performance, 1950–1960

1950–1960	West Germany	France	UK	USA	Japan
Real Output – Annualized	8.2%	4.7%	3.4%	3.6%	8.4%
Productivity – Annualized	6.9%	4.7%	1.9%	2.5%	6.1%
Inflation – Growth	21%	74%	49%	23%	50%
Nominal Wages – Growth	123%	126%	77%	62%	115%
Real Wages – Growth	102%	52%	28%	39%	65%

Sources:

Output & Inflation – Refinitiv: An LSEG Company

Productivity – author's calculations based on Total Economy Database: Output and Labor Productivity published by the Conference Board: www.conference-board.org/data/economydatabase/total-economy-database-about

Real wages (manufacturing) – BLS

due to ideological reasons. The main driver for this interest was that between 1950 and 1960 when Erhard was Minister for Economics, the West German economy outperformed on almost every measure.

As Table 4.1 shows, West German growth and productivity soared above other countries with the exception of Japan which was also recovering from extensive wartime destruction. Inflation was lower than in other countries, and while nominal wage growth was similar to France and Japan, real wage growth in West Germany was significantly higher than every other country.

For supporters of the price mechanism this was considered to be proof that it is only by unleashing markets can prosperity be achieved. For those in favour of greater government involvement, the view was that this would have happened anyway given the wartime economic dislocation of the German economy.

Naturally, Erhard took credit for this economic transformation in what was a relatively short space of time. His core argument was that the role of the state was to focus on creating the framework for the economy within which individuals could pursue their goals. And the results, as far as Erhard and his supporters were concerned, demonstrated that his social market economy was by far the most successful system when compared with other industrialized countries.

While this might appear to be a credible story at face value, simplistic narratives based on a government deciding to pursue a series of policies which then result in the expected outcomes across an entire economy is highly unrealistic. The limitations of knowledge in combination with the complexity of modern society in terms of how agents behave suggest the reasons behind policy successes will be multifarious including random factors resulting in both positive and negative unintended outcomes.

The idea that the causes of events can have simplistic narratives was precisely the reason why Tolstoy decided to write *War and Peace* (Berlin, 1953). The view that France invaded Russia because Napoleon gave the order and as a result, 600,000 people followed him across Europe, greatly exasperated Tolstoy. Hence, such a simple view that Erhard had a set of policies which was implemented that resulted in an economic miracle should be seriously questioned.

For example, the currency reform had been agreed by the Allies following a proposal submitted by the US occupation forces in 1946. After the Soviet Union walked out of discussions in London in 1947, the Allies made it clear that they could no longer preside over the economic and political deterioration of the Western zones (Bennett, 1950). The new notes began to be printed in the US and shipped to the vaults of the Reichsbank building in Frankfurt towards the end of 1947. As part of the currency reform process, the Bank Deutscher Lander was set up as an independent institution to control the future money supply.

However, the implementation of the currency reform was under Erhard's remit, which he pushed through with considerable success. On the afternoon of Friday 18 June 1948, after the banks had closed for the week, the first announcement of the new currency law to become effective on 20 June was made by press and radio to the German people of the Western zones. The conversion laws were published on 27 June, the day after the expiration day for the surrender of the old currency.

The conversion rate on saving and debts was 1 DM for 10 Reichsmarks but was limited in absolute terms. Every person received an initial entitlement of 40 DM with another 20 DM two months later (Giersch, Paque & Schmieding, 1992: 36). In July, Erhard abolished dozens of price regulations for most manufactured commodities, but decided to keep controls in place for iron and steel as well as basic foodstuffs given continued under supply. Wage controls were also subsequently abolished (Stolper & Roskamp, 1979).

The results of this overall approach surpassed most expectations with the level of German production rising from 61 per cent of 1936 production in July 1948 to 89 per cent in March 1949 (Bennett, 1950). This jump in production was driven by two thirds more hours worked and a third rise in labour productivity, indicating that the new system had provided sufficient incentives to work and innovate (Giersch, Paque & Schmieding, 1992: 39).

One striking effect of the currency reform was that it did have an equalizing effect improving the initial allocations for West Germans. The accumulated wealth for the richest who had been allied to the Nazi regime was significantly impacted. This was further pursued by the Equalization of Wealth Emergency Aid Law in 1949 and the Law for Equalization of War Burdens in 1952 where a 50 per cent wealth tax was levied which were paid in annuities until 1979 (Giersch, Paque & Schmieding, 1992: 80). Hence, a case can be made that Erhard appeared to have taken full advantage of the opportunity offered to him by the allies.

The guarantee of the rights of private property in the basic law wasn't inevitable but the result of a deliberate decision. In the immediate aftermath of the Allied occupation of Western Germany, the political debate between the two main political parties the *Sozialdemokratische Partei Deutschlands* (SPD) and the CDU, was about whether to use the market mechanism at all. The SPD led by Kurt Schumacher were focused on mass nationalization and a socialist economy. Indeed, the idea that the market might solve the sluggish production figures which were at half of the pre-war output before the currency reforms was not widely considered. In addition, the British Labour government were keen to see the SPD succeed. However, it is hard to see how the American occupying forces would have agreed to a socialist West German state that ignored private property rights. Indeed, the Americans appear to have been increasingly influential in terms of policy which included the ditching of nationalization plans (Giersch, Paque & Schmieding, 1992: 23).

Another important development of ordoliberalism that took place at the foundation of West Germany was the imposition by the allies of a federal political structure. This both decentralized power and also ensured that each area was responsible for its own economic destiny. West Germany has suffered less from regional economic imbalances compared with other countries, and communities have had a much greater say on the economic and political direction of their areas due to the decentralized nature of its political system.

But this idea of dispersing power was imposed by the allies at the Six Power Conference in London in April 1948 attended by the US, UK, France and the Benelux countries. As part of the post-war occupation, the allies had decentralized German administration with reconstruction starting at the local government level (Merkel, Kollmorgen & Wagener, 2019: 286). Alongside British and French concerns to avoid a strong central government, a federal structure was perceived as the best way of dispersing power.

Interestingly, the London agreements were not well received in Germany when they were presented to the *Ministerpräsidenten* of the individual German *Länder* in July 1948. The requirement to develop a democratic constitution to establish a federal government raised concerns that a constitution would cement the partition of Germany. The Allies eventually agreed that a Basic Law would suffice instead of a constitution. The view to disperse power across communities based on the principle of subsidiarity was largely down to the fear of a resurgent Germany by the British and French (Bumke & Vosskuhle, 2019: 2).

Although imposed allied policies had a positive effect on the West German polity, a number of other microeconomic policies implemented by Erhard did result in successful outcomes, but again it is hard to argue that this was purely down to Erhard. The equalization process was extended to the labour market when Adenauer's government passed two bills related to *Mitbestimmung* or co-determination, where workers would have a say in the running of firms. In 1951, this was applied to the coal and steel sector with representatives making up a half of the Supervisory board. In 1952, all companies, with the exception of family firms, were mandated to enable the participation of workers through works councils.

The trade union movement under the leadership of Hans Böckler decided to pursue a course of political neutrality, with the view that economic power was more important than political power. Hence, the unions were quite open to discussions with the CDU on co-determination. One effect of this was that the unions became less convinced of the value of strikes given they were now running sections of the economy with the managers of firms. Furthermore, this co-determination resulted in the unions accepting the reality that higher profits were needed to raise the rate of investment. This caused them to distance themselves from the SPD's nationalization dogma as they now had a financial stake in the West German economy (Hartrich, 1980: 190). Crucially, firm-level strategic decisions were no longer perceived as being class-based decisions based on whether capital or labour should benefit.

In addition, the unions did not seek aggressive pay demands during the 1950s. It is plausible that productivity growth was continually higher than expected; hence, the unions were always playing catch-up. But there is also evidence that the bargains struck contained elements of greater social responsibility. The unions could see the economy was improving the lives of their members, and given their greater leverage as part of the co-determination process, they could also argue that this was down to their negotiations with managers. Another hugely important step taken by the unions was to agree with government that the state should subsidize retraining for workers (Giersch, Paque & Schmieding, 1992: 121). This would enable workers to maintain greater parity in the labour market as the economy changed through time in terms of demand for certain skill sets.

Another market that the state intervened in to improve outcomes was in housing. Indeed, land reform had featured in the 1947 *Ahlener Programm*. During the Weimar Republic, private persons had been allowed to profit from land shortages in high-demand areas through speculation. This issue had been noted by Adam Smith in the *Wealth of Nations* who observed that monopolistic patterns of land ownership resulted in high prices and critically less capital investment (Smith, 1904, Vol I: 341–2). Erhard was convinced that the competitive system could function best if property was widely distributed which was incompatible with the existence of overmighty landowners (Nicholls, 1994: 74–5). Erhard was thus faced with two issues. The first was that there was a huge demand for capital to fund the new housing given the destruction of the war, but in post-war Germany capital was scarce. The second was how to implement new rules in the land market to ensure that speculation did not return and curb housebuilding efforts.

The housebuilding law was implemented to provide cheaper finance using a tax subsidy for private enterprise supported by the Marshall Plan through the newly founded *Kreditanstalt für Wiederaufbau*. In conjunction with this approach, the government published its land compensation law the *Baulandbeschaffungsgesetz* in 1953 to prevent landowners from profiting from speculative land values. The 1953 law precluded compensation from being paid to landowners based on the change or potential change of use of land, or what is often termed as 'hope value' in Anglo-Saxon countries. This avoided the profiteering characteristic of the Weimar period where 'owners of scarce land in urban areas demanded exorbitant prices from developers, thereby contributing to higher rents and discouraging construction' (Silverman, 1970). The impact of providing cheaper finance and preventing speculation in the land market led to a massive expansion in housebuilding, which in turn resulted in a further boost for employment.

Other factors that played a role in Erhard's success were down to luck. For example, only around 6.5 per cent of machine tools were destroyed in the war and Nazi investment in the war economy meant that Germany nearly had as many machine tools as the US (Nicholls, 1994: 125). However, Erhard's drive for freer trade, which was also supported by the US, played a key role in taking advantage of these factors. When things started to get tough for Erhard in 1950, the Korean War resulted in a huge demand for German-manufactured produce (Stolper & Roskamp, 1979).

Indeed, the shift in the structure of the West German economy through the 1950s and 1960s towards a greater share of higher value-added sectoral output was due to the rising demand for its manufactured goods. The demand for these products continued to grow in this period particularly across Western Europe, which in turn created a trade surplus (Giersch, Paque & Schmieding, 1992: 90). While this was indeed fortuitous, German managers working with the unions made the best of the opportunities, with a continual focus on investment and training and generally good industrial relations.

Despite what appeared to be a growing ordoliberal success story, increasing dissatisfaction arose within the sections of Adenauer's government that policy was far too interventionist. Co-determination was seen as restricting the freedom of contract. However, the ordoliberals had made it clear that a laissez-faire approach to markets would not lead to greater equalization of initial conditions. This shift in sentiment within the governing CDU Party began to signal that the ordoliberal movement was losing influence.

This was particularly the case when it came to the central plank of ordoliberal ideology which was to enforce competition. Erhard had argued that:

> One of the most important tasks in a country based on a free social order is, therefore, to secure free competition. It is no exaggeration when I declare that a law against monopoly is essential as an indispensable economic principle ... This principle means that no individual citizen must be powerful enough to suppress individual freedom, or, in the name of false freedom, to be able to limit it. (Erhard, 1958: 2–3)

But the anti-cartel legislation drafted by Paul Josten with recommendations to break up dominant enterprises was rejected. The reality was that political pluralism was back and vested interests were attempting to superimpose their views on the German government. The ordoliberal window of opportunity that had opened due to the collapse of German society was closing. By the time the anti-cartel law was finally passed in 1957, it was extremely light in terms of enforcing competition with merely the principle of banning cartels implemented. Franz Böhm was furious as he wanted to see rules established to ensure large firms treated their customers equally and did not use their power to cripple competition (Nicholls, 1994: 336).

The opposition from trade unions and big business, who were now working closely together in order to eliminate competition, resulted in the complete failure of this ordoliberal idea. The Ruhr industrialists had spent liberally to cultivate a large bloc of deputies in the Bundestag to ensure their view prevailed. Indeed, West German industry began to increasingly resemble the Weimar Republic with a set of oligopolistic firms with close links to the government. This close network of firms and government was documented at the time which indicated the lack of competition and the dominance of existing networks (Giersch, Paque & Schmieding, 1992: 75).

In March 1958, the ordoliberal *Aktionsgemeinschaft Soziale Marktwirtschaft* (ASM) asserted that 'we are still very far from our goal. The social economy has only been imperfectly realised.' Hence, it has been concluded by Nicholls that despite material improvement, the development of the new market-based system had stumbled to a halt (Nicholls, 1994: 359). The state was favouring too many special interests and a social market economy could not be achieved by trying to correct the market with piecemeal centralized planning adjustments.

Finally, as the threat of the Soviet Union increased, the CDU – just as had been the case with the Mont Pelerin society – drifted away from the notion of power dispersion towards a more conservative approach to policy. One important achievement of the ordoliberal movement, however, was related to cross-party interest in their ideas. This was confirmed when the SPD at their conference in Bad Godesberg in 1959 rejected its Marxist dogma of state ownership. They instead pivoted to what they called 'consumer socialism' which was really just another name for the social market economy (Hartrich, 1980: 241). This shift of the SPD towards the centre ground was instrumental in their electoral success in the mid-1960s.

The SPD economist Karl Schiller framed this policy as a logical continuation of the social market economy. The language was anti-monopoly, pro-market and virulently anti-communist. The conference deliberations emphasized that:

> The goal of social democratic economic policy is to ensure, for all, growing prosperity, fair participation in the national economy and a life of liberty without degrading dependence or exploitation ... Economic Policy must secure full employment, which together with a stable currency increases productivity and general prosperity ... Free consumer and job choice are crucial foundations in the social democratic economic policy, as are free competition and entrepreneurial initiative. Autonomy for employees and employers' associations through collective bargaining is also a substantial component of the liberal order ... Where markets are distorted by the supremacy of particular interests or groups, they require various interventions to uphold economic freedom. (Rittershausen, 2007)

The ordoliberal baton had been transferred to the SPD, with Schiller supporting genuine competition along the lines of Eucken and Röpke. His slogan, 'as much competition as possible, as much market regulation as necessary' (Nicholls, 1994: 319), was an ordoliberal gem as was his criticism of the CDU's shift towards a more traditional laissez-faire approach which has come to be associated with the contemporary neoliberal movement.

Schiller's attack on the CDU was that free consumer choice was absurd because of the unequal distribution of wealth. In essence, the CDU had ignored the basic notion of the ordoliberal economy which was to equalize power prior to voluntary exchange. When Schiller took over Erhard's ministry in the mid-1960s after the SPD's assent to power, he consistently refused to permit his party to tamper with the *Soziale Marktwirtschaft* (Hartrich, 1980: 243). But while Schiller endorsed the language of the social market economy, SPD policy related to the equalization process shifted away from constitutional style reforms towards direct intervention.

The equalization process that had kicked in during the 1950s through ordoliberal ideas to a certain extent led to an element of de-proletarianization. The framework of co-determination and the localized approach to community living played a significant role in reducing class conflict. One striking example was Heinz Nordhoff, the CEO of Volkswagen, who rather than separating himself from the rest of society lived in a small detached house in a housing settlement populated by his workers (Hartrich, 1980: 220). Ordoliberalism appears to be have been somewhat of an antidote to Tocqueville's warning that a business aristocracy would rise up and separate themselves from the rest of society.

Revisionism of *Wirtschaftswunder*

While an attempt has been made to briefly assess the ordoliberal drivers on the post-war German economy and society – which was a combination of Erhard's policies, the Allies and a degree of luck – a number of recent studies have suggested that the high growth rates of the social market economy were only to be expected. While these analyses do not contradict any attempt to assess the ordoliberal nature of the social market economy, they are interesting in that they question whether the West German economy did improve on public policy decisions that led to higher growth rates.

One theory expounded by the economic historian Werner Abelshauser has focused on the negative output shock resulting from the final phases of the war up until 1948, which merely pushed the economy off its long-term growth path. Hence, the post-1948 growth rates were merely the economy getting back on track and therefore had little to do with Erhard at all (Abelshauser, 2011). However, many of Abelshauser's points were subsequently taken on board by the authors of *The Fading Miracle* which argued that the idea of making markets work and allowing individuals to flourish was a strong factor in growth (Giersch, Paque & Schmieding, 1992).

Another theory postulates that the West German economy grew in the context of productivity catch-up and convergence, with the shift from Germany's higher level of agricultural workers to manufacturing explaining the jump in growth rates. Erhard's view of the unique factor of German institutions and policy explaining the difference has also been modelled. Eichengreen and Ritschl (2008) suggest that all three of these factors may have played a role in the West German *Wirtschaftswunder*. However, they subsequently discounted structural change and institutional arguments while emphasizing the post-war shock as a key determinant of German economic performance in the 1950s.

The economist Rudiger Dornbusch in his review of *The Fading Miracle* suggested that the nature of post-war construction might also be a major factor indicating that Japan in the 1950s had a similarly high rate of growth to West Germany. Furthermore, Japan rather than using free trade to expand, used industrial protection to develop its manufacturing sector (Dornbusch, 1993). While this is true, the difference in real wage growth does appear to stand out from the data despite the similarities in output and productivity growth.

A study by Wendy Carlin indicates that the level of German post-war growth in the 1950s was quite exceptional in terms of Germany's historical experience from 1870, and in comparison with other countries. Carlin also notes that there was no certainty that a post-war Germany would follow a free market path, thus enabling it to capitalize on its human and physical capital stock. Hence, she argues that the currency and liberalization reforms were meaningful. The West German economic recovery was initially constrained by institutional factors and not the destruction of the industrial capital stock or the labour force. Carlin also notes that the specific institutional characteristics of the German economy such as its industrial relations system and training may well have also been factors in higher productivity growth (Carlin, 1994).

Indeed, one of the key factors for German firms to accelerate investment was down to higher profits (Alt & Schneider, 1962), which in turn was closely linked to wage determination not being overly aggressive. Thus, the co-determination approach appears to have played a role in this higher rate of investment. Röpke's concern around trade-union leaders wanting to continuously raise money wages because they needed to demonstrate to their members they were providing tangible results for their efforts appears largely unwarranted. Röpke's point though is valid to the extent that it was quite possible for price reductions to further the true interests of trade-union members better than wage increases, which was the case during the 1950s (Röpke, 1960: 146).

Indeed, the stabilization of inflation is a key factor that helps explain the strength of the German economy. Although nominal wage growth in West Germany was akin to growth in France and Japan, because of subdued inflation, real wage growth was substantially higher. According to one study it was most unusual for a period of explosive growth to be combined with decreasing unemployment and strong wage growth where prices did not rapidly increase. Wage gains were therefore transferred almost intact to consumers. This approach was further entrenched by the law which transformed the Bank deutscher Länder into the Bundesbank, which enjoyed a high degree of independence and continued to focus on the primacy of a stable, non-inflationary currency (Rittershausen, 2007).

No doubt the debate about whether Germany's *Wirtschaftswunder* was the result of good policy or whether it would have happened no matter who was in power during the 1950s will continue. However, there appears to be sufficient evidence that the ordoliberal ideology and to the limited extent it was implemented is worthy of further exploration in an attempt to reinvigorate the liberal idea based on the principles of freedom and equality.

One further challenge is that the lens through which this *Wirtschaftswunder* has been analysed by those attempting to promote Erhard's ideology, and those wanting to disprove there was anything remotely different about West

Germany, is that it has largely been conducted using a traditional Pareto function of welfare maximization. An economy that is founded on high investment, productivity and high real wage growth will likely perform well using a utilitarian approach to optimize aggregated outcomes.

The argument the ordoliberals were making was to achieve liberty and equality through the dispersal of power; hence, economic outcomes can therefore be described as second-order variables. There is more to freedom than optimizing trades based on any given allocation of goods and a set of societal preconditions. It is fundamentally about power dispersion and the ability of individuals to lead a life of vitality in decentralized communities. It is worth emphasizing that the ordoliberal thinkers didn't necessarily see the maxim of power dispersal as a direct replacement for utility and hence the basis of all policy programmes, but it is not far away in policy discussions. While ordoliberalism is often described as a German version of contemporary neoliberalism, largely due to the focus on private property and the importance of the price mechanism, the fundamental distinction between power dispersal and maximizing utility results in significant differences in policy deliberations and hence potential societal outcomes.

The ordoliberal heritage combined with elements of Erhard's *Wirtschaftswunder* is also interesting as a potential alternative for the current utilitarian approach as they inspired the French philosopher Michel Foucault to explore these ideas in relation to the pursuit of freedom. In a series of lectures given at the Sorbonne in 1979, he relied heavily on the German ordoliberal movement as a way to theorize about liberty. This provides further evidence that developments in West Germany and ordoliberal ideology had the potential to take liberalism in a different direction.

The pursuit of freedom

Foucault makes it clear at the start of the lecture series that his interest is in contemporary German liberalism (Foucault, 2008: 22) and not what he termed the American anarcho-liberalism of Friedman that has come to be more associated with contemporary neoliberalism (Zamora & Behrent, 2016: 177). Moreover, while he notes there are similarities between the two forms of liberalism related to a dislike of a planning and state interventionism, he saw them as quite distinct ideologies with substantive differences. In particular, he saw the American version as proposing a more radical and complete theory which attempted to generalise the economic 'form of the market beyond monetary exchanges ... as, a principle of intelligibility and a principle of decipherment of social relationships and individual behaviour' (Foucault, 2008: 243). This is in stark contrast to the ordo notion of *Vitalpolitik* which argued that the market mechanism could not be used as a foundation for society.

The differences between the two versions appear to drive Foucault's interest in the German strand and its relevance for contemporary liberal debate, and why the lectures largely ignore the American neoliberalism that has become so ubiquitous today.

One of the central arguments of Foucault's series of lectures on German liberalism is that freedom is not static, but a process, which has to be constantly produced. Hence, Foucault argued that 'liberalism is not acceptance of freedom, it proposes to manufacture it constantly, to arouse it and produce it, with of course the system of constraints and the problems of cost raised by this production' (Foucault, 2008: 65).

The implication of this is that by not intervening, freedom cannot be realized. However, Foucault is also aware that the process of intervening can undermine freedom. Although Roosevelt's interventionist policies during the Great Depression could be construed as a way of producing more freedom, they also created the potential for a new despotism. As Foucault notes, 'in this case democratic freedoms are only guaranteed by an economic interventionism which is denounced as a threat to freedom' (Foucault, 2008: 68). Foucault sums up the crisis of liberalism arguing that the mechanisms for producing freedom actually produce destructive effects which prevail over the very freedom they are supposed to produce. States that violate the freedom of individuals cannot exercise their power legitimately.

It is noteworthy these reflections were made in the late 1970s after the *30 Glorious Years* had come to an end and during a period of economic stagnation for many industrialized countries. This is perhaps why the ordoliberal approach was of interest to Foucault given the relative success of the West German economy. Hence, Foucault indicates the importance of legitimizing the state on the guaranteed exercise of economic freedom. A successful economy can therefore help legitimize the state that is its guarantor, producing a permanent consensus among all the different agents involved in economic processes including investors, employers and workers (Foucault, 2008: 83–4).

Rather than the state attempting to define what freedoms it should leave to the economy, ordoliberalism instead asks the economy how its freedom has a state-creating function and role (Foucault, 2008: 95). The state is therefore legitimated as a key supporting function so freedom can be continuously manufactured within the economy. This fundamentally changes the idea of the relationship between the state and the market. Instead of accepting a free market maintained by state supervision, it is necessary instead to adapt the market as an organizing and regulating principle of the state. Hence the state becomes the mechanism to disperse power in order to maintain freedom.

This is why competition was so central to the ordoliberal argument. Competition has an internal logic and structure, but its effects are produced only if its logic is respected. The problem of ordoliberalism is therefore how the overall exercise of political power can be modelled on the principles of a market economy. This requires the state to be active, vigilant and to intervene if anything prevents the logical outcome of the market mechanism. The market, which is a general social and economic regulator, is a reliable mechanism when it functions well and nothing distorts it. Hence, the role of the state is to constantly ensure it is not distorted by interest groups (Foucault, 2008: 121, 131).

This leads to perhaps the most important distinction between ordo and contemporary American neoliberalism which is related to concentrations of private power. While the neoliberals saw the need to restrict the power of the state to intervene and directly address market outcomes, they did not see the concentration of private power as an issue per se. For Eucken, the problem of private power ultimately meant that an evolutionary process could not be relied upon. The state had to ensure constant competition to prevent any abuse of power, otherwise a centrally planned economy will materialize (Oswalt-Eucken, 1994). This is why, for Böhm, the individual and public interest could only be aligned where private power is constrained (Koslowski, 2000: 157).

Foucault raises the concern of the injustice of initial conditions highlighting how a wealthy or high-income family will have as its immediate and rational economic project the transmission of human capital of at least as high a level to its children. But if *homo oeconomicus* can increase market power, it is no longer clear that the invisible hand leads to an increase in the common good (Foucault, 2008: 244). In this instance society will have failed to maintain freedom, which is now in the hands of dominant private interests. This in turn begins to delegitimize society just as Tocqueville cautioned in the 19th century with the rise of a new aristocracy that begins to isolate itself from the rest of society. Unless all individuals feel that everyone has an equal voice, support for liberal ideas will falter.

Foucault then tackles the issue of social policy repeating Eucken's mantra that social policy needs to be central to economic policy and not a counterweight to it.

> Social policy will have to be a policy which instead of transferring one part of income to another part will use as its instrument the most generalized capitalization possible for all social classes, the instrument of individual and mutual insurance, and in short the instrument of private property ... this leads us to the conclusion that there is only one true and fundamental social policy: economic growth ... Only economic growth should enable all individuals to achieve a level of income that will allow them the individual insurance. (Foucault, 2008: 144)

But Foucault was clear that it has to be a certain kind of economic growth. Growth must be based on avoiding centralization, encouraging enterprise and trying to replace social insurance of risk with individual insurance. The more one encourages enterprise in decentralized communities, the more one multiplies the centres of formation of enterprise, which in turn reduces the need for governmental intervention. This pattern will then result in rules developing to maintain these interactions between multiple centres of dispersed power. To a certain extent this might be construed as similar to Hayek's common law approach in the *Constitution of Liberty*. However, this approach requires the state to constantly intervene and protect the mechanism from market abuse, something that Hayek did not countenance the need for (Foucault, 2008: 149, 240).

As part of this enterprise process, a crucial aim is to develop a worker's human capital which means making what are called educational investments in relation to the economy. But this support must be deployed alongside the moral and cultural values of *Vitalpolitik* so that the individual does not feel alienated from society. While *Vitalpolitik* requires society to organize the economy according to rules of the market economy, the cold mechanism of the market alone is not sufficient to legitimize society. Hence, the importance of the bonds of local communities taking responsibility for their own actions (Foucault, 2008: 229, 243).

It is doubtful whether ordoliberalism would have grabbed Foucault's attention in the way it did, if West German society from 1948 had not developed in the way it had. All the economic indicators were positive, there were few regional imbalances across the country and it did not seem to have had the social tensions that were beginning to surface in France, the UK, Italy and the US in the 1970s.

Foucault's reflections provide further evidence that West Germany's success was not just Erhard's successful propaganda campaign, and that there were some unique institutional developments that had arisen from the brief ordoliberal flourishing during the post-war reconstruction period. Despite this potential alternative to classical and social liberalisms based on a utilitarian construct, there has been little development of these ideas outside Germany. Although the *Walter Eucken Institut* has continued to keep ordo alive in Germany, the ideology of dispersing public and private power as a potential framework for public policy has largely faded from view.

The central task for an ordoliberal system is that of legal design backed by a strong and constitutionally limited non-discriminatory state. Its purpose is to create and cultivate an institutional framework that makes possible decentralized coordination among free individuals who are legal equals. This can be achieved by introducing policies that disperse economic power (Wohlgemuth in Labrousse & Weisz, 2001: 205). The threat to a liberal system thus comes from within, whereby power can be accrued by individuals resulting in the refeudalization of the economy, which is akin to the principle of rent-seeking. Crucially, the accrual of private power enables individuals to influence the rules of the game.

One of the initial weaknesses for this framework was the challenge indirectly raised by Hayek on the knowledge question. Given that an ordoliberal system requires the state to constantly intervene to manufacture freedom at the rules level, how can the state develop such knowledge and adapt to ensure that freedom is indeed the desired outcome? Furthermore, the adoption of superior rules needs to assume that the world is not populated by fully rational agents.

According to a former director of the *Walter Eucken Institut*, the ordoliberal approach appears more practicable as the framework starts 'from the recognition that the human agents that populate the world of our experience are imperfect agents, with limited knowledge and limited mental capacities', in contrast to the Walrasian tradition of perfectly rational beings (Vanberg, 2005). Moreover, to counteract the knowledge question Vanberg has argued there is a critical difference

> between an economic policy that requires knowledge of all relevant welfare effects of specific interventions and an economic policy that requires knowledge of the general working properties of alternative rules. Knowledge of the latter kind can be gained and systematically improved in a cumulative, experience-guided process of trial-and-error learning. By contrast, an interventionist economic policy that considers 'each case on its own merits' cannot equally benefit from such cumulative learning, since its major knowledge-problem is that of identifying the relevant particular circumstances and the specific contingencies in ever-new, unique situations. (Vanberg, 2005)

While ordoliberals made it clear that their arguments to guarantee freedom were fundamentally different to the outcome of a utilitarian calculus, their ability to translate this into an objective policy function that can be implemented and measured empirically remains a challenge. Vanberg has argued that the outcomes of the rules of the game can be measured in terms of better service to consumers (Vanberg, 2005), but there is no empirical analysis to show how policymakers might be able to systematically improve on rules.

It is important to emphasize that the concept of a constitutional rule does not necessarily mean that the constitution of a country needs to be amended, but rather that the rules that govern an area of public policy need to be altered. Furthermore, these rules should be subject to democratic scrutiny, which is in contrast to claims made that so-called constitutional rules are an attempt to remove key aspects of economic policy from democratic control (Gill & Cutler, 2014: 38). Any institutional framework is required to be legitimated by a democratically elected assembly. This is crucial given that the rules might be wrong and be required to change.

For example, in the UK there is nothing stopping Parliament debating and passing a new mandate for the Bank of England's monetary policy target. Moreover, embedding rules in a constitution might result in the continuation of underperforming existing rules due to the challenge of making constitutional amendments, despite the existence of evidence that they are no longer fit for purpose. The current European Central Bank (ECB) mandate for monetary policy which is embedded in the Treaty on European Union is one such example.

The guidelines that the ordoliberal theorists produced were qualitative in nature, which is one reason why utility continues to be used by economists and policymakers as a key benchmark. Hence, Eucken's argument that the problem of the structure of economic systems is not a quantitative one appears flawed, as qualitative judgements cannot practically measure the success or failure of an ordoliberal set of policies. The task at hand, therefore, is whether it might be possible to develop an alternative normative objective function to replace the utilitarian benchmark of utility maximization and to remove arbitrary interference in making changes to the rules of the game.

The maxim of dispersing private and public power and how it improves the equality of initial conditions could be used as an alternative foundation of liberalism to utility if quantitative values of such a function could be developed to measure these effects. From a public policy perspective, this does not mean that attempts should be made to deduce specific policies from ordoliberal principles. Instead, policy should continue to approach complex problems in a practical way but instead use an alternative benchmark of whether policies result in greater or lesser power dispersion instead of income or more elusive concepts such as well-being.

Such a function should also be used to challenge existing ordoliberal policies that have been implemented historically. The underlying superstructure of an economy and society is subject to change; hence, the rules required to disperse private and public power may need to be altered through time. For example, the ordoliberal implementation of currency stabilization was to stabilize the price level. This policy has been adapted by most developed market central banks as the key monetary policy target. However, there is increasing evidence that stabilizing the price level creates unequal power relations rather than contributing to the dissipation of power as discussed in Chapter 5.

While rules for monetary policy were put into practice albeit with potential negative effects on the distribution of power, it is less obvious what rules might be implemented with regards to the liability of firms. The Global Financial Crisis raised the issue that the directors of companies no longer have skin in the game which has resulted in the privatization of gains and the socialization of losses. Furthermore, it is unclear how such a rule how might deal with increasingly complex arguments on patents and innovation.

Other policy areas that need to be addressed include how one might be able to strengthen community ties enabling citizens to live a life of *Vitalpolitik*. In addition, policymakers need to develop rules to deal with environmental challenges such as the loss of biodiversity and climate change. Other policy areas that also need to be addressed include how it might be possible to reverse the decline in purchasing power of middle- and low–middle-income groups, and how should antitrust policy deal with mergers that increase consumer welfare but reduce competition. Finally, an alternative framework needs to address how rules for international trade can be developed which provide guidance on trading with authoritarian countries that have no desire to see liberalism succeed.

As modern liberal societies continue to struggle with these daunting issues, further exploration of how power might be dispersed across an economy, enabling freedom and equality to thrive may well generate some positive developments in public policy. The challenge is how such a maxim of dispersing private and public power could be quantified to help guide future policymaking.

This challenge has been greatly facilitated by Hanna Pitkin's work which distinguishes power over another individual which is by nature relational, from the power to accomplish something which has no bearing on anyone else (Göhler in Clegg & Haugaard, 2009). The ability of an agent to exercise power over another by definition restricts freedom. Or as Rowley and Peacock (1975) argued, the aim of a liberal welfare function is to minimize the degree of coercion of some individuals by others. Hence, the public policy challenge is to prevent the accumulation of 'power over' to be continuously dispersed between economic agents. To achieve this requires an active state to intervene at the rules level to prevent imbalances across the economy and society.

Eucken stipulated that a number of foundational policies were prerequisites for a liberal society. First was the need for a stable currency to ensure wages maintain their purchasing power, savings their value, while providing incentives to invest. The second was that an ordo system must also be founded on private property, providing incentives for individuals and firms to innovate and make profits. However, the existence of private property requires individuals and firms to be liable for their actions thereby preventing the privatization of profits and the socialization of losses.

Eucken also highlighted the importance of labour markets which had to address freedom of contract and unequal power relations between capital and labour, as well as open product markets between firms both at home and internationally. For Eucken, the price mechanism plays a central role in the dispersion of power and therefore must be protected at all costs. In addition, these rules must have social policy embedded in them rather than developing social policy as an afterthought if outcomes are construed as unfair. For example, rules to strengthen the power of labour without any provision for unemployment insurance would not be effective given that this would merely increase the power of capital.

The other area of public policy that ought to have a central role in any ordo framework is the need to address unequal power relations between central governments and communities. While Eucken did not address this issue, it remained central to the idea of *Vitalpolitik* expounded by Röpke and Rüstow, as well as a key constitutive principle for Böhm.

No doubt the list of ordoliberal policy fields could be expanded; however, for these purposes the approach is to assess how a framework might be developed using the maxim of dispersing private and public power across these five areas.

In terms of public policy, one way to think about rule development is to assess which fields are continuous in nature and which ones are more discrete. For example, enshrining private property rights is more likely to have discrete outcomes whereas the labour market design in relation to human capital development is more likely to be continuous in nature.

By splitting out the discrete from the continuous rules-based approach, it might be feasible to come up with a framework as to how an ordoliberal framework could operate and potentially replace a utility-based system. The framework laid out in Figure 4.1 proposes that monetary policy and private property and liability are the discrete pillars of an ordoliberal framework.

Figure 4.1: Ordoliberal framework for public policy to achieve freedom and equality through the dispersal of public and private power

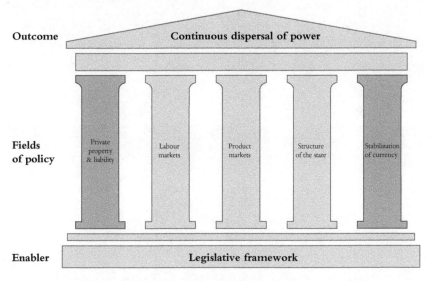

These can be thought of as largely binary in nature to the extent that monetary policy can be considered neutral in terms of power relations, and whether private property rights exist in conjunction with an appropriate liability regime.

These foundational pillars provide support for the three core policy pillars which are more continuous in nature. These include decentralization enabling *Vitalpolitik* to thrive, a functioning labour market with equal power relations between labour and capital, and equalization across product markets both domestically and internationally through protecting the price mechanism.

In the chapters that follow, an attempt will be made to assess the extent of current policy across OECD countries that is in accordance with the ordoliberal objective of the dispersal of public and private power. While no quantitative analysis has been undertaken to assess the nature of the discrete variables, an attempt is made to quantify the dispersion of power for the three continuous pillars. Such an approach may help address one ongoing challenge for ordoliberalism which has been its failure to provide suitable alternatives to Bentham's felicific calculus for policymakers.

Monetary Policy: The Illiberal Practice of Inflation Targeting

A misplaced obsession with stable prices

Concern about inflation in Germany has a long history. The onset of the Thirty Years War in 1618 triggered an inflationary spiral which contributed to living standards plunging in towns across the Holy Roman Empire. Between 1619 and 1622, real wages fell by more than two thirds in Augsburg in Bavaria, in contrast to just a 5 per cent decrease in Southern England. Furthermore, this dramatic fall in real wages took place largely before the outbreak of hostilities (Kindleberger, 1991).

A plate published in 1620 by Daniel Mannasser and now in the Germanisches Museum provides an indication of the causes of the inflationary spiral. It appears to depict a German mint deliberately debasing coins designed to be taken into other city-states and exchanged for good coins. The good coins could then be brought back and re-coined with greater seignorage – the difference between the face value of coins and their production costs.

This perceived opportunity by principalities to profit and increase their war chests led to a massive increase in the money supply through mint production of an ever-falling value of coinage across the empire. Contemporary accounts depict children playing games in the streets with the worthless coins due to the debasement of the currency (Kindleberger, 1991).

The more recent hyperinflation experienced in 1923 under the Weimar Republic was of a similar origin. The debt burden of war and the onerous reparations imposed at the Treaty of Versailles led the Reichsbank to permit other public authorities and industrial concerns to issue emergency money tokens. This process was exacerbated by the French occupation of the Ruhr which removed a third of industrial output from Germany (Desai, 1981: 18). Once again this resulted in a massive expansion of the money supply and an appalling fall in the standard of living, which stoked calls for rising wages backed up by strikes.

Although the inflation of World War One had been responsible for a 15 per cent fall in real wages for skilled workers, by the end of 1923 this had fallen by nearly 40 per cent (Bry, 1960). The first 100 billion note was soon printed, resulting in worthless paper money burned as fuel due to the widespread shortage of coal.

Foodstuffs began to replace currency as farmers did not see why they should exchange their goods for worthless paper money. This resulted in food shortages with one historian noting that Berlin's daily milk consumption of 1.8 million litres fell to just 130,000 during this period. German industry also suffered. Widespread bankruptcies drove up unemployment to 2 million by 1926, dragging the German economy into depression. Living conditions deteriorated significantly as indicated by a letter sent by the women of Cologne to the women of the British Empire pleading for help due to starvation (Fergusson, 1975: 118). Set against this historical backdrop and the rise of national socialism, it is unsurprising that West Germany, influenced by ordoliberal ideology, placed such an emphasis on currency stabilization.

The idea of stabilizing the price level stems from Eucken's concern that abuse of the monetary system leads to inflation (Eucken, 1959: 161–3). When the Deutsche Bundesbank was founded, countering inflation was central to its monetary policy, which subsequently developed into an inflation target that has become so ubiquitous today. Hence, the Bundesbank has come to be seen as a bastion of ordoliberal ideology. However, this approach to monetary policy is at odds with principle of power dispersion and improving the initial conditions prior to voluntary exchange. This chapter explores the relationship between inflation targeting and the concentration of power and argues that targeting nominal wages is more in keeping with the underlying ordo principle.

The monetary economist Ralph Hawtrey noted that 'the policy of currency stabilization might be interpreted to mean either the stabilization of the wage level or the stabilization of the price level, but it cannot mean both, for they are not consistent with one another' (Hawtrey, 1930). Given Germany's history of inflation, it is unsurprising that West Germany opted to focus on the stabilization of prices in an attempt to stabilize the currency. In its first annual report published in 1958, the Bundesbank made it clear that nothing would deter it from 'acting against the price rises with all means available to it' (Deutsche Bundesbank, 1958: 47).

When the Bundesbank was founded in 1957, taking control of monetary policy from its forerunner the Bank deutscher Länder, its main duty as an independent institution of the state was to safeguard the value of the currency. This was to be achieved by regulating the amount of money in circulation and the supply of credit to the economy. The success of the independent Bundesbank and its forerunner in controlling inflation was a highly significant factor that increased real wages during the 1950s. As was shown in Table 4.1, while nominal wage growth in West Germany was similar to that in France and Japan, real wages grew almost twice as fast due to relatively lower inflation. This success in fighting inflation continued after the break-up of the Bretton Woods Agreement in 1973 up until 1989. During this period, West Germany's annualized rate of inflation remained the lowest across the entire OECD (Clarida & Gertler, 1997).

According to Otmar Issing, a former board member of the Bundesbank, this success was driven by providing a quantified guidepost to help manage expectations. This consisted of an inflation goal and a target growth rate of a broad monetary aggregate that was expected to be consistent with the inflation goal. This signalled the intention of controlling inflation and also to guide those involved in wage bargaining of the potential outcomes of excessive nominal wage growth (Issing, 2005).

In the initial phase after the break-up of the Bretton Woods Agreement, the experience of monetary targets and influencing the wage-bargaining process was not particularly effective. The high increase in nominal wages in 1974, which was an attempt to compensate for the loss in real income, was followed by higher unemployment and inflation. This changed towards the end of the 1970s with more subdued wage settlements. Issing believed this success was only possible due to public support which was linked to the German public's historical concern about the value of their currency.

From 1986, the Bundesbank set a goal of 2 per cent annual inflation, and when the ECB took control over monetary policy for the eurozone in 1999, its mandate was to maintain the rate of inflation below 2 per cent. This was amended in 2003 to maintain the rate of inflation below but close to 2 per cent over the medium term, and in 2021 it adopted a symmetrical target of 2 per cent over the medium term. With the exception of the Federal Reserve which has a dual mandate of maximum sustainable employment and price stability, a 2 per cent inflation target has become the de facto monetary policy target of central banks across advanced economies. This ubiquitous influence of the Bundesbank was summed up by a former president, Otmar Emminger, who noted that 'price stability is not everything, but without price stability everything is nothing' (Deutsche Bundesbank, 2012).

However, the notion that price stability will necessarily stabilize the currency is problematic in both theory and practice. Furthermore, there is increasing evidence that price stability has instead facilitated greater concentrations of power, rather than dispersed it thereby contravening the ordoliberal maxim.

Over the last 20 years the policy of a 2 per cent inflation target has resulted in a tendency for large swings in the relative purchasing power of currencies, as shown in Figure 5.1. The yen has moved within a 60 per cent range, sterling within 41 per cent, the US dollar 36 per cent, Canadian dollar 35 per cent and the euro in Ireland 35 per cent, although it has been more stable for Germany with an 18 per cent range.

The main reason for these dramatic fluctuations was, of course, the Global Financial Crisis, which occurred despite a 2 per cent inflation target being achieved by these central banks. But if a 2 per cent inflation target results in monetary instability, then it is a cause of the very issue it has been designed to curb in the first place. This is something that the Bank for International Settlements warned about prior to the financial crisis, although their concerns were mostly ignored (White, 2006).

Ever since the idea of stabilizing prices as a means to maintain a monetary equilibrium was developed by the Swedish economist Knut Wicksell in his 1898 classic work *Interest and Prices*, a substantial body of monetary theory has developed to demonstrate why this cannot be the case. Wicksell's pure credit economy was a theoretical construct to understand why prices had fallen during a period when metallic money was dwindling into insignificance, thereby reducing the relevance of the quantity theory of a cash economy (Leijonhufvud, 1997). Wicksell thought this so-called paper standard might function internationally if the world's central banks could cooperate their discount policies to stabilize international currencies (Laidler, 2004).

For Wicksell, the goal of monetary policy was price stability which he thought could be achieved by the central bank increasing or decreasing the discount rate or money rate of interest relative to the marginal productivity of capital which he called the natural rate of interest.[1] By influencing the cost of credit across the banking system, Wicksell thought the central bank could induce the two rates towards equilibrium.

Wicksell's Swedish colleague, David Davidson, pointed out that stabilizing prices would not necessarily maintain an economy at equilibrium. Productivity growth, which raises the marginal productivity of capital, might result in falling prices. Wicksell's response would have been to lower the money rate of interest, but this would push the two rates further apart and hence would not result in a monetary equilibrium.

For Davidson, a necessary condition for monetary equilibrium was that the volume of money in an economy be permitted to increase in proportion to population and real capital, or factor inputs. Any positive changes in productivity would therefore result in a proportionate fall in the price level (Uhr, 1975: 21, 92). In essence, when productivity increases, stabilizing the value of money requires prices to fall. Davidson's approach to maintain a monetary equilibrium is generally described as a productivity norm.

Davidson also argued that the issue of fairness and distribution was highly relevant to monetary policy, which from an ordoliberal perspective can be thought of as ensuring that monetary policy avoids concentrations of power.

Figure 5.1: Comparison of real effective exchange rates (Index 2010 = 100)

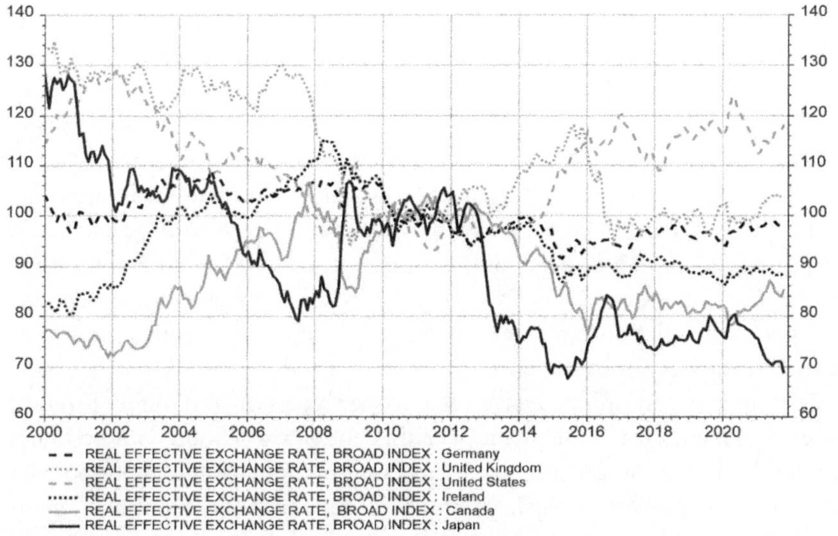

REAL EFFECTIVE EXCHANGE RATE, BROAD INDEX : Germany
REAL EFFECTIVE EXCHANGE RATE, BROAD INDEX : United Kingdom
REAL EFFECTIVE EXCHANGE RATE, BROAD INDEX : United States
REAL EFFECTIVE EXCHANGE RATE, BROAD INDEX : Ireland
REAL EFFECTIVE EXCHANGE RATE, BROAD INDEX : Canada
REAL EFFECTIVE EXCHANGE RATE, BROAD INDEX : Japan

Source: Refinitiv Datastream, an LSEG Company

He asserted that if productivity were to increase by 25 per cent and the price level were kept constant, money incomes such as wages and profits would rise by 25 per cent, but incomes fixed in terms of money would stay the same resulting in a lower standard of living for certain sections of the population. In view of social injustice he disagreed that it was desirable to stabilize the price level (Thomas, 1935). Monetary policy can have a significant impact on how income and wealth is distributed; hence, the most appropriate monetary policy for a liberal society is one that does not favour one group or another. This would be in alignment with the ordoliberal maxim of dispersing power to ensure that no specific interest group benefits at the expense of another.

But not only can stabilizing prices cause unfair distributional effects, a 2 per cent inflation target can also favour capital at the expense of labour. The idea of supporting a gently rising price level to stimulate production stems back to David Hume in *On Money*. Nicky Kaldor reiterated this argument that a slow and steady rate of inflation provides a most powerful aid to the attainment of a steady rate of economic progress (Thirlwall, 1974: 18–20). While this argument supports a higher rate of profit, it largely ignores the question as to whether labour will be rewarded for its contribution to rising productivity.

Since 1990, when inflation targeting started to become the norm for monetary policy, the returns to capital have increased at the expense of the returns to labour. This generally reflects more rapid growth in labour productivity compared to average labour compensation, and hence an increase in the returns to capital relative to labour. Between 1990 and 2009, the share of labour compensation in national income declined in 26 out of 30 advanced countries for which data were available. The median labour share of national income across these countries during the period fell from 66.1 per cent to 61.7 per cent (ILO & OECD, 2015).

While an increase in profits might increase investment thereby boosting job creation, which was the case in West Germany, the study found that in developed economies the shift in income away from labour towards capital has not produced the expected increase in investment. Between 2000 and 2007, the capital share in advanced G20 countries grew by close to 2 percentage points. In contrast, investment as percentage of GDP remained stable. Hence, a 2 per cent inflation target has merely accentuated the concentration of power among economic agents.

Furthermore, in order to stave off a deeper recession and higher levels of unemployment during the financial crisis, central banks floored interest rates and embarked upon quantitative easing programmes. While these policies did have some positive effects on the economy enabling economic agents to refinance at lower costs in addition to supporting new projects at the margin, the significant fall in real and nominal interest rates had additional distributional effects that have entrenched wealth and power.

The fall in the cost of borrowing for nonfinancial corporations resulted in a jump in income of $710 bn in the US, UK and eurozone between 2007 and 2012 (McKinsey Global Institute, 2013). This increase in profits supported higher equity valuations in conjunction with a lower discount rate. In the US the top 10 per cent of the wealthiest households own 84 per cent of all stocks (New York Times, 2018). In the UK over the same period, the cost of housing services fell by 15 per cent for high-income households due to lower interest rates while they *increased* by 13 per cent for low-income households.[2] This is due to the fact that there are almost three times as many wealthy households who own a house with a mortgage than low-income households. The rise in the value of real assets such as housing has also exacerbated intergenerational fairness due to the relative high cost of acquiring housing assets.

Davidson's productivity norm was taken up by a number of other Swedish economists including Erik Lindahl and Gunner Myrdal. Lindahl emphasized the practical nature of a productivity norm which he argued was much easier to implement than price stability. Furthermore, if a change in productivity is compensated by a shift in the price level, this is not only more easily rectified but also minimizes the disturbance of output (Lindahl, 1970: 225–6, 231). Indeed, Lindahl shows that it is more straightforward to forecast the factor inputs of demographic change and normal capital growth, but it is very hard to forecast productivity growth which is required to maintain price stability. Furthermore, he thought that 'keeping the price level stable requires fairly large interest rate movements determined on the basis of a profound knowledge of the situation' (Fregert, 1993: 134).

Lindahl also focuses on the fairness angle of monetary policy between borrowers and lenders, arguing that a productivity norm generates the best outcome as it neutralizes the effects of productivity changes. For example, cheaper energy which might be the result of productivity improvements is good for debt holders due to a lower price level and for entrepreneurs who can generate the same output with lower inputs. In addition to the productivity norm generating equity between borrowers and lenders, it also ensures that the benefits of productivity gains are shared between labour and capital, rather than just benefitting capital. Employers base their wage offers on an estimate of the value of labour in money terms for the period when the work is done. If productivity increases during the period, then workers will not be able to benefit from the improvement until the next round of wage agreements. Even then, it is not certain that employees will be able to fully receive the increase as employers might argue that the outlook has changed. However, a fall in prices enables workers to receive those benefits instead through higher real wages when money wages are held at a constant level (Fregert, 1993: 136).

Lindahl's colleague Gunner Myrdal provided additional colour why price stability is incompatible with monetary equilibrium, noting that agents in an economy often make use of multi-year fixed contracts. In addition, there is a general inertia to the adjustment of prices over time and finally there exist opportunities for price manipulation due to the lack of competition. Myrdal thus concluded that price stabilization and the elimination of the business cycle are to some extent competing and contrary objectives.

Although a number of important theoretical developments related to the productivity norm originated in Sweden as a reaction against Wicksell's price stability approach, these ideas also developed independently in the Anglo-Saxon world. The monetary economist George Selgin has argued this extends back into the first half of the 19th century and the writings of Samuel Bailey (Selgin, 1995).

Central to Bailey's argument for an appropriate monetary policy was the concept of fairness. He noted that although benefits from a rise in the price level originating on the side of money might stimulate industry, in reality this is an unjust transfer of income and wealth in favour of entrepreneurs and speculators. Furthermore, Bailey could not see why creditors should not bear their share of losses arising from increased difficulty of production any more than they should not partake in the advantages derived by the community at large from improvements in production.

Arthur Pigou also favoured a productivity norm arguing that the goal of credit regulation ought to be to stabilize adjusted real income per head. The productivity norm was also supported by Dennis Robertson, who insisted upon the need for such a norm to avoid windfall profits flowing to entrepreneurs when productivity increases or losses to entrepreneurs when productivity declines (Selgin, 1995).

Ralph Hawtrey also pursued a similar line of argument. He thought that the government had to take responsibility for regulating credit to prevent monetary disturbances leading to a vicious circle of the expansion or contraction of credit. But he argued that it was a mistake to base credit regulation on either the quantity of money or on movements of the price level. Instead, he proposed that credit be regulated to maintain a specified wealth value of the unit of wages. With nominal wages held fixed, the central bank 'would aim at so regulating credit that the flow of money would just allow full employment at this wage level' (Hawtrey, 1967: 186). Fiscal measures, according to Hawtrey, are too slow and cumbrous to effect credit with the bank rate providing a prompt and flexible approach (Hawtrey, 1967: 203).

Such a solution to monetary stabilization would also avoid various disorders which unregulated variations in the value of the monetary unit may cause, including the injustice between debtor and creditor, disturbances of the values between wages and profits as well as the effect of monetary expansions and contractions upon productive activity. The idea of equity is also central to much of Hawtrey's thinking which is compatible with the notion of dispersing power so no specific group is able to benefit from monetary policy. Hawtrey notes that in the event of increased productivity, a stable price level means increased profits. But as increases in wages lag behind productivity improvements they may be obtainable only at the cost of friction and possibly of industrial disputes. Hence, Hawtrey argued that the most appropriate solution was to stabilize the wage level with the advance of real wages coming about through a fall of prices (Hawtrey, 1930).

Hawtrey attacked the view of those who supported price stability such as Keynes arguing that their use of a retail index was an inappropriate target as it ignored the price of capital goods. Furthermore, he thought that price indices were liable to be disturbed by non-monetary causes which can be considerable in nature. Indeed, this was exactly the mistake made by the Federal Reserve in 2008 when inflation was driven by a negative exogenous supply shock due to rising commodity prices, and therefore was not related to monetary disturbances that the Fed should have been focused on.

Hawtrey also put to rest the naïve view that falling prices always cause a depression whatever the cause. He argued that in so far as the fall is due to diminished real costs or increased productivity in some industries it has no restraining effect on enterprise. Moreover, if price falls are not related to a fall in demand then there is no motive to postpone purchases.

Despite this body of evidence in terms of theory and practice, the stability of Germany's effective real exchange rate over the last 20 years suggests that perhaps the Bundesbank's obsession with price stability has paid off. But this victory has come at a significant cost. What works for Germany has not worked for peripheral eurozone countries who have experienced more volatile real currency movements accompanied by much lower growth and significantly higher unemployment. In its attempt to conduct monetary policy across the eurozone, the ECB has neither satisfied the demands of the peripheral countries nor it seems those of the most powerful economy, Germany.

The ECB vs an irritating German idea?

In 2019, the Bundesbank president Jens Weidmann openly criticized the ECB's low interest rate policy on a number of fronts including that it was undermining Germany's savings culture (Reuters, 2019). The issue of fairness and who benefits from monetary policy remain critical issues for public policy. Such criticism should also not be surprising given that the Bundesbank is entitled to promote Germany's interests within a *Staatenverbund* or union of states. This criticism was subsequently followed by the publication of a memorandum by a group of former central bankers, including three former senior executives of the Bundesbank, criticizing the ECB's 'ultra-loose' monetary policy.

In addition to criticizing quantitative easing they argued that the ECB was keeping interest rates low to ease the debt burden of profligate and highly indebted eurozone countries. This approach they noted has also kept zombie firms afloat, which in turn may be contributing to weaker productivity growth. The effect of maintaining ultra-low interest rates, they emphasize, is therefore only increasing the risk of financial instability by enabling counterparties to continue to fund themselves which under normal conditions would not have been possible (Bloomberg Newswire, 2019).

The increasing fractious debate between the Bundesbank and the ECB with respect to the implementation of monetary policy highlights the well-known but potentially intractable issue of whether the eurozone is an optimum currency area, and whether without a full fiscal and banking union the euro can be sustained. Most analyses of the eurozone have never been particularly positive that optimal conditions exist. Eichengreen argued that Canada and the US were more of an optimal currency area because labour mobility was greater, the return on capital was similar and real exchange rate disturbances were less than in Europe (Eichengreen, 1991). Analysis by the author demonstrates a substantial variation in the return on capital across the eurozone (Aubrey, 2012: Ch 6).

Friedman argued whether a common currency is good or bad depends primarily on the adjustment mechanisms that are available to absorb the economic shocks on individual countries. He thought the advantage of lower transaction costs requires there to be sufficient labour mobility greased by a common language, flexible wages and prices, as well as the freedom of movement of goods and capital. Critically, it also requires a central government that directs monetary policy to be able to use fiscal transfers. While he argued that these conditions existed in the US, he did not think they existed within the prospective eurozone states. Interestingly, he noted that:

> As of today, a subgroup of the EU – the Benelux countries ... Austria, and perhaps Germany – come closer to satisfying the conditions favorable to a common currency than does the EU as a whole. But they already have the equivalent of a common currency. Austria and the Benelux three have, for all intents and purposes, linked their currencies to the Deutschmark. However, these countries still retain their central banks, and hence can break the link at will. (Friedman, 1997)

Given that flexible exchange rates are a powerful adjustment mechanism for managing shocks that affect each country differently, the economic benefits of new currency zones appear to have been overstated.[3]

This Anglocentric view of the eurozone is, however, not shared by many European technocrats. Indeed, a strong argument has been made by an ECB board member that there is in fact very little difference between the European project and how a common currency emerged in the US (Mersch, 2011). As noted in a blog by David Beckworth there was very little labour mobility between the north and south in the US until the 1930s. Beckworth suggests that the US isn't really an optimum currency area even today (Beckworth, 2010). But what really matters for currency zones is not whether they are optimal but whether they are backed by a unified political organization with a common fiscal and banking policy.

Hence, when the Global Financial Crisis hit, the lack of a single political body in the eurozone clearly exacerbated the issue. Furthermore, the rigid Maastricht criteria of fiscal constraints, such as limiting budget deficits to 3 per cent of GDP and ensuring a debt limit of 60 per cent of GDP, made the situation far more complicated. In 2011, the Stability and Growth Pact was amended by two regulations for eurozone economies, known as the two-pack, which facilitate the monitoring and assessment of draft budgets. In addition, six directives and regulations were passed which focused on improving compliance with the Stability and Growth Pact and to address macroeconomic imbalances. In 2012, the Fiscal Compact was introduced to further strengthen the Stability and Growth Pact which included debt brakes with the view that this would encourage faster structural reform and greater convergence. Germany, having passed its own debt brake in 2009 to balance its budget, played a leading role in pushing these fiscal reforms at the European level.

During the eurozone crisis, southern European countries were unable to use monetary policy to stimulate their economies as they were eurozone members. They were also unable to use fiscal policy as they were up against the single currency debt ceiling rules. Some labour did move out of Greece and Spain; however, it is unrealistic to expect this would equalize unemployment rates. In 2012, at the height of the eurozone crisis when unemployment in Greece and Spain was close to 25 per cent, emigration flows were 1 per cent of the population of Spain and 1.4 per cent for Greece, but just 0.5 per cent for Portugal that had around 15 per cent unemployment. The average across the EU was around 0.8 per cent (European Commission, 2014).

To leave one's community behind and go in search of work should not be underestimated, particularly given the language and cultural barriers across the EU. Even in the US in the absence of language and cultural barriers, labour is not particularly mobile, although it is important to note that the US does not have such large disparities in unemployment rates. The median distance between where adults live and their mother in the US is just 18 miles, with only 20 per cent of adults living more than a two-hour drive away (New York Times, 2015).

The quickest solution to the eurozone crisis would have been for heavily indebted countries to have restructured their debt; however, this would have most likely resulted in the collapse of the French and German banking systems given their exposure. Hence, it is the lack of a political union alongside a banking and fiscal union that makes the eurozone fundamentally flawed, not whether it is an optimal currency area. What ultimately matters for a single currency is the willingness of wealthier areas of the union to support a substantial redistribution of their income to poorer areas. Given this is not currently the case, nor is there support for a federal union, the economist Steve Keen has argued that the eurozone is essentially a suicide pact (Brave New Europe, 2019).

In his book on the eurozone crisis, the former Greek finance minister Varoufakis noted that Erhard had ignored France's attempt to create a common currency arguing that it would have to be preceded by political integration. Kaldor had also argued that it was dangerous to start with monetary union prior to a political union. Intriguingly, President Mitterrand conceded to Delors that the next financial crisis would find the euro wanting, but the issue would then resolve itself in a political union (Varoufakis, 2016: 61, 66, 93, 94). However, the requisite political union has not come to pass.

A recent argument in favour of strengthening the eurozone is for Germany to lead the charge for a greater fiscal and banking union (Vallee, 2021). The result of such a move would begin to resemble a federal state; however, there is not any desire for a federal union at the moment.[4] This raises the question how the current impasse might be resolved, if at all.

The ECB is obliged to meet its mandate by law of maintaining inflation at 2 per cent over the medium term; hence, it could attempt to pursue an expansionary monetary policy generating above-average inflation in Germany, thereby encouraging a greater movement of labour and capital investment out from Germany towards peripheral countries. Alternatively, member states could agree to large fiscal transfers from north to south or enable peripheral countries to turbocharge fiscal policy which would mean breaking the rules of the Treaty on the Functioning of the European Union (TFEU) or agreeing to amend them.

The COVID-19 public health crisis has resulted in some fiscal transfers from north to south through the Recovery Fund. The European Commission will for the first time borrow from financial markets to the tune of €750 bn, of which €312.5 bn will be distributed in the form of grants to member states, and the remainder to top up the EU budget and to be distributed as loans (European Commission, 2020). In addition, the fiscal rules for eurozone members were suspended as a result of the pandemic.

Despite strong support from Germany for this proposal, it has been argued that Germany has been resistant to reforming the eurozone due to an adherence to ordoliberal ideas (Dold & Krieger, 2019: 31). The ideas of price stability and liability, where economic agents must be held responsible for their actions to prevent costs being imposed on others, were both embedded in the Treaty on European Union that all members signed up to. In addition, it has been argued that the fiscal austerity imposed by Germany was due to a dogmatic adherence to ordoliberalism, which destroyed livelihoods across the eurozone. Hence, ordoliberalism has been politely portrayed by critics as an irritating German idea (Hien & Joerges, 2017).

Matters have been made worse as there rarely appears to be any acknowledgement from the German authorities that its participation in the euro has maintained an artificially undervalued currency, thereby stimulating its exports and accumulating a large current account surplus. Thus, the criticism has stuck. Germany is destroying the eurozone due to its obstinate adherence to an ordoliberal outlook.

The challenge with this narrative is that the eurozone is not compatible with a number of fundamental ordoliberal principles. First, the ongoing distortion of the real German exchange rate is a clear transgression of the need to maintain an efficient price mechanism. Second, the imposition of a singular economic and social construction across diverse countries ignores a fundamental aspect of how one might be able to live a life of *Vitalpolitik*, with the eurozone via the ECB *centralizing* public power rather than dispersing it.

Third, although Eucken argued for rational automatism for a central bank target, it is not clear whether there is sufficient knowledge to stipulate at the constitutional level the central bank target. This lack of knowledge suggests that targets should be set by the central bank in response to changing conditions to achieve a specific constitutional goal such as currency stability or stabilizing wage levels. The Bundesbank was given a free rein to meet its constitutional goal of stabilizing the currency, which it did more successfully than any other central bank. Indeed, the economist Adam Posen warned that that the blind pursuit of price stability may not necessarily result in a successful outcome given that central banks might have to act in a more flexible manner in response to events. The important issue is that targets are conveyed transparently to the market. For Posen, this indicates that the constitutional rules created for the ECB learnt nothing from the Bundesbank's success given the complexity of the economy (Posen, 1997).

Finally, there is nothing inherent in ordoliberalism that dictates fiscal austerity. The debate on whether fiscal austerity, as supported by then finance minister Wolfgang Schäuble and Jens Weidmann of the Bundesbank, was part of an ordoliberal crusade or rather just a set of bad policies due to the fundamental architectural flaw of the eurozone has become highly contentious. Authors such as Mark Blyth see this an ideational-driven set of policies (Blyth, 2013), whereas Brigitte Young argues that 'critics are right to take Germany's handling of the Eurozone crisis management to task, but it is simply incorrect to hold that ordoliberal ideas are responsible for this' (Young in Hien & Joerges, 2017: 206).

Fiscal austerity per se has little in common with the underlying principles of ordoliberalism, which are related to the dispersion of power and using rules to frame economic conduct (Bonefeld, 2017: 2). Moreover, the success of the Bundesbank in managing inflation during the 1970s was achieved in conjunction with the Stability and Growth Act from 1967 which included a fiscal policy component. Prior to reunification in 1990, Germany rarely adhered to fiscal austerity as noted by Adam Tooze. Germany's gross public debt as a percentage of GDP was higher than France, and in 2007 was the eurozone average. Tooze suggests that the application of the debt brake in 2009 to reduce the deficit appears to be more related to political manoeuvring, including concerns around environmental sustainability (Tooze, 2017).

While it is true that Eucken was sceptical about fiscal policy driving full employment due its corporatist overtones, as had been the case in fascist Italy and Nazi Germany, Weale argues that Eucken hadn't had the opportunity to explore how such a policy might be achieved in a democracy (Weale in Hien & Jorges, 2017). Eucken, in the early 1930s, had been in favour of the Lautenbach plan, which was a fiscal stimulus package designed to overcome the Great Depression in Germany (Feld et al, 2018). Röpke also advocated strong fiscal and monetary stimulus as part of a short-term measure when faced with an economic contraction (Dyson, 2021: 25).

While Erhard, during the 1950s, did not pursue an aggressive fiscal policy, the cancellation of 50 per cent of West Germany's debt in 1953 played a significant role in supporting growth, enabling greater spending on investment and social policy than otherwise would have been the case (Dyson in Dold & Krieger, 2019: 151). It is also important to note that capital was severely constrained at the time; hence, there was no real alternative for West Germany. Any attempt to raise more debt via fiscal policy would have merely driven up interest rates to punitive levels. By 1967, West Germany was actively embracing fiscal policy following the passing of the Economic Stability and Growth Act.

Hence, there is nothing inherent in ordoliberalism that is opposed to fiscal expansion in both good and bad times, particularly given the central role played by investment. If fiscal expansion were to destabilize the currency then this would certainly be in contravention of a fundamental principle, or if it were to only benefit a certain section of society. But fiscal expansion would only have such an effect if it were inflationary due to an excessive demand shock leading to increased competition for increasingly scarce resources, which in turn might de-anchor inflation expectations. Hence, fiscal expansion is constrained by its ability to generate a positive real return on specific projects.

What is critical, however, for an ordoliberal fiscal policy is that it should not be centralized, but instead be communally driven. This is perhaps the most important distinction with Keynes' centrist approach. This is related to the rejection of the *Herrschaftsstaat* (centralizing state) and the favouring of a *Gemeinschaftsstaat* (community-based state) (Dyson, 2021: 25, 40). Centralized states that raise large amounts of money are more likely to struggle to spend it wisely, thereby preventing the asset side of the balance sheet from growing, which in turn is likely to be more inflationary.

Localized fiscal policy is more likely to resolve the challenges posed by the knowledge question, particularly given that borrowing via the bond market is often tied to specific projects. This provides additional transparency with regards to any shift in inflation expectations given that bond yields will tend to rise if investors believe that fiscal policy has become inflationary. A good example of this is the *Société du Grand Paris* project which is investing in new transportation lines and the built environment, including housing and office space. The project has a debt ceiling of €35 bn to redevelop large sections of Paris, which is managed locally but is ultimately backed by the French state. If the project were to create inflationary pressures, the yields on its outstanding bonds would begin to rise. While this might place pressure to reduce fiscal policy in the Paris region, it would not necessarily stop other local areas from tapping the capital market if there was less inflationary pressure.

The *Gemeinschaftsstaat*, therefore, more effectively resolves the knowledge issue ensuring that projects are financed and managed by those closest to them. These projects benefit from the state's balance sheet which can be used to stand behind the debt and maintain lower borrowing levels. While fiscal policy is clearly important for raising the rate of investment, it is less useful in immediately counteracting falls in demand as fiscal policy can be cumbersome, as noted by Hawtrey. There can be long delays in creating sufficient 'shovel-ready' projects to make a difference to employment in order to increase aggregate demand. If there are projects that require workers who are unemployed and who have the right skills, this is not an issue. However, it is rare that such a dovetailing of supply and demand of specific skills is possible given the elapsed time of such projects.

Planning decisions for small infrastructure projects generally take between one to two years to consider,[5] although it took eight years for Terminal 5 at Heathrow Airport to be approved which was completed in 2008 employing 7,500 workers on site. The tendering process for the Hornsea Wind Farm in the North Sea began in 2008, with stage 1 receiving planning permission in 2014. The project created 2,300 jobs – many of which were highly specialized.[6]

In practical policy terms this largely leaves monetary policy to try and address ongoing issues with the eurozone, but it is monetary policy that has been the focus of the greatest clash between German and European authorities. It is perhaps understandable that Germany, for historical reasons, does not want to see relatively higher inflation, nor permit the eurozone to pursue monetary financing. In 2013, Weidmann as head of the Bundesbank argued in the German Constitutional Court that the ECB's bond-buying programmes amounted to monetary financing which the ECB is not permitted to do under Article 123 of TFEU. In 2020, the German Constitutional Court ruled that the Public Sector Purchase Programme (PSPP) of the ECB, which was set up to acquire government bonds and other marketable debt securities, was in breach of its mandate. According to the Court, 'by unconditionally pursuing the PSPP's monetary policy objective – to achieve inflation rates below but close to 2% – while ignoring its economic policy effects, the ECB manifestly disregards the principle of proportionality' (Bundesverfassungsgericht, 2020). While the Court recognizes that it doesn't have jurisdiction over the ECB, which is the role of the European Court of Justice (ECJ), it believes that it is within its rights to comment on such issues in rare cases.

Although the ECB has exhausted the traditional avenues of monetary policy by reducing the discount rate, pursuing open-market operations such as buying bonds and reducing the reserve requirements for banks, these are not the only tools that might be used for monetary policy. Indeed, it was the Bundesbank who were often at the forefront of such experimentation including using a forward-looking inflation expectation management framework to influence actual inflation in the 1970s. Hence, the challenge is how the ECB might pursue other strategies to increase the volume of money in the economy.

The economist Willem Buiter, following Friedman's classic 1969 paper, has argued that helicopter money, or the injection of money into an economy, always works. Such an approach to monetary policy should not be thought of as anything unusual given that central banks regularly inject more money into the economy as demand for cash increases when the economy grows. For Buiter, it just requires determination to keep doing it until the effects can be observed against a specific target (Buiter, 2014). But this requires care to be taken how. As Richard Cantillon noted, 'I conceive that when a large surplus of money is brought into a state, the new money gives a new turn to consumption, and even a new speed to circulation. But it is not possible to say exactly to what extent' (Cantillon, 1932: Pt II, Ch 7).

For example, the pursuit of a continuous quantitative easing is unlikely to result in the outcome Buiter seeks, which would also lead to unfair distributional outcomes. One approach advocated by the economist John Muellbauer is for the ECB to send each adult citizen a €500 cheque (Muellbauer, 2014). This is in effect the same approach taken by the US government as part of the CARES Act passed in 2020, which sent out stimulus cheques to Americans to counter the effect of the global pandemic. In this instance an increase in the volume of money placed into the economy was funded by increasing debt. But managing the volume of money in an economy is the role of monetary policy; hence, it is not obvious why new money needs to be borrowed. Indeed, when the central bank injects new money into the economy due to increased demand for cash it does not have to borrow this money, it just creates it.

Following Muellbauer, the fund manager Eric Lonergan has argued that a greater volume of money can be inserted into the economy by maintaining a differential between the interest rate on bank lending and the rate on bank deposits. Hence, no matter what the money market rate is – even if it is zero – the central bank can lend money to banks on certain conditions at negative rates while increasing the interest rate paid on deposits (Lonergan, 2019).

This is effectively what the targeted longer-term refinancing operations (TLTRO) of the ECB have been doing. One key challenge remains that investment rises when expectation of future profits rise, so while this might help some projects at the margin of viability, it is unlikely that this will change Keynes' insight of animal spirits to being positive about the future so consumers start spending again. Lonergan argues though that the TLTRO approach could be used to deposit money directly in individuals' bank accounts (Lonergan, 2016). Following Buiter, these deposits should keep on coming until they start to have an observable effect on animal spirits.

By depositing money in everyone's bank account in equal absolute amounts rather than a tax cut funded through fiscal policy avoids any unfair redistribution as tax cuts tend to be targeted at specific income groups. Low-income groups whose income isn't high enough to pay tax rarely benefit from this approach to fiscal stimulus. For the unbanked, payment cards could be provided via firms that hold a settlement account at the central bank. These solutions are already in place in many jurisdictions which reduces the need for a central bank digital currency to be created for this purpose. While an absolute amount is mildly progressive, the effect on individual liability is muted to a certain extent given that those who were more in debt are still more in debt on a relative basis for each part of the income distribution. Such payments would continue until the appropriate monetary effects can be observed against an agreed target.

This approach to monetary policy would avoid the unfair distributional aspects of aggressive interest rate moves to combat recessions, which in recent years have been significant and have been one of the great causes of the concentration of wealth and power across developed economies. Furthermore, it would also curtail the negative effects of excess credit creation when interest rates are floored which tends to result in greater monetary instability at a point in the future. The easing of monetary policy through lower interest rates relative to the marginal productivity of capital between 2002 and 2006 and from 2012 has merely led to excess credit creation resulting in poor lending decisions and hence greater financial instability (Aubrey, 2014). As such, any shift away from using large changes in interest rates to counteract recessions towards tools which treat individuals equally should be supported.

While it might be theoretically possible for the ECB to embark upon delivering money to households through TLTRO schemes as Lonergan suggests, the focus on an inflation target would still result in increased monetary instability. Some monetary economists have recommended that instead of an inflation target, a price level target ought to be used which requires a central bank to target an inflation index (Svensson, 1996). However, a price-level target prior to the financial crisis due to the positive labour supply shock would have potentially resulted in even greater monetary instability forcing procyclical variation in interest rates. The downward pressure on inflation, due to the massive expansion of the global labour supply,[7] would have required monetary policy to have been even more expansionary, potentially resulting in an even worse build-up of private debt.

Hence, exploring how a productivity norm might be implemented without recourse to using large moves in interest rates remains a key plank of an ordoliberal monetary policy to maintain monetary stability and ensure that monetary policy does not benefit specific interest groups. Any move towards a new target is very much in keeping with Vanberg's view that constitutional rules can be changed based on accumulating evidence over time.

Such a shift also requires voters to be convinced that whatever target is chosen is easily understood and appears beneficial. During the early 1990s a consensus formed that central banks should adopt an inflation target, partly because of the political saleability of the idea given that inflation was a real issue for voters. President Reagan once described inflation as violent as a mugger, as frightening as an armed robber and as deadly as a hit man. Consumers understood this story and appeared comfortable with the anti-inflation approach central banks took given the history of inflation in the 1970s.

Which nominal target

For Selgin, a productivity norm can be thought of as either a total factor productivity norm or a labour productivity norm. The distinction matters because in the real world the capital–labour ratio is not static. Selgin argues that given the labour input is less subject to measurement errors than the input of capital services, a labour productivity norm might be put into effect with greater accuracy than its total-factor productivity counterpart and would come closer to achieving an 'optimum' money stock (Selgin, 1997: 65). Earl Thompson also proposed a labour standard as the monetary target which is close to Hawtrey's proposal to target low nominal wage growth to stabilize the exchange rate and maintain full employment at that wage level (Thompson, 1982).

One of the challenges of the focus on nominal targets is that it is more likely to increase real wages through falling prices. However, for the last 30 years politicians have been claiming, via central bank 2 per cent inflation targets, that falling prices are by definition bad. This remains a potential hurdle, despite the fact that the Bank for International Settlements (BIS) has found no broad correlation between depression and price falls (Borio, Erdem, Filardo & Hofman, 2015). The debt deflationary spiral of the Great Depression highlighted by Irving Fisher is a special case of deflation that must be avoided. Data from the US information technology sector demonstrates that falling prices have resulted in a rapid increase in profits, and an expansion of employment (Aubrey, 2016a). Hence, there is no reason why these positive outcomes shouldn't be applied to other sectors experiencing productivity growth.

More recently there has been increasing support for nominal GDP level targeting (Sumner, 2012; Beckworth, 2019). While stabilizing total nominal income instead of nominal wage levels is not too dissimilar given wages account for over half of GDP, they are not the same. One challenge for economists promoting a nominal GDP level target is that it is more abstract for consumers than wages, and thus may not engender support among voters. Indeed, at a conference in 2019, the economist Olivier Blanchard suggested that a nominal wage target might be far more politically saleable given that it would force the central bank to care about wages. Given the sluggish nature of wages over the last few decades, such a shift may well be welcomed by politicians looking for votes.[8] Hence, a more engaging narrative can be developed that enables the returns to labour to grow with productivity through falling prices, instead of unanticipated gains flowing to capital.

The economist David Glasner also notes that 'maintaining a stable wage level would ensure that the labour market was always in some reasonable balance. In particular, falling wages in one location, occupation or industry would be offset by rising wages elsewhere' (Glasner, 1989: 238). Given the central importance of the labour market to an economy, this would not only provide a clearer signal to workers but would also demonstrate politically that monetary policy is focused on workers' wages.

Glasner has also argued that a nominal wage target is superior to a nominal GDP target given that in the event of a negative supply shock a nominal GDP (NGDP) target would not provide sufficient monetary stimulus offsetting the contractionary tendency of the shock (Glasner, 2011). Furthermore, targeting either NGDP or nominal wages may result in potentially different outcomes across the income distribution, thereby effecting the initial conditions of voluntary exchange.

An analysis of the UK shows that household income grew much faster than wages between 1998 and 2017 for the lower two quintiles. The difference is largely explained by a significant increase in employment participation across lower-income households. Attempting to stabilize nominal income as opposed to nominal wages may have resulted in a premature tightening of policy after the financial crisis. Rising costs experienced by lower-income households is one reason behind the increase in employment participation, particularly for women. In this instance monetary tightening may have harmed their ability to find work. Conversely, wage growth over the 20-year period has experienced far less variation across the income distribution, as highlighted in Figure 5.2, which has partly been due to the introduction of the minimum wage. Besides nominal wages being more stable than household income for use as a potential monetary target, it is also much closer in terms of ensuring that no section of the income distribution benefits more than another.

Hence, a nominal wage target appears to be more closely aligned with the ordoliberal maxim to disperse public and private power, given that no section of the income distribution is favoured. Moreover, the focus on wages is more likely to facilitate engagement with the electorate that the economy should be managed to stabilize wages. When it comes to public policy, narratives matter. The challenge is therefore more related to the narrative of the benefit of price falls in terms of driving up real wages. As a recent

Figure 5.2: Wage vs household income growth by quintile 1998–2017 (UK)

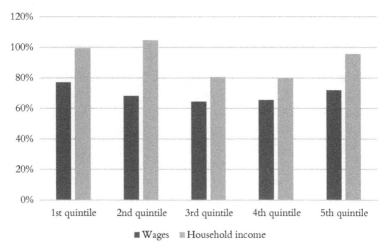

Source: HBAI, ASHE

paper in support of targeting nominal wages based on gross labour income has pointed out, 'Americans want a bigger paycheque, not a higher cost of living' (Armanath, 2019).

The introduction of a new monetary target does raise potential operational issues. For instance, targeting expected NGDP based on the economy's long-term nominal growth rate is affected by the fact that NGDP data often lags by two months with frequent sizeable adjustments (Goodhart, Baker & Ashworth, 2013). One way of potentially removing this issue is to base it on NGDP futures contracts whereby the market is used to forecast NGDP which in turn can be used as an objective function for central banks to loosen or tighten monetary policy accordingly (Sumner & Roberts, 2018). But this supposes that markets are good at forecasting at the macro level. However, there is a great deal of evidence to indicate that while markets are micro-efficient they are not macro-efficient. This forms the basis of what has been described as Samuelson's dictum (Samuelson, 1998), where the efficient markets hypothesis works well at the stock level, which is why it is hard for stock pickers to consistently beat the market, but works less well at the aggregate level (Jung & Shiller, 2006).

There appear to be fewer operational challenges with regards to targeting nominal wages given that wage data is published monthly and is subject to far fewer revisions, and the rate of growth of labour inputs is easier to forecast as Lindahl noted. Despite this, care needs to be taken to ensure the wage target used is adjusted to take into account self-employment and tax effects that might affect the value of a unit of labour. Hawtrey argued that the central bank should target basic wage stabilization (Hawtrey, 1967: 198), which might correspond to a lower quintile target. Armanath in his 2019 paper advocates using gross labour income which can be seen as an aggregate of wages which is a function of workweek, compensation per hour and employment. As wage growth has been reasonably stable across the income distribution, the decision of which wage data to target is less likely to result in unfair distributional issues.

While the ordoliberals were right to single out monetary policy as central to the success of a free and equal society, inflation targeting is not necessarily the most effective way to stabilize a currency. Indeed, inflation targeting may have been a contributory factor to the rising inequality and concentration of power across liberal democracies since it was introduced in the 1990s.

Despite the Bundesbank appearing to wave the flag for ordoliberalism in its fight with the ECB and raising important questions on the distributional effects of monetary policy, price stability is not in tune with the ordoliberal maxim of dispersing power, and therefore it should be replaced. Instead, a nominal wage target appears to be more in keeping with this maxim as it does not advantage any specific interest group. In the event of downward movements in wages, rather than lowering interest rates to increase the volume of money, central banks should instead explore alternative monetary tools such as distributing money directly to households. This should not be seen as some technocratic exercise based on an optimization function, but rather as a way of selling to voters how to progress the principles of freedom and equality that underpin the liberal order.

Liability and Private Property: Confronting the Perfect Externalizing Machine

The limited liability company: greatest invention ever?

One of the items in the collection of the United States Holocaust Memorial Museum in Washington, DC is a machine manufactured by IBM. The machine, known as a Dehomag Hollerith Machine, used punch-card technology enabling information to be sorted and arranged before computing the required outputs.[1]

During the late 1930s and early 1940s, more than half of the profit of IBM worldwide was likely derived from the sale of these machines to Nazi Germany and occupied Europe.[2] The machines were used to classify who was Jewish, which facilitated the mass incarceration and ultimately extermination of 6 million Jews. Without these machines it would not have been possible for the Nazis to have carried out genocide on the scale that they did (Black, 2001: 352).

The concept of private property that emerged within liberal societies protects a company's right to contract with other agents in order to generate an income stream from its assets. Since the 19th century this legal framework has been accompanied by the development of the limited liability of shareholders. In 1911, the Nobel Peace Prize winner Nicholas Murray Butler, who was then the President of Columbia University, said in a speech that the limited liability corporation is the greatest single discovery of modern times. He noted that even steam and electricity were far less important as they would be reduced to comparative impotence without it (Micklethwait & Wooldridge, 2003: 9).

The key success factor of this change was to dramatically increase the amount of investment, which arose as shareholders were no longer liable for claims arising from the result of poor decisions taken by the company directors. Although this increase in investment has been central to economic growth and the improvement in living standards, limited liability has also created a dilemma given that company directors may act in ways that are ultimately not in the interest of the company, and more importantly not in the interests of a liberal society.

Eucken was hostile towards the concept of limited liability as he thought directors ought to be accountable for their decisions, thereby reducing power concentrations and promoting a free society maintained through personal responsibility. While Eucken promoted the concept of private property, the ordoliberals argued that such rights were contingent on benefiting society, which required competition to eliminate the extraction of economic rent. Hence, where competition was not possible, natural monopolies ought to be communally owned. The ordoliberals were also somewhat sceptical of patents which conveyed a temporary monopoly, thereby increasing the concentration of power. This chapter explores how ordoliberal ideas can be applied to the contemporary debate on corporate governance, the regulation of public utilities and the issue of intellectual property.

The debate on liability is an old one, which Adam Smith raised in *The Wealth of Nations*. Smith noted that 'the directors of such companies, however, being the managers rather of other people's money than of their own, it cannot well be expected that they should watch over it with the same anxious vigilance with which the partners in a private copartnery frequently watch over their own' (Smith, 1904: Vol II, 190). Thus, Smith highlights the importance of having skin in the game in order to rein in immoral behaviour.

Eucken's implicit criticism of limited liability is along similar lines.

> The purpose of the unlimited liability of the entrepreneur in a competitive economy is to make him careful in the disposition of his resources, and in investing and producing, and automatically to eliminate him if unsuccessful. Unlimited liability is part of a competitive system, and its destruction by legal policy endangers the functioning of this system. (Eucken, 1950: 316)

The financial success of IBM derived from supplying machines, punch cards and services to Nazi Germany raises an important question. To what extent should liberal societies permit the directors of companies to engage in behaviour that might undermine the fundamental values of freedom and equality? This issue is summed up by Röpke's critical stance of German firms trading with the Soviet Union during the post-war period. He argued passionately that such trade merely strengthened those countries who were fundamentally opposed to freedom. For Rüstow, international economic integration could only be sustained if those engaged in international trade had similar ethical principles where self-interest is restrained by sympathy, virtue and approbation.

Thomas Watson, who was the President of IBM during this period, unsurprisingly thought that fascism was good for business (Black, 2001: 69). While this might have been the case for IBM's sales and crucially Watson's personal fortune, the Nazi regime was fundamentally opposed to the premises of liberalism. While Watson benefitted financially from dealing with the Nazi regime, more than 400,000 American servicemen during World War II lost their lives in fighting for freedom.

Such an outcome is in direct conflict with Eucken's mantra that whoever stands to benefit must also bear losses. This was central to his concept of *Haftung* or liability (Eucken, 1959: 172). *Haftung*, which translates as liability in both its legal sense and accountability for one's actions, was central for all societal stakeholders. According to Eucken, liability plays a major role in the structure of a competitive economic order. It is intended to ensure that capital is managed effectively and that senior personnel are responsible and liable for their investments. Eucken thought that liability acts as a prophylactic against the squandering of capital, and crucially can hinder the incorporation of firms striving for power.

For example, if the shareholders of a firm were liable for a newly purchased company, they would think twice about expansion through acquisition, thereby curtailing concentration. Eucken argued that the economy was increasingly being controlled by directors who were not liable for their actions. Eucken stressed that this in turn was impairing the price system through increased concentration. Liability then was not only central for economic order but also for a social order in which freedom and personal responsibility prevailed (Eucken, 1959: 173–4).

The introduction of Sarbanes Oxley in 2002 was precisely the outcome that Eucken was trying to avoid. The collapse of Enron and Worldcom alongside the bursting of the dot com bubble had created a situation where 60 per cent of Americans called corporate wrongdoing a widespread problem (Micklethwait & Wooldridge, 2003: 148).

In a speech soon after the default of Lehman Brothers, Jürgen Stark who was then a member of the executive board of the ECB reflected on Eucken's principle of liability.

> The CEOs of large financial institutions are right in seeing their role as one of entrepreneurs. However, this implies that they should assume unlimited liability for their decisions. Would this hamper financial innovation? I don't think so. But it would certainly be a strong safeguard against excessive risk-taking and procyclical behaviour during financial booms. (Stark, 2008)

The bailout of the banking systems across Europe and the US during the Global Financial Crisis once more triggered a tendency towards a centrally administered economy due to the social imperative to intervene. This raises the policy challenge whether Eucken's framework for a free society requires a dramatic shift towards the unlimited liability of firms or whether directors of limited liability firms can be made liable for their actions through other avenues.

The idea that shareholders cease to be liable for the actions of a corporation raised a number of concerns when it was introduced in the 19th century. Lord Curriehill raised three main points in the British Parliament as the 1856 Joint Stock Companies Act was debated. First, he thought creditors would be subjected to fraud. Second, he thought speculation would increase given that risk would have been transferred from investors to creditors. Finally, he thought that this would create unfair competition between those that did have limited liability and those that didn't (Boyle, 2016).

J.S. Mill thought that such concerns were overblown as creditors were not forced to deal with limited liability firms and there was no obligation to provide firms with unlimited credit. Furthermore, he thought that creditors were perfectly capable of taking care of themselves. However, this depended that no false representation was given and that transparent accounts were made available if necessary with penalties for non-compliance. As long as this transparency was safeguarded, Mill saw no reason why any number of persons should not 'freely desire to unite their funds for a common undertaking … [and] any body of persons ought to have the power of constituting themselves into a joint stock company' (Mill, 1994: 276–7).

During this contentious debate, the Deputy-Governor of the Bank of England argued in favour of limited liability given that unlimited liability was resulting in excessively lax credit decisions as creditors could claw losses back from shareholders (Saville, 1956). The result of the 1856 Act was that although the huge legal privilege of limited liability had been granted, the classical liberal outlook of the day did not require that anything 'should be conceded in return for it, in the shape of accountability, disclosure provisions or particular governance structures to ensure that companies acted in the public interest' (Parkinson, Gamble & Kelly, 2000: 34).

The debate during the 19th century in America is illuminating in that attempts were made by states to address some of the implications of the new-found privileges of managers and shareholders. Some states, including Pennsylvania, attempted to make shareholders liable for the payment of outstanding wages to employees. Massachusetts attempted to make shareholders of banks liable to creditors for the mismanagement of firms by its directors. In 1836, this morphed into double liability for the shareholders of banks who were liable for their initial investment, as well as the value of the asset holdings of the bank which were used to determine the value of the outstanding shares. Hence, shareholders would need to pay additional compensation to depositors and creditors. In addition, directors were held liable for the illegal payment of dividends which was defined by any impairment of the capital stock (Kempin, 1960).

While attempts to ensure that the goals of limited liability intersect with the common good have not always succeeded, this does not mean that the experiment of limited liability is a bad thing. Indeed, there is a reason why Butler thought it the greatest invention ever given the transformation it has presided over. But it has not done everything expected of it.

An analysis of whether it would be more efficient to continue with limited liability or move towards an unlimited liability system with insurance contracts largely comes down on the side of limited liability, particularly for larger firms. While there is evidence that unlimited liability might be more efficient for smaller firms with few shareholders, it is worth noting that smaller firms are less likely to have demand for credit. In addition, the banking system has already developed the institutional framework to manage these risks, whereas the insurance sector is relatively undeveloped in managing unlimited liability contracts at scale (Halpern, Trebilcock & Turnbull, 1980).

Furthermore, given the importance of investment in ordoliberal thought to improve equalization in the labour market, there is a strong economic argument in support of limited liability. According to one writer, 'limited liability is best understood as a subsidy designed to encourage business investment' (Millon, 2007). Albeit a subsidy that comes with certain costs due to the behaviour of a small minority of directors.

Given that limited liability is now so widespread across multiple jurisdictions it suggests that the benefits of maintaining the current system are likely to outweigh the costs of moving the legal basis of the global economy towards unlimited liability. However, any society that ignores the costs arising from limited liability will find itself being forced to intervene through societal pressure to rectify negative externalities. It was this tendency towards centralization that Eucken was worried about.

While directors have a duty of care towards the company, there is some evidence that the moral values of virtue, sympathy and approbation that Smith thought would rein in errant behaviour do not work without skin in the game. Nor do they appear to work without strong communal ties where individuals might have to confront their peers on a regular basis. Directors who place an excessive focus on profit maximization can lead to misjudgements in ethical behaviour. A series of experiments in North America indicates that the executives of limited liability firms place profits before moral beliefs, whereas this is not necessarily the case for the partners of firms that are not covered by limited liability (Boyle, 2016).

Furthermore, as limited liability has made capital easier to pool, investors have acquired a diverse portfolio of shares which makes the owners of public firms increasingly anonymous and therefore less interested in the day-to-day operation of firms that they own a small percentage of.

As a result, fewer shareholders directly engage with firms and monitor the behaviour of directors, although this is less of an issue for privately owned firms. For the minority of directors who do not feel their decisions and actions should be tempered by sympathy, virtue and approbation, the link between corporate irresponsibility and limited liability has resulted in the corporation turning into what has been termed the perfect externalizing machine (Gerner-Beuerle & Schillig, 2019: 814).

This potential divergence between the interests of firms and the broader interest of society has become a central issue with respect to the liberal ideas of freedom and equality. Market-oriented liberals such as Milton Friedman argued that as long as firms maximized their profits within given constraints, there shouldn't be any divergence (Friedman, 1970). But as Böhm noted, an economic system that entrenches private power as part of a profit-maximization strategy will reduce the equality of starting conditions thereby reducing the freedom of firms to compete. Hence, the interests of firms can be in contradiction with the interests of society.

Parkinson has advanced the idea that the public interest is the foundation of corporate legitimacy. Hence, where private decisions result in public discontent the foundation of this legitimacy is questioned. Despite Friedman's claim that the only role of business is to maximize profits, the private sector is aware of this broader legitimation issue as noted in a trade association publication where more than 90 per cent of firms agreed that companies had obligations which went beyond the pursuit of profits (Parkinson, 1993: 287).

The challenge is therefore to prevent a small minority of directors behaving in way that undermines the liberal principles of freedom and equality. This would require the legal obligations upon directors to be tightened such that directors and their advisers would err from pushing the boundaries of the framework from increasing profits at the expense of the public interest. A point noted by a former chair of the European parliament's Economic and Monetary Affairs Committee (Bowles in Aubrey, 2017).

Goodhart and Lastra argue that the basic problem is managers' remuneration is dependent on the level of equity prices, and equity holders have limited liability.

> With unlimited upside potential, but limited downside, this puts an equity holder into the position of having a call option on the residual assets of the enterprise. The value of such options increases with risk. This is because when the downside risk occurs, those with limited liability can shift the risk onto the other creditors, depositors, bond holders, trade creditors and taxpayers. (Goodhart and Lastra, 2019)

The result of this effect is that it can be argued that shareholders and managers can 'enjoy income rights without having to worry about how these income streams are generated' (Gerner–Beuerle & Schillig, 2019: 48). Hence, there is little incentive to ensure that directors are behaving in an appropriate way. In the instances where this kind of behaviour results in significant negative externalities, it creates a demand by society to intervene. However, such interventions rarely resolve the underlying issues which are caused by directors having accumulated an excess of power. This raises the question how an ordoliberal system of corporate governance might be implemented to ensure directors are held liable for their actions and what might be done to make shareholders care more about the long-term success of firms.

Goodhart and Lastra argue for the introduction of double liability to act as a break on the errant behaviour of directors. They propose to distinguish between different classes of shareholders with outsiders retaining limited liability, and insiders, including all directors, would be subject to double liability which tapers down over time (Goodhart and Lastra, 2019). To what extent this system would be straight forward to implement and would curb director behaviour remains to be seen. Whatever system is put in place it is important to note that any director behaviour that negatively affects the long-term success of the company is a breach of the duties of directors. The challenge here is that in many countries there is almost no enforcement of these duties.

In the UK according to the 2006 Companies Act, directors are obliged to promote the success of the company, which includes having regard for the long term as well as the interests of employees, the environment and other stakeholders. At face value this would appear to provide the right framework to instil these values. However, as noted by J.S. Mill, there needs to be sufficient penalties for non-compliance. Indeed, one of the central requirements of the OECD Corporate Governance principles is that legal and regulatory requirements that affect corporate governance should be enforceable (OECD, 2015a).

Evidence compiled by the World Bank suggests that without a general enforcement environment, few corporate governance mechanisms are effective. The effectiveness of any corporate governance framework therefore hinges upon a government's commitment to enforce the existing rules, particularly as private enforcement is inherently limited. The paper notes that as shareholders appoint boards, 'little independent corporate governance should be expected from the board in a firm with a controlling owner' (Berglöf & Claessens, 2004).

In the UK there is no public enforcement of directors' duties, thus contravening the basic corporate governance enforcement framework. Any breaches of section 172 which relate to the duties of directors of the Companies Act are to be enforced by the board of directors, but this is highly unlikely to happen given the conflict of interest. It is possible that if the board doesn't take action, shareholders can exercise a private action;

however, this has generally been ineffective and very few actions have been initiated (Keay, 2014).

In his paper on the public enforcement of directors' duties, Keay rebuts the view that as law is private it should just rely on private enforcement. Such an argument rests on the view that private law has no negative effect on society. However, it is a central tenet of ordoliberal thought that any private concentrations of power can and do negatively impact society as was argued by Böhm. This is why directors must be held liable for their actions.

Hence, a central tenet of a successful corporate governance framework must be that the state enforces the rules that are in place. This will ensure that directors are subsequently held liable for their actions where they do not support the long-term success of the company. As Jürgen Stark highlighted in relation to the Global Financial Crisis, bank directors should have been held liable for their actions. Instead, the net result of these actions has been an expensive and ongoing set of interventions that has impaired the price mechanism.

In the UK, the Financial Reporting Council (FRC) which sets the UK corporate governance code for listed firms requires companies to go through a self-assessment process in terms of addressing key corporate governance concerns. Unsurprisingly, this has merely resulted in 'achieving box ticking compliance at the expense of effective governance and reporting' (Financial Times, 2020a). The FRC is therefore not in a position to enforce the code, which makes its role largely useless. As Keay notes, 'it was due to the inadequacy of private enforcement of breaches of duties that the New Zealand government empowered the Financial Markets Authority to bring actions in relation to breaches of duties' (Keay, 2014). This follows Australia which already has public enforcement through the Australian Securities and Investments Commission (ASIC). Thus, Keay recommends that the UK moves towards public enforcement and also dropping the distinction between public and private firms.

Removing this distinction is critical as one of the major drivers of company failure is excessive leverage. While there have been a number of high-profile UK-listed firms that have defaulted under the weight of excessive debt, such as Carillion and Thomas Cook, according to one paper leveraged buyouts funded by private equity groups are more likely to default than a control group (Ayash & Rastad, 2019). Analysis of the probability of default of firms issuing leveraged loans by the author indicates that private equity-owned firms are nearly three times riskier than publicly listed firms (Wall Street Journal, 2019). The greater transparency provided by public markets appears to act as a management constraint to limit excessive leverage. One reason is that when a listed firm's debt to earnings before interest, taxes, depreciation and amortization (EBITDA) ratio is too high, the firm's equity can be shorted by investors. Private firms do not provide this option. According to the rating agency Moody's, in H1 2020 across the non-energy sector in the US, 58 per cent of all the defaults recorded were private equity-sponsored firms (Moody's, 2020).

When highly leveraged firms default, whether they are privately or publicly owned, it can often result in bankruptcy and job losses. Hence the directors who made the decision to increase leverage to unsustainable levels have not performed their duty towards the company. A recent court ruling in the US on the bankruptcy of the retail firm Nine West stated that creditors could pursue misconduct charges against the previous board of directors for over-leveraging the firm leading to its bankruptcy (Financial Times, 2020b). At this stage it is unclear what the effect of this ruling will be on director behaviour. What is clear is that public enforcement of directors' duties is a central component of any corporate governance framework. Directors ought to be held liable for their actions in any event where they have contravened their duties towards the company.

In tandem with public enforcement, it is also important that shareholders are engaged in the long-term success of the companies they own. In 2007, 94.5 per cent of RBS shareholders voted for the acquisition of ABN Amro despite the fact that the market signalled it would be value destroying (Aubrey, 2013a). And yet when RBS collapsed, its shareholders were bailed out by the UK government. This was fundamentally different to the bailout of the Swedish banks in the early 1990s where shareholders were not compensated (New York Times, 2008).

One issue reducing the oversight of directors by shareholders is that many investors might have short-term time horizons, and investors with long-dated liabilities such as pension and insurance funds have reduced their asset allocation to equities. As highlighted in the Kay Review of UK equity markets, the ownership of UK firms by pension and insurance funds was around 52 per cent in the early 1990s. However, by 2010 this had fallen to just 14 per cent, along with the dramatic rise of intermediation in the investment process (Kay, 2012).

One drawback of the pensions and insurance sector exiting equities has been the reduction of ownership in companies by shareholders with long-dated liabilities. This shift may well have been a factor in the increasing detachment between the underlying owners of public companies from the executive management teams who run them. This dynamic has been characterized by Andy Haldane as the era of the 'ownerless corporation' (Haldane, 2015). This divergence between sustainable long-term growth and executive management teams is well illustrated by the dramatic rise in executive pay without any associated performance. This was noted by the UK government in its consultation on corporate governance reform (BEIS, 2016).

In many jurisdictions, fund-management companies manage large chunks of pension assets; however, the mandates they receive from pension funds are often quite short with one report indicating that 25 per cent of mandates are for less than three years (NAPF, 2014). A fund manager given a target to drive returns over a three-year period is going to care less about long-term investment and the longevity of the firm. Only just under a third of pension assets have a mandate longer than ten years. Another challenge for the asset-management sector is that corporate governance analysis can be expensive which would increase fees, thereby potentially reducing returns. Moreover, those firms who do decide to play an active role would end up sharing the rewards with others who chose to do nothing.

The economist John Hicks thought that shareholders did have a role to play in acting as a break on the managers of firms. 'There is something to be said for the system ... in which the shares of large companies are held in large blocks by ... pension funds ... which have a sufficient stake in the company to keep in close touch with its affairs' (Hicks in Ornhial, 1982: 20). This suggests there might be some benefit for encouraging pension funds to become long-term investors directly. This would better align the needs of savers to generate long-term returns and provide the appropriate governance structure for management teams to invest for the long run. But to do this pension funds would need to have scale.

Research on the Canadian pension sector indicates that funds need to have at least Can$15 bn under management to attract sufficient expertise to bring in-house. This approach tends to reduce costs and better align incentives between the investor and firm (World Bank, 2017). This suggests there is potentially a corporate governance premium for long-term investors given they can exert greater control on firms in the long run. Indeed, there is considerable evidence that private equity-owned firms outperform public firms in terms of R&D intensity and job creation given the closer relationship between investors and directors (Akguc, Choi & Kim, 2015).

With regards to the pensions sector there are some encouraging examples in Canada such as the Ontario Teachers' Pension Plan (OTPP). The OTPP has a high level of public equity investment at 45 per cent. The fund tends to invest in firms with 5–30 per cent of total shareholding as well as large stakes in private firms. This permits the fund to have a much larger impact on corporate governance and to reap the rewards of that governance.

A comparison of the annualized returns of the five largest Canadian pension funds over the decade ending in 2019 demonstrates returns of 10.2 per cent compared with 8.1 per cent for UK private personal pensions which tend to have a high equity asset allocation.[3] High asset allocation to bonds within UK-defined benefit pension funds indicate far lower returns over the last decade, which also negatively impacts pension fund deficits. The large Canadian pension funds also benefit from the ability to invest in alternative asset classes such as infrastructure, in addition to the corporate governance premium.

In the UK, there are around 46,000 workplace pension schemes in both trust-based and contract-based schemes (defined benefit and defined contribution). In terms of size, nearly 60 per cent of these schemes have fewer than 100 members. These are just too small to manage investments in-house and therefore it is unrealistic that they can have any effect on corporate governance issues. The Australian pensions regulator has the capability to force mergers where there is insufficient scale to provide value for money (Aubrey, 2015).

Creating an investment and governance framework which provides incentives for shareholders to rein in errant behaviour of directors, alongside the public enforcement of breaches of directors' duties, would significantly reduce the need to socialize losses. As a result, there would be more support for a liberal economic system. An economic system where individuals are not held liable for their actions is unlikely to be a sustainable one.

While an ordoliberal system requires obligations to be imposed on individuals in the way they act to avoid concentrations of power and societal losses, it is crucial that property rights are maintained so firms can feel secure they will reap the rewards of their investments. The demise of the Soviet Union and Deng Xiao Ping's reforms in China indicate an almost universal acceptance of the central importance of private property for a successful polity. However, where firms and individuals are able to use private property rights to generate unearned incomes, this conflicts with the underlying ideas of freedom and equality.

Individual or communal property rights

Ronald Coase in his pioneering work on the nature of the firm highlighted the importance of clearly defined private property rights. Furthermore, he thought that the market would establish the most efficient owner of those rights. Coase's approach is embedded in new welfare economics, which accepts the initial allocation as a given and then attempts to optimize the outcome via a bargaining process (Coase, 1960).

In an attempt to avoid the public versus private debate, Coase argued that Pigou's view where private gains might impose public costs or externalities such as pollution was false. He thought that what might be termed externalities were merely mutual costs that are reciprocal in nature, and therefore are embedded in the transaction process itself (Getzler, 1996). The implication appears to be that government intervention should therefore not be necessary. And even if it were, it would still need to demonstrate that it was able to improve on Pareto efficiency where the market had failed.

This has led to a general criticism of state-owned property rights within contemporary neoliberalism emphasizing that resources will always be more effectively used when they are privately owned. Communal assets, it is asserted, will often be overused resulting in the destruction of those assets or the tragedy of the commons. In addition, it is argued that state-owned resources are inefficient due to the lack of incentives of managers.

However, transaction costs may be too high to ensure Coase's mutual reciprocity functions between polluters and non-polluters; hence, often the government has had to step in due to this failure by providing environmental legislation (Alchian, 1993). Furthermore, privately owned assets can also result in the destruction of those assets as has been demonstrated through excessive leverage. In addition, evidence collected on lobster fishing in Maine suggests that it is possible for communal assets to be managed effectively, in this instance to prevent overfishing (Coyle, 2020: 143). Although this has not been the case for the oceans which have been affected by both pollution and overfishing (Dasgupta, 2021).

From an ordoliberal perspective, private property rights work well when there is competition to help prevent abuse of those property rights. Hence, where competition is not possible, exploring public ownership of property rights is necessary. This is the basis of the arguments made by both Henry Simons and Alexander Rüstow in that natural monopolies such as utilities should be publicly owned. As far as they were concerned, the allocation of private property rights for natural monopolies such as energy and water distribution was not commensurate with the common good, given that private concentrations of power must be avoided.

One interesting historical case study was the acquisition of private utility firms by Birmingham City Council under the leadership of Joseph Chamberlain in the late 19th century. When Chamberlain became Mayor, he acquired the Birmingham Gas Company and Staffordshire Gas Company in 1875 using municipal debt. Importantly, he persuaded the council to run the acquired entities like businesses. Profits went to the community instead of flowing as dividends to shareholders. According to Chamberlain, 'all monopolies which are sustained in any way by the state ought to be in the hands of the representatives of the people … and to whom the profits should go' (Nettlefold, 2017: Ch 2). Chamberlain saw water in the same light as energy production and he municipalized local water firms through the Birmingham Water Corporation in 1876.

However, natural monopolies do not have to remain monopolies if technology advances, enabling greater competition. Energy production has been under private ownership for decades in many countries and the recent development of small-scale solar and wind energy production units will only increase competition further. The contemporary neoliberal consensus that developed through Bork and Friedman, argued that government ownership of utilities results in worse outcomes; hence, natural monopolies such as water should be privatized. While the privatization of electricity generation can be considered a success, the recent trend towards the re-municipalization of water supply and sewage suggests that it has been a failure for water (Kishimoto, Lobina & Petitjean, 2015). This is unsurprising given water retained its natural monopoly status whereas electricity, with the exception of the national transmission infrastructure, has been subject to competition.

While undertaking international comparisons of water utilities is fraught with challenges, there is growing evidence that the municipal ownership model of Sweden has outperformed the private model of England. While charges prior to taxes such as VAT are 25 per cent lower across Sweden for the supply of 100 m³, levels of investment remain higher in Sweden and profits much lower (Lobina & Hall, 2001; International Water Association, 2014). This indicates that simplistic binary arguments that state is bad and the private sector is good are unhelpful and sometimes wrong.

One important aspect of the privatized natural monopolies in England is to understand to what extent the interests of shareholders and directors has overlapped with those of society. According to the Financial Times, privatization has led to a divergence between society and the interests of the directors and shareholders (Financial Times, 2017a). Such an outlook from an ordoliberal perspective is unsurprising given that without the regulating effect of competition, the private concentration of power will not result in outcomes that promote freedom and equality.

An analysis of Thames Water which supplies water to the London region suggests that water bills might have been 25 per cent lower had it remained under municipal ownership. Higher bills appear to be merely paying for higher profits. Indeed, one owner received returns of between 15.9 and 19 per cent during the 11 years it controlled Thames Water, which is twice what an investor might expect from a private utility (Financial Times, 2017b).

A report published by the Public Services International Research Unit indicates that the 40 per cent increase in real household bills since privatization was mainly driven by continuously growing interest payments on debt rather than investment (Yearwood, 2018). Hence, accelerating debt levels are primarily the result of disproportionate dividend pay-outs, indicating that all of the investment could have been paid for out of operating costs without taking on any debt (Financial Times, 2018).

This has led to calls for the water regulator to improve its performance. While it is feasible that better regulation can generate improved outcomes, it needs to be recognized that continuous intervention by the state is less likely to be successful due to the complexity of behaviour across markets. The ordoliberal approach was instead for municipalities to run these organizations on behalf of the community in order to avoid private concentrations of power.

Property rights are therefore not absolute but contingent upon them providing value to a society. Ordoliberals did not believe that providing property rights to private agents to manage natural monopolies was expedient to a liberal society. The same is true for land. As has been argued by Alchian and Demsetz, 'to own land usually means to have the right to till (or not to till) the soil ... What are owned are socially recognized rights of action' (Alchian & Demsetz, 1973). This idea is important when thinking about the development of private property rights in land.

Liberalism's ideas on property rights have largely followed on from Locke's definition of private property which is based on labour rather than any absolutist sense of ownership. Locke thought that 'whatsoever then, he removes out of the State that Nature hath provided, and left it in, he hath mixed his Labour with, and joyned to it something that is his own, and thereby makes it his Property' (Locke, 1993: 274). The implication is that a liberal society should recognize the rights to property based on labour adding value to something. Therefore, ownership that is not contingent on added labour is not necessarily recognized as private property.

Locke's focus on labour provided the backdrop for Adam Smith who argued ownership incentivized individuals to increase capital accumulation. Thus, private property is a key driving force of wealth creation, resulting in an increase in living standards. Smith did not believe in the sacredness of property, but rather saw it as a means to an end. He used the example of the Duke of Cornwall not taking rent for mining projects in order to stimulate industry, which for Smith had a higher priority (Smith, 1904: Vol I: 162).

Mill further disputed the idea of the sacredness of property rights particularly when it came to land. 'No man made the land. It is the original inheritance of the whole species. Its appropriation is wholly a question of general expediency. When private property in land is not expedient, it is unjust' (Mill, 1994: 40–1). This point logically follows from Locke given that ownership was developed to protect labour inputs and not to protect a person's ability to claim land and extract value from the labour of others.

Mill's point on expediency has been central to the development of property rights within liberal democracies where from time to time the public authority needs to expropriate land for the public interest. Property rights are therefore merely a function of the legal relations agreed and accepted by the polity. As part of the expropriation process, liberal democracies generally assert that it is right to pay an appropriate level of compensation to the landowner. This concept has become enshrined in Article 1 Protocol 1 of the European Convention on Human Rights, where land can be expropriated for the public good so long as market compensation is paid (Reid, 2012).

As was discussed in Chapter 4, the West German government introduced its 1953 land compensation act to avoid the rampant land speculation of the Weimar period. Compensation for landowners therefore excluded speculative values that might arise from alternative planning uses, or what is sometimes described as hope value. This in effect implemented Locke's idea of private property where rising demand from the community, which increases land values, benefitted the community as they were the cause of the rise and not the landowner.

When the municipality acts as a master planner for a large-scale residential housing project, the rise in land values is generally used to pay for community infrastructure. That way local entrepreneurs and workers as well as education and healthcare professionals benefit from improved infrastructure and access to housing from their hard work. Liberal property rights are clear on this issue. They do not permit landowners to derive unearned income from the labour of others, a point emphasized by Lippmann in *The Good Society*.

Given the challenge of rising land values across the world in economically buoyant areas, ensuring that a liberal theory of property rights is adhered to remains a major challenge for public policy. While these issues to a large extent have been resolved in Germany and other countries such as France through its Urban Code (Renard, 2006) and the Land Readjustment Acts in the Netherlands (Hong & Needham, 2007), they remain problematic in most Anglo-Saxon countries where the approach to property rights in land remains at odds with freedom and equality.

Although landowners benefitting from the hard work of others has been recognized as an issue in countries such as the UK, rather than addressing the problem at source as advocated by Lippmann, the UK has instead embarked on a continuous series of complex tax reforms that have resulted in a constant stream of policy failures (Jones, Morgan & Stephens, 2018). The net result of this is that the state has maintained its protection of a landowner's economic rent.

This is a classic case of the refeudalization of an economy resulting from the ability of a specific interest group to ensure the rules of the game are biased in their favour. In the UK, what amounts to state subsidies are provided in law to landowners at the expense of labour in the form of future speculative values. Analysis by the author indicates this subsidy is worth about £10 bn per annum for England alone (Aubrey, 2016b). A similar argument can be made to ensure that existing residential and business property is taxed effectively to curtail unearned income from rising land values.[4]

The lack of support for liberal property rights is also likely to result in fewer incentives to increase investment as highlighted by Adam Smith. Lower investment is likely to result in lower productivity and lower living standards. The excess profits siphoned away due to the refeudalization of the economy could have been used to invest in infrastructure and housing that would enable real wages to rise rather than fall by reducing the cost of transportation and ensuring that housing supply remains constant and high.

The current socially recognized rights of action related to property rights in many Anglo-Saxon countries contravene liberal ideology with unearned profits flowing to vested interests in private natural monopolies as well as through speculative land values. A similar issue can also be observed under the broad banner of intellectual property, where socially recognized rights of action are also largely contrary to liberal values.

Intellectual property that is not really property

Intellectual property is a broad concept that covers numerous areas of law that has come to include patents, copyright, trademarks and trade secrets. According to the judge and jurist Richard Posner, although there are similarities between physical and intellectual property there are importantly a number of striking differences (Posner, 2006).

Crucially, intellectual property rights tend to be limited in duration – 20 years for most patent rights and life plus 70 years for copyrights owned by individuals. A patent is therefore merely a temporary legal right conveying a monopoly position on to a firm to prevent other firms from making and selling an invention for a period of time. Posner argues that trademarks are not intellectual property but rather an identifier. Intellectual property doesn't apply to trade secrets either which can be reverse engineered as long as contract and tort law is not violated.

In addition, intellectual property ideas are not exclusive whereas as physical property rights are, as two people cannot own the same piece of land. Property rights also need clear boundaries to function and patents do not have clear boundaries at all. For example, for firms selling online there are thousands of patents that they could be violating, and even if a firm could check them, it would largely be impossible to know what the boundaries are (Bessen & Meurer, 2008a: 8–9).

Finally, an idea is not just the product of an individual's labour but rather the product of all the accumulated information available to that person in addition to their labour. In the example of a piece of land, an individual would have paid for this accumulated labour, but in the event of intellectual property, the other inputs are free. According to Thomas Jefferson, 'inventions cannot, in nature, be a subject of property'. The question for Jefferson was whether the benefit of encouraging innovation was 'worth to the public the embarrassment of an exclusive patent' (Lemley, 2004).

Ideas, therefore, ought not to be owned as they are part and parcel of a civilized society. Patents should instead be understood as something akin to a transient monopoly privilege that offers innovators financial incentives for their ideas. However, monopoly privileges act as an impediment to the freedom of exchange and merely result in the growth of market power.

Eucken argued that patents fostered the concentration process, thereby hindering competition, which is why he thought that modern patent law and the ordoliberal competitive order were mutually incompatible. Eucken accepts that although the original intention was to further innovation, the reality is 'that patents grant exclusive and monopolistic privileges, that they clothe private interest groups with power and that they therefore close markets, cause and corroborate the politico-economic concentration process and enhance the emergence of cartels and concerns' (Wörsdörfer, 2012).

Hayek had similar views arguing that patents had assisted the growth in monopoly; hence, 'in the field of industrial patents in particular we shall have seriously to examine whether the award of a monopoly privilege is really the most appropriate and effective form of reward for the kind of risk-bearing which investment in scientific research involves' (Hayek, 1958: 114). The question for society then is whether firms require the entrenchment of transient monopoly power to generate income streams? According to Schumpeter, an early champion of innovation as the driver of the economic process, patents were largely unimportant. What mattered instead was the benefit of the first mover advantage and continuous innovation to stay ahead (Guichardaz & Pénin, 2019).

Furthermore, there is increasing evidence that patents rather than being a driver of innovation have now become a hindrance to innovation (Boldrin & Levine, 2005) and, therefore, are merely leading to increasing concentrations of power. According to Posner, sectors like pharmaceuticals might need support given the very high costs of bringing new products to market, but other sectors don't really need patent protection (Posner, 2012). This conclusion is generally supported by the academic literature where patents in the pharmaceutical sector 'provide strong positive incentives to invest in innovation. But in many other industries ... they may actually discourage innovation' (Bessen & Meurer, 2008c).

Intriguingly, analysis on the development of aircraft suggests that patents may have acted as an initial barrier to innovation. After the Wright Brothers successfully patented their invention, no further aircraft development took place between 1903 and 1906. However, fortunately for the sector, 'the Wright brothers had little legal clout in France where airplane development began in earnest in about 1907' (Boldrin & Levine, 2005: 97). The software industry, which is one of the most innovative sectors, developed without hardly any protection of intellectual monopoly. According to Bill Gates, 'if people had understood how patents would be granted when most of today's ideas were invented, and had taken out patents, the industry would be at a complete standstill today' (Boldrin & Levine, 2005: 18). Schumpeter appears to have been spot on in his analysis.

Since the 1990s, the number of patent applications soared in the US reaching 345,000 by the end of the 1990s, rising more than threefold from a value which had oscillated around 90,000 during the 1960s (Boldrin & Levine, 2005: 79). Despite this rise in patents there has been no increase in productivity – indeed, if anything the rate of productivity growth has slowed (Sainsbury, 2020). A senior vice president from Oracle stated in 2003 that 'our engineers and patent counsel have advised me that it may be virtually impossible to develop a complicated software product today without infringing numerous broad existing patents' (Boldrin & Levine, 2005: 80).

When Boldrin and Levine undertook their research, they indicated that Nokia was sitting on 12,000 patents, while Microsoft was adding at least 1,000 a month to 20,000+ patents. A senior executive from Intel stated that 'we have 10,000 patents – it's an awful lot of patents. Would I be happy with 1,000 patents rather than 10,000? Yes, provided the rest of the world did the same thing' (Boldrin & Levine, 2005: 81).

The effect of what has come to be known as a patent thicket has created a number of major challenges. Given that the boundaries of these patents are not clear, it acts as an impediment to R&D, thereby slowing innovation. It has also created a new form of business that accumulates patents to deliberately catch out firms that end up infringing a patent, often known as patent trolls.

The cost of searching existing patents is extremely high and the lack of boundaries makes patents difficult to interpret. Indeed, firms appear to be damned if you do and damned if you don't. Kodak built a competitor product to Polaroid working with legal counsel to work around their patents, whereas RIM did not appear to have searched to see whether existing patents might have affected their business given the lack of clarity of the patents. Both firms lost in court (Bessen & Meurer, 2008a: 50).

It has also been found that the majority of patents filed for business methods are at least partially invalid, as are close to half of all software patents (Miller, 2013). Indeed, patenting business methods and software has resulted in attempts to prevent firms from improving their online checkout services. Following the Amazon one-click patent controversy, Jeff Bezos proposed that the patent life for software and business method patents be reduced from the standard 20 years to only three to five years (Jaffe & Lerner, 2006). This suggests that patents are not really necessary at all for software development. Moreover, most software patents are not filed by software companies, and firms that acquired more software patents tend to reduce their level of R&D spending relative to sales (Bessen & Meurer, 2008b). In addition, the more a firm spends on R&D the more likely it is to be sued for infringement (Bessen & Meurer, 2008a: 124).

Even the Federal Trade Commission (FTC) concluded that 'questionable patents are a significant competitive concern and can harm innovation' (Federal Trade Commission, 2003). The FTC has recommended a series of changes to patent policy, but no coalition has emerged that is capable of pushing through significant legislative reform (Bessen & Meurer, 2008a: 215). Although European law did not initially recognize patents for software and business methods (Economic and Social Committee, 2002), this appears to have been relaxed somewhat in terms of case law, potentially exacerbating the situation (Carpmaels & Ransford, 2019).

Besides acting as a brake on innovation, there are more fundamental reasons to oppose patents when thinking about the broader potential effect on society. One patent attorney argues that 'it is arbitrary and unfair to reward more practical inventors and entertainment providers, such as the engineer and songwriter, and to leave more theoretical science and math researchers and philosophers unrewarded. The distinction is inherently vague, arbitrary, and unjust' (Kinsella, 2008). This approach also disregards what might be in the common interest of society. Kinsella postulates what might have happened if the first person to invent a house had been able to patent it. This would have then prevented others from building houses on their own land unless they paid the required licence fee. And if the terms of patents were made perpetual, 'no one would even be able to build a house without getting permission from the heirs of the first protohuman who left the caves and built a hut' (Kinsella, 2008).

Even in the pharmaceutical sector, which is the one sector where patents have been of value, there is increasing concern that patents are beginning to act as a disincentive. The excessive and broad nature of patents is potentially leading to fewer useful medicines being developed downstream from the patents, which has become known as the tragedy of the anti-commons where agents underuse scarce resources because owners block each other. Prior to the 1980s, the federal government sponsored premarket or upstream research and encouraged broad dissemination of results in the public domain. As a result, unpatented biomedical discoveries were freely incorporated in downstream products for diagnosing and treating disease. The unintended consequence of the privatization of biomedical research is that the proliferation of upstream patents is stifling new downstream innovations (Heller & Eisenberg, 1998).

Furthermore, the cost of the drug-discovery process is increasingly being driven by the costs of clinical trials rather than research and development. Data suggests that around two thirds of the costs for new drugs are taken up in clinical trials and being in compliance with regulatory requirements (Bessen & Meurer, 2008b). As such it appears there is less logic than there once was for using patents to enhance innovation even in the pharmaceutical industry (Heller & Eisenberg, 1998).

Another challenge related to the current policy approach to patents is that all of the issues arising from the ability of patent owners to generate rents and block innovation are now enforced at the international level. When the WTO was launched in 1995, following the completion of the Uruguay Round Agreement, one of its founding legal texts was the Agreement on Trade-Related Aspects of Intellectual Property Rights or TRIPS. TRIPS has, in effect, embedded the system of patents and intellectual property rights into the global trading system.

According to one of the leading advocates of globalization, Jagdish Bhagwati, the success of corporate lobbying during the Uruguay Round has turned the WTO into a royalty collection agency for firms. Bhagwati notes that the rules sought by pharmaceutical companies are unnecessarily harmful to poor countries and hence argues that 'TRIPS should not be in the WTO at all' (Bhagwati, 2004: 185).

The current system of intellectual property protection appears to have partly developed into a rent extraction system for powerful firms; hence, following the FTC's concerns, urgent action is required to restrict the use of patents. However, there is still an argument to provide some kind of protection for intellectual property to encourage innovation. This is of particular concern with regards to the ongoing issue of microbial resistance to the current generation of antibiotics, and one which the current patent system does not appear to be able to solve. The challenge for the pharmaceutical industry is that other drugs are likely to be more profitable, raising questions as to what the right business model of development might be.

The anti-microbial resistance review in the UK led by Jim O' Neill has recommended that a global fund be set up in to which the pharmaceutical sector should also contribute (O'Neill, 2016). Others have argued that longer patents ought to be awarded to enable pharmaceutical firms to enjoy an extended period of monopoly (Laxminarayan, 2011). It may well be that the initial discovery process of antibiotics provides a clearer way to incentivize innovation without creating monopolies and increasing the concentration of private power. Indeed, the transformation from growing mould in a laboratory into a mass-produced drug in a matter of years to treat soldiers in World War Two is quite remarkable (Quinn, 2013).

While the British and American governments provided the funding for the basic research, the demand for the drug made it profitable for firms to participate in the project. However, it was the lack of patents and the early involvement of government in penicillin that enabled a broad licensing of streptomycin at low prices. Ironically, the lower profit margins appear to be one reason why firms transformed themselves into vertically integrated companies in order to capture the patents further upstream in the research process. However, it is largely agreed that the lack of patents or exclusive licences further supported follow-on innovation, just as was the case with aircraft and software (Sampat, 2015). Further research suggests that introducing a variety of antibiotics can reduce resistance to each drug, which suggests that if patents are to be used then they should be set extremely narrowly (Eswaran & Gallini, 2018).

From an innovation standpoint this suggests that a successful policy is one where basic research is undertaken by the public sector which then licenses the outputs on a narrow basis to more than one firm to ensure that some form of competition is present. This appears to be in keeping with Rüstow's ideas that monopolists or patent holders should be forced to license their technology to smaller firms while the research is effectively run by public authorities.

The reality is that the cost of innovation is high and risky and something that the public sector can do well. Indeed, the state's ability to leverage its balance sheet for these kinds of risky projects is unique. Mariana Mazzucato's research has demonstrated that many of the components in the iPhone were the result of various military research projects including those conducted by the Defense Advanced Research Projects Agency (DARPA) (Mazzucato, 2013: 109). When new upstream technologies are developed through state-sponsored research, the state can therefore ensure that the licensing of such technologies can facilitate greater competition. Limited liability companies can then do what they do best. Such an approach, however, would require a reversal of the Bayh–Dole Act in the US which has since become embedded in the global trading system (Mazzucato, 2018: 204).

In conclusion, Butler is correct to highlight the importance of limited liability given that it has improved the outlook for investment and job creation, and hence supported the pursuit of freedom and equality. However, the state needs to make it clear to directors that they do have obligations and they must be held liable for their actions through public enforcement, supported by the creation of an investment framework that better aligns the incentives of long-term investors and firms.

Alongside the enforcement of individual liability, the ability of firms and individuals to generate unearned income streams must be curtailed. Private property rights developed to protect the value of labour, not to support the extraction of economic rent through the increasing concentration of power as is currently the case in many parts of the economy. Private natural monopolies, the abuse of the patent system to restrict innovation and the ability to extract income from speculative land values all hinder the price mechanism. Without a functioning price mechanism, the ability to curtail the concentration of power is limited resulting in the inequality of initial allocations and the refeudalization of the economy. Thus, implementing these foundational principles is central to a free and equal society.

7

Structure of the State:
Community and *Vitalpolitik*

The state, society and community

In the courtyard of the district court in Altona, which is now part of Hamburg, lies a memorial to four men falsely accused of murder. On 17 July 1932, a major confrontation between thousands of extremists took place leaving 18 dead as a result of police intervention with firearms: 16 were communists and two were fascists. Street fighting between radical left- and right-wing groups by the late 1920s had become an increasingly common occurrence in large urban conurbations across the country (Rosenhaft, 1983). When the Nazis took power, four communists were sentenced to death and beheaded for the alleged murder of the two national socialists.

These violent skirmishes are to a certain extent the epitome of the massification that Rüstow and Röpke railed against. The breakdown of community ties along with the rise of mass production, anonymity and the onset of high levels of unemployment left workers unfulfilled and resentful of the liberal system of the Weimar Republic. Many turned towards embracing the faith of a greater nation or towards class war to fill this vacuum.

Rüstow and Röpke attempted to counteract the threat of societal alienation by arguing that communities had to be the foundation for social and economic development or *Vitalpolitik*. This community would be based on individuals and their families in a decentralized economic system, taking into account the natural environment. To support individuals and their families, the state had to provide a basic level of welfare to all citizens given that individual insurance was not always practicable. This foundation would also serve as a basis for closer international economic interaction with other like-minded states. This chapter explores how the ideas of community-based living provide a positive theory of a liberal state, and help inform the contemporary debate on the built environment and relationship with the natural world. It also explores questions on the nature of the welfare state, and how liberal states might decide to enter into voluntary arrangements to legitimate supranational organizations such as the European Union.

The state, therefore, has a positive role to play in equalizing power to maintain freedom and equality across different communities and can be understood as a rejection of a centralized polity. In his great work *The Leviathan*, Thomas Hobbes argued that certain types of communities posed a grave threat to the Commonwealth including towns that had the potential to organize armed resistance and corporations who he likened to 'wormes in the entrayles of a natural man' (Hobbes, 1985: 375). The logic of Hobbes' idea to enable a peaceful society to flourish was to tear apart traditional communal ties and replace them with direct ties between the state and the individual based on the social contract. However, societal contractual ties, as argued by the German sociologist Tönnies, are neither natural nor sufficient to legitimate a polity and history suggests will merely result in the ascendency of greed and ambition (Tönnies, 2002: 202).

Tönnies noted there was a contrast between a social order based upon a consensus of natural wills grounded on folkways, mores and religion, and a social order based upon a union of rational wills. The natural will which dominates *Gemeinschaft* (community) is an artistic spirit from which springs feelings – while the will that is rational dominates *Gesellschaft* (society). The latter defines how a society can function resting on agreement, finding its ideological justification in public opinion (Tönnies, 2002: 223). But there is no inevitability that the public will come to an agreed opinion. Indeed, there is nothing to prevent societies becoming highly polarized as can be observed across many advanced economies today.

Writing in the early in 1930s, the political theorist and prominent Nazi Carl Schmitt thought that for a political theory to facilitate a legitimate social order it had to have protection and obedience at its centre. Schmitt had been deeply influenced by Hobbes, and thought that the lack of a positive theory of the state remained a fundamental weakness for liberals who had merely placed restrictions on the power of the state while subjugating it to economics. This did little to resolve what Schmitt called the political, which can be understood as the situation where individuals within a society have the conviction that only they possess the truth leading to conflict. The liberals' negation of the political, which is inherent in individualism, leads necessarily to a political practice of distrust towards political forces, which in turn weakens the state to maintain liberty. The role of the state for Schmitt is to maintain order and obedience by its citizens to prevent the destabilization of society. Schmitt also makes the point that economic antagonisms can arise within a state and hence the political may be reached from the economic as well as from any other domain (Schmitt, 1996).

One major challenge for liberalism is that while the ethical underpinning of virtue and approbation might function at a communal level, social and economic phenomena, as noted by the author Taleb, do not scale well (Taleb, 2018: 58–9). Hume assumed that society would be self-legitimating in that it would be able to adjust and eliminate excess in the system (Hume, 1994: 208). Hume did not appear to countenance the potential of an anonymous society which would reduce the impact of approbation and the obligation for virtuous behaviour.

This is one reason why liberalism at the societal level remains challenging, and why it has proven even less effective internationally. Taleb argues that one reason behind this is because 'bureaucracy is a construction by which a person is conveniently separated from the consequences of his or her actions' (Taleb, 2018: 12). This leads Taleb to argue that for good decisions to be made, the person needs to have skin in the game, or be liable for their actions which is the same as Eucken's idea of *Haftung*. In essence, the greater the distance between where administrative decisions are taken and the people whom it affects, the less likely those decisions will be beneficial. This separation also increases the incentives for centralized politicians and officials to abuse power given that there are fewer drawbacks from such behaviour. The ability of elites to enrich themselves was at the heart of the ordo critique of the Weimar Republic, and remains a concern across liberal democracies today.

The idea of certain phenomena not scaling was demonstrated in a paper by Mandelbrot and Taleb through the distinction between mild and wild randomness. While mild randomness is largely the case for phenomena like height or weight which result in predictable standard deviations, it is not the case for things like wealth or power. Wild randomness is related to instances where 'a single observation or a particular number can impact the total in a disproportionate way', thereby increasing the probability of extreme outcomes (Mandelbrot & Taleb, 2010).

This is why history jumps. Society is too complex to directly manage, resulting in unpredictable outcomes. This matters for liberalism as it indicates that Hobbes' Leviathan has a higher probability of failing, resulting in precisely the opposite effect that Hobbes desired. The lack of scaling within socio-economic systems suggests that freedom and equality can only be sustained at a more devolved political and economic level, which was precisely the argument made by the ordoliberals.

Freedom through living spaces

Placemaking took on a pivotal role for ordoliberals in the development of West Germany. This can be seen through the need to equalize power between places across the country as well as a balance between industrial and environmental concerns. Urban planning thus became a central plank of the social market economy.

During the reconstruction phase in the 1950s, the haphazard growth of industry and transport networks resulted in a chaotic development of the built environment. This approach disregarded what Müller-Armack called the 'natural form of life', or the environment in which people live and its relation to the natural world. Müller-Armack, a former advisor to the Nazi regime, became intimately involved in the creation of the social market economy working with Erhard. Müller-Armack argued the state had to provide an order in which urbanization develops. This is needed to ensure that infrastructure is integrated with businesses and the environment where people desire to live. Müller-Armack was critical of long commutes between home and work which he thought created unnecessary tension, and was in stark contrast to the benefits of increasing prosperity (Müller-Armack, 1976: 280–2).

The idea of a natural form of life where humans live in harmony with the natural world has increasing ramifications in relation to pollution, biodiversity and the sustainability of communities for policymakers today. In particular, a greater understanding of the shifting of the balance of power between humans and the biosphere is required and to what extent it is undermining the fabric of the built environment. A recent report on biodiversity by Partha Dasgupta argues that natural capital must be adequately taken into account as part of spatial planning. Hence, there is a strong argument that humanity must strive towards a balance of power between the development of society and the maintenance of natural capital. The current rate of depletion of natural capital indicates that power concentrations need to be reversed if our societies are to be sustainable (Dasgupta, 2021).

As Röpke argued, an economic system that not only destroys the natural fabric of society but also prevents humans enjoying what it means to be human is a major challenge to the legitimation of any liberal democracy. Policy should therefore attempt to focus on power imbalances to deal with policy issues around biodiversity and environmental degradation. This approach may also alleviate the challenges government face when dealing with vested interests who may claim that overall utility will fall as a result of any reform, as the polluting sector will have to pay for some of the costs of transition. For example, following an announcement in 2006 by the British government to move towards a zero-carbon homes policy, the new administration in 2015 decided to override this policy by relaxing 'regulation on housebuilders' (HM Treasury, 2015). In essence, the profits of the housebuilding sector trumped all environmental considerations leading to a greater concentration of power.

This issue is even more acute when it comes to the import of fossil fuels, the bulk of which originate from authoritarian regimes who have little interest in promoting liberal values. For example, the Nord Stream 2 pipeline, which will connect Russian gas directly to Germany, will effectively double gas imports from a government that has been trying to undermine the existing liberal order (Lampe & Gabidullina, 2019). This highlights the issue where utility-derived outcomes not only result in concentrations of power for authoritarian regimes but also greater imbalances between the biosphere and humanity.

Hence, policies related to the built environment need to take account of the balance between urban and the natural environment. Müller-Armack argued that placemaking required authorities to take account of business, residential and recreational areas which might extend *beyond* traditional local government boundaries. And that the spatial environment should not be viewed statically but instead must adapt to changing conditions through time with a particular focus on the movement of people. For Müller-Armack this meant that the public authority ought to focus on creating a public environment as being both meaningful and harmonious, particularly given that once consumption needs are less pressing, the broader context in which people live takes on a more important role in life (Müller-Armack, 1976: 282).

The German planning system was heavily influenced by a report published in 1961 by *Sachverständigenausschuss für Raumordnung* (SARO) or the Expert Committee for Spatial Planning. *Raumordnung* refers to the economic, social and cultural needs corresponding to the order of space. The committee was set up by Adenauer in 1955 under the context of a general disdain for both centralized planning and a complete free for all under a laissez-faire system. It took into account the economic principles of full employment and economic growth, as well as the idea of the *Gleichwertigkeit der Lebensverhältnisse* or the equality of living conditions, and employment opportunities across West Germany (Mäding, 2017). This concept also attempted to remove any imbalance between urban and rural communities through infrastructure investment and job-creation schemes (Strubelt, 2009: 204). Planners were required to work across departments and areas of policy to ensure that the competition for space did not result in settlements with poor transport links and low-quality living spaces (Mäding, 2017).

The West German planning system was ultimately successful in ensuring that no particular urban centre dominated the rest of the country. Power was effectively dispersed across multiple urban centres with low unemployment. This aim was supported and enabled by the federal constitutional settlement. Article 72 of the Basic Law requires the establishment of equivalent living conditions throughout the Federation and Article 109 that the *Länder* should be autonomous and independent of each other. To achieve this financial independence Article 106 stipulates to which authority specific taxes should be allocated to, so each *Land* is held liable for its actions.

In addition, a revenue-sharing mechanism was embedded in the Basic Law with regards to VAT revenues as a way of maintaining some form of equalization across the different regions. Article 107 requires VAT revenue to be apportioned to *Land* with lower revenues per capita, although the formula used also prevents a *Land* from lowering tax rates and then attempting to receive extra money through the equalization process.

This is different to the US where the federal model sees states in competition with each other. This has resulted in poorer states becoming dependent on federal grants with Congress favouring narrow programmes to achieve specific goals. However, such an approach to policy is anathema to ordoliberalism as it becomes an attempt by the Federal Government to intervene in the market, instead of ensuring that the rules are fair for everyone, and that each state is responsible for its own actions. According to Larsen, 'it is not clear that competition among [US] states for tax revenues leads to either more equivalent living conditions or more efficiency in the creation of goods and services generally' (Larsen, 1999).

Since German reunification, this dispersal of power has begun to reverse. Berlin is now twice the size of Germany's second city, Hamburg, and appears to be more closely aligned with the trend towards megacities where power is increasingly concentrated. Research by the physicist Geoffrey West indicates that larger cities are more productive, wealthier and grow exponentially faster than smaller conurbations. West found that even walking speeds in larger cities are faster (West, 2017: 29, 335). According to Ed Glaeser, the rise of big cities is a function of globalization and new technologies which increase the returns to urban proximity due to smart people hanging around with other smart people, thereby becoming hubs of innovation (Glaeser, 2009).

While this might sound like a basis for a successful polity, these higher growth rates are also accompanied by higher levels of inequality, crime, congestion, homelessness and pollution. Furthermore, West's research also indicates that if large cities are unable to sustain these growth rates, they can also shrink at similar rates too. To sustain the rate of a city's growth requires innovation to speed up; however, as cities become larger, they are less able to adapt to external shocks because of their size, and hence may stagnate and eventually collapse (West, 2007: 215, 415).

To highlight the challenges that megacities face in their quest for more growth, research by the consultancy firm McKinsey shows that megacities since the late 1990s have not been the driver of global growth with many megacities not even growing faster than their host economies. The research concludes that this trend is expected to continue. The constraint in growth is an indication of the problem for large cities attempting to adapt to changing conditions (McKinsey Global Institute, 2011).

The implications of West's research are striking in terms of thinking about the challenges to liberalism. A utilitarian form of liberalism is more likely to be wedded to extreme urbanization as on average this increases total utility, despite the fact that such growth results in more crime, more inequality and more pollution. While social liberal utilitarians might argue these issues can all be fixed by redistribution, this requires an all-knowing state to not only solve all social problems but also achieve this without affecting the growth element. Neither of these claims is sufficiently well substantiated in theory given a Pareto optimal output is almost impossible to achieve, and in practice lump-sum transfers do not address the issue of unequal power.

In essence, megacities begin to function more akin to centralized states. In addition to the coordination issues of localized knowledge in a central body, as an economy changes authorities need to be able to adapt their policies, but this becomes harder to achieve, the larger the organization. While public policy failures have always happened in liberal democracies, until the last decade or so public authorities were generally able to control the narrative of events due to their monopoly of information. The rise of the internet, however, has broken this monopoly. Hence, it has become increasingly harder for public authorities to be able to justify their decisions when things go wrong, which has exacerbated the issue for larger political organizations.

Public displays of incompetence and collusion has led to a collision between the traditional hierarchical, top-down approach of government with an egalitarian and bottom-up movement who no longer automatically accept the authority of elites. As Martin Gurri notes in his book *The Revolt of the Public*, this is having a destabilizing effect on modern liberal democracies (Gurri, 2018: 128). Hence, a more concerted effort is needed to dissipate public power to maintain legitimacy, enabling the public sector to better adapt to changing conditions. This is no different to the move away in the corporate world from hierarchical bureaucracies to more decentralized and flat structures. As Drucker noted, individuals and teams closer to production are best placed to recommend improvements due to their local knowledge.

This suggests that megacities are unable to provide the conditions to enable freedom and equality and merely result in concentrations of power within a country as well as the localized eradication of nature. Berlin is now beginning to suffer from the increased complexity of large urban conurbations. Rent has doubled in the last ten years, which has been exacerbated by the privatization of 200,000 social homes. The city government's response has been to interfere directly in the market mechanism and impose a rent cap for five years.

The benefit of a federal or devolved system is to enable a functional economic geography to adapt to changing social and economic conditions.[1] This means that decision-makers should reside in the localities, enabling them to better adapt to changing local conditions. Hence, a federal or devolved system of government should not be seen as merely a practical system to rule larger countries. While it is true that large countries such as the US, Canada and Australia are federal, so are small countries such as Switzerland and Austria.

For such a system to operate effectively, local leaders at the functional economic geography level must have the requisite tools to take decisions for their regions. This requires these regions to have sufficient autonomy including tax-raising powers and to be able invest appropriately to ensure that citizens can live in a pleasant environment with access to good jobs. Clearly, there are significant benefits to some agglomeration given that it enables the specialization of labour and knowledge transfer which remain key building blocks for *Vitalpolitik*. The point here is that a large agglomeration should not be pursued as an end in itself. A traditional liberal utilitarian approach tends to ignore the downsides of large agglomerations and does not care whether concentrations of public power exist. Instead, it merely attempts to maximize utility based on parameters such as income per head.

The founding of federal systems has generally been facilitated by a significant break in politics such as revolution, war or independence. This suggests that devolution is more likely to be the process by which public power can be further dispersed, although there are different reasons why devolution has been pursued by governments.

The UK's reason for embarking upon this journey was originally related to trying to maintain its union of nations. Gladstone twice tried to pass an Irish Home Rule bill only to be thwarted by a combination of Ulster Unionists and the House of Lords. By the time the third bill was finally passed in 1914, there was little desire by the Irish to remain, and the War of Independence between 1919 and 1922 resulted in the southern counties of Ireland seceding from the union.

In 1999, the Blair Administration devolved power to Northern Ireland following the signing of the Good Friday Agreement, as well as the devolution of powers to Wales and Scotland. Blair's view appears to have been that this was necessary to maintain the union as the smaller nations felt they were increasingly being dominated by the Westminster Parliament.

More recently the Cameron Administration embarked upon a limited devolution of powers to England's city regions starting with the Greater Manchester Combined Authority in 2011. However, fiscal powers remain limited, resulting in a political culture that remains dependent on central government grants – precisely the opposite approach required to engender responsibility and liability.

The experience in France has been quite different. The first wave of devolution in France in 1982 was driven by a 'belief in proximity, democratic empowerment, citizenship and local self-reliance' (Cole, 2006), rather than any focus on identity, as was the case in the UK. The desire to devolve power in the hope that this might improve policy outcomes due to local capacity building appears in many respects to be close to the social market economy of West Germany. Indeed, Giscard d'Estaing had argued for the creation of a few large regions to be compatible with the German *Länder* (Cole, 2006).

The 1982 reforms created elected regional assemblies followed by a law in 1983 that described those responsibilities. Twenty years later, in 2003,

Prime Minister Raffarin changed the constitution introducing the principle of financial autonomy, as well as devolving skills, transportation, housing, health and education. From a placemaking perspective, this has been highly successful with the regeneration of urban conurbations such as Montpellier, Lille and Strasbourg linked to these devolved powers (Hall, 2013).

Indeed, the ability of city regions to take responsibility for their future is central to the idea of new localism as described by Bruce Katz and Jeremy Nowak. This new localism is a pragmatic way of getting businesses, educationalists and local government officials together to make decisions to improve their local areas. One crucial point made by Katz and Nowak is that for decades the myth of national power has meant that when there is a local issue there has been a tendency to go begging to the federal government for help. The reality is that the answers lie at a local level, but this requires a new level of institutional development. They use the case study of Indianapolis to illustrate their point where, 'collaboration is treated as a serious business that advances the broader prosperity of the city', which has enabled stakeholders not only to discuss policy but also to decide on it (Katz & Nowak, 2017: 34, 102).

While this argument is persuasive, it is still limited by institutional and constitutional structures. For example, devolution in France has enabled city regions to thrive, and crucially for Indianapolis, the city was integrated with the county in 1970 from an administrative perspective. Both these solutions resolve the border issues raised by Müller-Armack. While it is still possible for local authorities to cooperate across local borders, evidence from the UK suggests this is impracticable (Shepley, 2017). Hence, just letting local communities resolve the issues is unlikely to work unless they have the jurisdictional powers to take decisions across the entire functional economic area.

The dispersal of public power is a central component of an ordoliberal theory of the state. Devolving social and economic development enables more meaningful interactions between members of the community and helps eliminate legitimation issues that arise with a greater focus on societal systems. To support individuals and their families in a decentralized economic system, the state also needs to step in and provide a basic level of welfare when such circumstances arise and where individual insurance is not practicable.

The welfare state

The ordoliberal welfare state is predicated on a dynamic economy, where power is dispersed between workers and managers, and competition among firms is robustly enforced to increase productivity and drive prices down. Together these forces result in rising real wages, which in turn support unemployment, health and pension provision. Eucken's view was that social policy had to be embedded into the fabric of economic policy, and this included a requirement for the state to provide a safety net to protect individuals against economic calamity beyond their control. Crucially, this safety net had to be universal and is central to the concept of a free society (Karsten, 2005).

Ordoliberals thus oppose an all-encompassing welfare state based on the concern that a culture of dependency or direct cash transfers impairs the virtues of self-reliance, independence and responsibility that are central to *Vitalpolitik*. Habermas has raised similar concerns of the ever-increasing power of the state and its erosion of the private sphere and civil society (Rothstein, 1998: 171). Instead, a welfare system should be enabled through a combination of insurance markets to mitigate the risks of ill-health, unemployment and an income for retirement, alongside the provision of a universal safety net provided through general taxation. The welfare states in parts of Continental Europe today resemble this ordoliberal framework with many services such as unemployment, health and pensions provided through compulsory insurance schemes backed up by a universal safety net.

With regards to pensions, policymakers have had to address a number of factors related to increasing costs such as rising life expectancy and a society with a greater proportion of older citizens. To ensure individuals have higher income levels in retirement, many pension systems have introduced compulsory employee and employer contributions which are invested either collectively or individually. There are also strong arguments to require those who are self-employed to contribute into a pension.

According to a recent report on pension fund sustainability, the Netherlands, Denmark and Australia have by far the most sustainable pension systems (Melbourne Mercer Global Pension Index, 2019). This includes a sustainable universal payment through pay-as-you-go taxes in conjunction with a retirement age related to longevity and well-funded employee/ employer contributions. An analysis by the OECD shows that the long-run levels of real returns from Dutch, Australian and Danish funds – along with Canada – are among the highest across the OECD countries (OECD, 2019b). Furthermore, the Dutch and Danish systems largely operate a collective risk-sharing principle which spreads risk across all members. As the investment horizon of the fund extends beyond an individual member's life, it therefore has a greater risk tolerance to generate higher returns. Such an approach is closely aligned with the basic notion of an ordoliberal insurance principle operating across a community of individuals.

The collective contribution scheme in Denmark is run by ATP, which is a government monopoly, whereas in the Netherlands, schemes are run by a number of large non-profit pension funds. In Australia, the superannuation system of individual defined contribution schemes is run by both public and private sector organizations. However, the private sector funds charge much higher fees to savers which leads to lower retirement income.

According to one report on the Australian system, the majority of the best-performing superfunds are public sector or industry funds which generally charge lower fees and are non-profit. The worst-performing superfunds were all managed by private sector institutions, which is mostly related to high fees (Brycki, 2019). The Australian Royal Commission into Misconduct in the Banking, Superannuation and Financial Services Industry has recognized there is a conflict of interest of trustees, particularly within for-profit firms, stating that 'trustees are not always discharging those obligations, often causing financial detriment to members' (Royal Commission, 2019). However, it stopped short of recommending that for-profit firms be prohibited from providing such services.

While there is sufficient competition in the investment management sector, there is an information asymmetry that has resulted in the sector generating higher profits due to higher fees. According to one study in the UK, high fees have resulted in the value of future pension pots falling by up to a third (Norman in Aubrey, 2013b). Such an outcome results in a negative incentive to save and increased probability of pensioner poverty, which in turn erodes the concept of self-reliance and individual responsibility.

Fees in Australia have been slowly coming down due to forced transparency and are now 1.1 per cent (Rainmaker, 2019), compared with around 0.8 per cent for the Netherlands (Baxter, 2018). While this difference of 0.3 per cent might appear small, a study by the Netherlands Authority for Financial Markets found that a reduction in costs of 0.25 per cent would result in a 7.5 per cent increase in collective pension assets over 40 years (CWC, 2018). The benefits of scale within the pension sector not only result in lower fees and higher returns, but also enable pension funds to invest in firms directly for the long term. As argued in Chapter 6, this is an important part of keeping tabs on the managers of limited liability firms.

An ordoliberal pensions policy requires there to be sufficient competition to ensure that the ability to extract economic rent is curtailed including information asymmetries which appears to impact private provision. If a sufficient level of competition is not possible, then the least-worst option is for it to be owned by the community but run like a business. The logic of this argument is that the Dutch system, where there is some competition between not-for-profit pension funds appears to be closest to an ordoliberal framework. Pension funds can still contract out mandates to private fund-management firms, but the scale of Dutch pension funds means they have the ability to negotiate more competitive fees, hence higher returns.

While public policy mistakes will always be made, the benefit of using a constitutional or rules-based approach is that over time it is possible to assess the success of policy through the acquisition of information as noted by Vanberg. For example, in the case of pension reform, there is a strong case that for-profit funds in Australia create a power imbalance between the saver and the fund provider due an information asymmetry, something that the Dutch system has managed to resolve effectively.

As with pensions, countries have developed different approaches to healthcare. The UK developed the Beveridge model where healthcare is financed through general taxation and provided directly by the state. Bismarck's model for Germany was based on employer and employee contributions, which is both universal and non-profit. Canada has a universal public insurance system although healthcare is provided by mostly non-profit providers, whereas the US system consists of both profit and non-profit providers based on a for-profit insurance system.

The key ordoliberal framework requires that healthcare be universal but that the system should encourage individuals to look after themselves through individual contributions. While the lack of universality discounts the US system, the lack of relationship between funding and responsibility also discounts the UK model.

While theoretically health insurance systems might engender greater individual responsibility, it is unclear to what extent it actually does. OECD data suggests that the rate of heart disease in Germany is 102 per 100,000 whereas in the UK it is slightly lower at 84 per 100,000 (OECD, 2019c). Cultural factors such as diet are likely to play a role here. Hence, it is unclear whether it makes much difference how the healthcare system is set up in terms of individual behaviour. Analysis of different healthcare systems indicates that social insurance models do result in better health outcomes although they are more expensive. In addition, citizens are more satisfied with the health outcomes of social insurance systems (Van der Zee & Kroneman, 2007).

Just as with pensions, the issue of a potential conflict of interest between consumers and for-profit providers arises. One issue with for-profit healthcare systems is that according to Kenneth Arrow, the profit motive acts as a signal that denies trust relations suggesting that private for-profit health insurance cannot resolve entirely a nation's healthcare problems (Arrow, 1971: 208). One study that appears to support Arrow's concern is the effect on cataract operations in the US as a result of declining Medicare fees for both complex and non-complex operations.

When fees were reduced between 2005 and 2009, the volume of non-complex cataract services fell roughly in proportion, but the volume of higher paid, complex cataract operations more than doubled. Such a response to shifts in the price for services is often theorized by the view that clinicians will increase the volume of higher paid work to offset lost income elsewhere (Gong, Jun & Tsai, 2017). While there are potentially many reasons for the substantial increase in complex cataract services which took place at the same time as the price change, it is hard to entirely dismiss the point of trust and the profit motive that Arrow raised. Particularly as government expenditure as a percentage of GDP in the US according to OECD health spending data is 45 per cent more than in Germany which spends the most in Europe.

While these conflicts of interest can exist at the primary delivery end of healthcare, all healthcare systems rely on private providers to a large extent given they need to acquire medical devices and equipment. This is no different to the pensions sector where assets are mandated out to for-profit investors. What matters ultimately is not necessarily whether providers are public or private but whether there is a sufficiently competitive environment to ensure that private and public interests overlap. This suggests that the primary delivery of healthcare ought to be in the non-profit domain to avoid conflicts of interest.

The same principles of universality and contribution have also found their way into the unemployment benefit system. An unemployment insurance system should aim to encourage unemployed workers back into employment while providing them with a guaranteed income through this temporary period. The idea of the guaranteed income is to address the highly unequal power relations when trying to return to the labour market.

To qualify for such payments, workers need to have contributed into the system for a period of time, which is related to the idea of individual responsibility. These payments are generally limited over a specific period, after which a lower level of universal income support generally kicks in. However, the result of these schemes is that not all workers are covered by these benefits. The average across the EU is that around a third of workers are covered by unemployment insurance with ranges from just 10 per cent in Romania to two thirds in Germany (European Commission, 2017). Policy measures to either increase the duration and level of benefits, as well as who it covers, cost extra money but without any necessary improvement in the employment outlook. One of the key success factors in improving re-employment is that firms need to be creating jobs in the first place.

The European Commission has also highlighted the variation in sick leave benefits across EU members, noting that few countries focus on the longer-term aspect of retraining and rehabilitation benefits to avoid a permanent exit from the labour market (European Commission, 2016b). Finally, while most advanced economies have developed some form of non-contributory minimum income benefit, the level where this is set also has an effect on power relations and the ability to return to the labour market. The rising use of food banks in the UK indicates that the basic level of income is insufficient to buy food. Furthermore, many users of foodbanks are working, indicating that the power imbalances between labour and capital needs to be addressed (House of Commons, 2021).

While a number of European welfare states have developed along ordoliberal lines, consisting of contributory insurance schemes alongside universal welfare benefits, other welfare ideas continue to be proposed including a jobs guarantee scheme as well as a universal basic income (UBI). A jobs guarantee which makes work available at the national minimum wage (Minsky, 1965) is, however, less helpful for those experiencing temporary unemployment from higher wage employment. While most governments are in need of more infrastructure investment and more care workers, these require specialist skills and hence are less suited to temporary employment which is needed for such schemes (Summers, 2018).

More recently there has been a great deal of excitement that a UBI is the silver bullet to solve current welfare issues. The argument in favour of a UBI is that a regular income grant generates the security and freedom to choose diverse lifestyles, particularly if individuals become disentitled to certain welfare benefits (Haagh, 2019: 15, 25). A study of UBI in Madhya Pradesh in India indicated that it improved health, agricultural yields and resulted in higher rates of school attendance (Schjoedt, 2016). While this success should be celebrated, this appears to be related to counterbalancing the lack of a universal benefit to support people at the bottom of the income distribution. Minouche Shafik notes that while using universal cash transfers in poorer countries that don't have strong welfare states is beneficial, this approach is less suited to developed economies. Hence, she questions the need for universality given that individuals higher up the income distribution are not in need of additional government money (Shafik, 2021).

A more recent basic income experiment in Finland demonstrated limited impact of getting individuals back into work, although there were results indicating an increase in well-being. The result showed that skills and health issues were more important barriers to employment than financial incentives (Hiilamo, 2019). Hence, public policy may be better served by increasing expenditure in these areas, further enabling access to the labour market. Furthermore, the well-being benefits may have been due to the attention created by the study itself. A famous study by the Western Electric Company at their plant in Hawthorn, Illinois sought to understand whether workers were more productive under higher or lower levels of light. The results showed that productivity improved under both scenarios, which has come to be described as the observer-expectancy effect.

If skills and health issues are more important barriers to employment, it suggests that a universal basic income may not be the best way to structure a welfare state in order to reduce unequal power relations across society. Other factors such as retraining, specialist healthcare, affordable housing and child support may be far more impactful in improving conditions prior to voluntary exchange. In light of this complexity, Coyle has argued for a universal basic infrastructure which provides equal access to key public services including transport, health, education and training (Coyle, 2017).

Devolved institutions with welfare systems that combine individual responsibility with a universal safety net provides individuals with the foundation for *Vitalpolitik*. This foundation also enables communities across countries to converge economically with other like-minded states through supranational organizations.

The EU: an ordoliberal institution after all

Given the focus on community and devolved power by ordoliberals, it has been argued that supranational authorities such as the EU contradict an ordoliberal outlook. Indeed, Erhard himself was sceptical of the creation of the European Economic Communities, preferring instead to pursue a free trade agreement with the UK and US. However, there was a clear political imperative operating from many sides to have some integration in order to prevent another European war.

The main concern from the ordoliberals was that the European Communities would evolve into French dirigisme writ large. This resulted in Röpke cautioning that such dirigisme at the supranational level commands rather than enables a free common market and was in effect a betrayal of Europe. Such a path he thought failed to comprehend the dangers of increasing centralization and harmonization to both peace and prosperity (Wandel, 2019). However, there is nothing inherently contradictory in being a member of a supranational organization in relation to the dispersal of power, it is more related to how that organization might function and be legitimated.

The attempt by many of Europe's leaders to create a federal state commenced with the French civil servant Jean Monnet. Monnet in a speech to the National Press Club in Washington, DC in 1952 advocated a United States of Europe with its own army that would be strong, free and prosperous. Despite Monnet's optimism, the French National Assembly rejected the idea of a European army. This led Monnet to focus on economic integration which he thought would eventually lead to political union.

The top-down approach to creating a European federal state is reminiscent of the enlightenment rationalists who thought they had divined the most appropriate form of political and economic organization for the peoples of Europe. Such an approach to public policy, however, ignores notions of culture, tradition and language. But the enlightenment rationalists did not consider these aspects of identity. It has been argued that one reason why enlightenment leaders ignored identity is that they were socially secure and firmly rooted in their cosmopolitan society so problems of identity status and position were much less likely to arise (Hauskeer in Mali & Wockler, 2003). The supporters of a European federal state, as suggested by the philosopher John Gray, appear to have a similar outlook to the enlightenment project. Gray notes that 'the EU is an attempt to create a state for a nation that does not exist' (Gray, 2020).

While this might be considered a negative Anglo-Saxon view of the EU given that the UK has decided it no longer wishes to continue to be a member, there does not appear to be a groundswell of opinion towards greater political union. As noted in Chapter 5, polls from 2017 recorded only a minority in favour of Schulz's proposed United States of Europe, although there remains broad support for continued membership of the EU.

Given this backdrop it was unsurprising that in 2019 the new President of the European Commission, Ursula Von der Leyen, stated her goal was not to pursue a United States of Europe but rather to promote unity from diversity, which she suggested was different to federalism (Weise, 2019). This repositioning is a much more realistic outlook given that the single currency has created serious legitimation issues across the eurozone.

This step back from imposing a federal state on the peoples of Europe is more in keeping with ordoliberal principles which are fundamentally opposed to an increase in the concentration of power and a rationalist Condorcet-style enlightenment project overriding community ties. However, the idea that the market might be extended beyond national boundaries with countries of similar value systems is a central component of this strain of liberalism.

Indeed, the European Economic Community prior to the Maastricht Treaty achieved a truly remarkable feat that has been largely ignored by contemporary political theory. It created a unique political structure that disentangled power from authority. This is in contrast to the state whose authority is backed by power or legitimate violence. While Montesquieu went to great lengths to argue in favour of the separation of powers between the legislative, executive and judiciary, they are all ultimately backed by the same power and authority of the unitary state.

Such a development in the structure of a polity should have been embraced by those who believe in freedom and equality. The process whereby like-minded nation states come together, and through a system of law, agree to supranational rules which are not backed by force is the triumph of the voluntary principle and crucially a new form of polity.

Hence, the single market ought to be seen as the pinnacle of this achievement with its equalizing tendencies for firms and workers across similar countries. The decision by the UK to exit the single market, therefore, ought to be understood as an illiberal policy which places costs on international trade and also attempts to distort the price mechanism through potential regulatory divergence thereby undermining the principle of the equality of starting conditions.

One challenge for this structure is that a legitimation theory was never put forward to justify this new form of political organization. Instead, it was perceived by some member states as being legitimated by the nation state, just like any other international organization.

The legal authority of a sovereign state derives from its coercive power, or an order backed by a threat. The jurist H.L.A. Hart in his book *The Concept of Law* argued that law ought to be seen as a body of rules which restrains agency by creating obligations. He argued that if the rules of a society reflect its morality, then social pressure to conform will be high. However, as Hart noted, while this generally works in a close-knit community, it has not been able to scale effectively to a larger community. Hart argued that legal systems have traditionally only been apparent within states because those are the institutions that have enabled what he called a secondary rule of recognition to develop. A secondary rule of recognition can be thought of as a system that confers legitimacy on a body to make new rules (Hart, 1994).

That European Community law has a direct effect on individuals across the Community was developed in the 1963 with the famous *Van Gen den Loos* case where the ECJ ruled that Article 12 of the EEC Treaty was directly effective. And one year later the *Costa v Enel* case gave priority of community law over the provisions of Italian law (Van Middelaar, 2014: 50–2). While direct effect has been conceded by national courts, the rule of recognition has not been conceded by all states.

For dualist states such as the UK, Parliament conceded in the 1972 Accession Act not to override Community Law demonstrating a clear rule of recognition. However, for monist states such as France and Germany, this rule of recognition has never been made clear. Indeed, the *Bundesverfassungsgericht*'s interpretation of the Treaty on European Union (TEU) in the *Brunner* case suggested that Community law was just another body of international law and hence that Germany was merely behaving in a highly monist way by agreeing to the TEU. The German court used the concept of *Staatenverbund* or union of states to describe the new organization, making it clear the legitimation of the institutions created by the Treaty was bestowed by the legal sovereignty residing within the nation state (Bundesverfassungsgericht, 1994). Such an approach fails to directly recognize the reality of a higher law, which puts the very existence of a legal system into question.[2] The French court's ruling on TEU was in a similar vein although less detailed and required amendments to be made to the French constitution enabling sovereignty over certain issues to be ceded.

This approach to the legitimation of the EU has been proven to be flawed, particularly for monetary union. First, by stipulating in the treaty that the ECB pursue price stability via a 2 per cent inflation target has created a highly inflexible system that can only be resolved through a Treaty amendment. However, as Treaty changes require unanimity, the direct link between democratic accountability through national parliaments to ensure that monetary policy is appropriate for their country has been broken. Irish or Spanish voters can no longer vote for how monetary policy ought to be conducted with regards to their own economies, but instead only through a compromise with all other eurozone countries.

The German Court at the time noted that:

> It has been pointed out by important contributors to the debate that a currency union, especially between States which are oriented towards an active economic and social policy, can ultimately only be realised in common with a political union (embracing all essential economic functions) and cannot be realised independently thereof or as a mere preliminary stage on the way to it.' The Court argued that this was not a legal issue but rather a political one stating that, 'if it emerges that the desired monetary union cannot in reality be achieved without a (not yet desired) political union, a fresh political decision will be required as to how to proceed further. (Bundesverfassungsgericht, 1994)

The only other major treaty change since Maastricht was the Treaty of Lisbon signed in 2007 which granted additional powers to the European Parliament, moved a number of policy areas away from unanimity to qualified majority voting in the Council of Ministers and institutionalized the European Council chaired by the President to set the direction and priorities for the EU. Once again, the constitutional courts of both France and Germany maintained the same outlook that had been set for the Maastricht Treaty in that the legitimation of the EU still stems from member state parliaments.

The German court noted that:

> The concept of *Verbund* covers a close long-term association of states which remain sovereign, a treaty-based association which exercises public authority, but whose fundamental order is subject to the decision-making power of the Member States and in which the peoples, i.e. the citizens, of the Member States, remain the subjects of democratic legitimation. (Bundesverfassungsgericht, 2009)

This approach requires any integration programme to be precise; however, the court did recognize that there might be occasions that give rise to a conflict between the competencies of the EU and member states. In the event of such occurrences, the German court made it clear that it had the right to *ultra vires* reviews. Hence, its recent opinion on the ECB's bond-buying programme.

The German court also made it clear that if the 'threshold were crossed to a federal state and to the giving up of national sovereignty, this would require a free decision of the people in Germany beyond the present applicability of the Basic Law' (Bundesverfassungsgericht, 2009). For it to be in keeping with democratic legitimation, the electorate of Europe would need to be able to vote out the European Commission, the Council and the European Council. As this is currently not the case, the court is comfortable to argue that national sovereignty remains the central legitimating mechanism.

The structure of the EU is thus left with a conundrum. Its legitimation stems from member state parliaments and the concept of national sovereignty due to the refusal of monist states such as France and Germany to accept a higher authority (Aubrey, 1995). And this will continue to be the case until the EU stops being a union of states and becomes a new federal state. But this approach appears to be completely inappropriate for the EU given that there is no demand for a federal superstate.

It is plausible that the pre-Maastricht European Community could have developed a robust legitimation mechanism using the ideas of group theory that were developed in the 19th century by the German legal theorist Otto von Gierke. Gierke argued that law develops in groups rather than being imposed upon the people by the state. While the state effectively enforces a body of secondary rules or a system of law subject to the primary rule of the constitution, behind the organized legal state there runs the life of national society where custom and rules form the basis of law. As such the groups involved in developing these customs have legal personality and exist without the need for sovereign authority. These groups can be seen as part of the web of voluntary arrangements that form the basis of civil society (Gierke, 1934).

These ideas were further developed by the political pluralist movement including the philosopher John Figgis into an alternative theory of the state. Central for Figgis was the idea that the state is unable to monopolise authority. Authority rather, 'springs up spontaneously wherever in society men find value and light' (Hocking, 1926: 390). Figgis refused to accept the idea that in every state there must be a body that is politically supreme. Hence, what matters for sovereignty is legal supremacy in terms of ruling on disputes so that there is no conflict. Legal sovereignty, therefore, just means that judges ought not to question an Act of Parliament, but it does not mean that law is merely a command of parliament (Nicholls, 1975: 47, 49).

Such an approach is similar to the ideas of *Vitalpolitik*, where groups within a state see the benefits of voluntary cooperation which can be recognized explicitly through the acceptance of a higher law in a specific area. However, such a bottom-up or group-theory approach would have likely slowed integration and may even have prevented the single currency from being introduced. Crucially, this is a better way of resolving the potential lack of transitivity between subnational groups and elitist national decision-making, and hence can only improve the legitimation of such a *sui generis* organization.

But for this to have come about, constitutional courts would have needed to accept the *sui generis* nature of the EU which would have meant ditching absolutist theories of sovereignty, and that such legitimation can be derived from groups accepting higher law in certain areas. While this would reduce the influence of national constitutional courts as the arbiter of such issues, there is no reason why the same courts could and should not continue to provide *ultra vires* opinions on such matters. Indeed, such opinions are central to group theory, and hence should be treated by the Court of Justice of the European Union (CJEU) as another group within the community instead of noting that they 'place in jeopardy the unity of the EU legal order' (CJEU, 2020).

It is hard to see how the EU can maintain the legitimacy of its current structure due to the single currency, particularly with regards to Italy (Varoufakis, 2018). Indeed, it is hard to conceive that the Maastricht Treaty's shift in policy has much in keeping with the underlying principles of freedom and equality. At some stage something will have to give unless Treaty changes explicitly permit countries to exit monetary union through a parallel currency alongside eliminating the requirement for new EU members to join the single currency. While these two Treaty changes are clearly both desirable and plausible, there appears to be little appetite within EU institutions to recognize this issue, with all the focus placed on further integration to solve the existing problems. But further integration does not have popular support.

The future of the EU does not necessarily need to be either a federal superstate or a confederation of states. The ability of the European Community to separate power and authority should be recognized as a major step forward in liberal ideology. In many respects it achieved the ultimate dispersion of power, something which a European federal state or a loose confederation of states would, of course, reverse, thereby undermining freedom through the centralization of power once more.

An ordoliberal approach might be expected therefore to embrace such a *sui generis* political organization which extends the single market between a community of liked-minded states with its legal system recognized as creating higher law. However, even with a *sui generis* political organization that completely separates power and authority, each member state would still remain a key building block in terms of cultural and social factors as emphasized by *Vitalpolitik*.

As was noted in Chapter 4, a weakness of the ordo framework was that it did not provide quantitative measures to benchmark the success of a public policy programme. Given that the dispersal of public power is not binary but is more continuous in nature, the development of such a benchmark could provide helpful guidance to policymakers. One simple metric that can be used to measure the dispersal of public power is to what extent taxing and spending powers are devolved as a percentage of central government revenues and expenditure. Countries that have a greater share of centralized taxing and spending powers have a greater concentration of power.[3]

As shown in Table 7.1, federal states such as Canada and Switzerland unsurprisingly perform well on this measure but so do the unitary states of Sweden and Denmark who in the last few decades have devolved a significant amount of power. Even Iceland, with a small population, has a significant amount of devolved power in contrast to Ireland which is one of the most centralized states in the OECD.

The devolution of power by the unitary states of Denmark and Sweden is of interest to an ordoliberal framework and provides some insight as to how and why countries have pursued this path.

The Swedish corporatist model backed by a large redistributive welfare state broke down in the 1970s due to the perception that the power of labour had become too strong (Rothstein, 2004). This ushered in a wave of market-oriented reform, but the implementation of competition and commercialization was markedly different to that in Anglo-Saxon countries, particularly due the focus on decentralization. In Denmark the Social Help Act in 1976 resulted in municipalities becoming the single point of contact for services, who were given significant discretion in determining clients' needs. This change in the delivery of the welfare state resulted in a shift away from universalism towards selectivism, enabling the state to deal with the specific needs of individuals (Kurachi, 2016).

In 1982, the Swedish Social Democrats developed a decentralization programme (taken from the Agrarian Centre Party) to make public authorities more accessible to influence by citizens. This also required municipalities to think about the welfare state in terms of market efficiency and hence run themselves as effectively as possible. This followed on from an initial period of devolution in the 1960s which led to regional and local governments expanding healthcare and child support programmes along with tax-raising powers (Olsson, 1990: 120–2, 276–7).

The effect of this process of devolution not only enabled those closest to social issues to take responsibility for them, but also after Sweden's banking crash, the government encouraged entrepreneurship in the delivery of public services. As a result, a publicly financed private welfare system emerged in education, health and personal social services, including a labour exchange, which has focused on service delivery to citizens (Hort, 2014: 117–18). These examples indicate that it is possible to disperse public power in a unitary state, although in this instance a fiscal crisis was the trigger for reform.

While such a measure can provide a quantitative benchmark of the dispersal of public power, it can also be used to ascertain whether there are growth benefits from dispersing power. Growth for ordoliberalism should be understood as a secondary variable as it is more important to prevent concentrations of public and private power. This view has been specifically articulated within competition policy by the *Bundeskartelamt* who note that in the long run, economic freedom does improve consumer welfare

Table 7.1: Comparison of power dispersion across OECD countries (structure of the state)

Country	Structure of the state power dispersal 2018 (%)	Rank order
Canada	61.57	1
Switzerland	52.95	2
US	46.40	3
Denmark	45.68	4
Sweden	41.46	5
Australia	39.48	6
Germany	38.48	7
Spain	35.92	8
Belgium	34.65	9
Korea	34.61	10
Finland	34.13	11
Japan	29.69	12
Iceland	28.28	13
Mexico	28.12	14
Poland	25.40	15
Norway	24.91	16
Czech Republic	24.04	17
Latvia	23.70	18
Austria	21.25	19
Italy	20.86	20
Netherlands	19.65	21
France	17.81	22
UK	15.68	23
Slovenia	15.46	24
Estonia	14.31	25
Lithuania	13.52	26
New Zealand	11.98	27
Portugal	11.74	28
Israel	11.65	29
Hungary	10.93	30
Slovak Republic	10.91	31
Ireland	7.57	32
Greece	5.28	33

Source: OECD

Figure 7.1: Public power dispersion vs GDP per capita

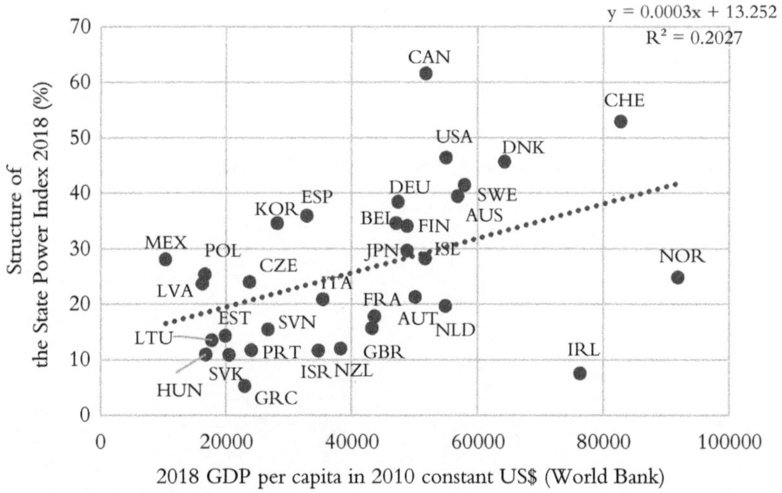

Source: OECD, World Bank

(Gormsen, 2007). This is important given that a system that does not have a positive growth outcome is unlikely to be able to sustain *Vitalpolitik* and provide sufficient employment opportunities. Hence, if the dispersal of power resulted in negative growth then this would impact the ability of the economy to provide sufficient employment opportunities.

The analysis in Figure 7.1 based on OECD data demonstrates that there is a positive relationship between the level of the dispersal of public power and GDP per capita, or there is a tendency for countries with a greater dispersal of public power to have higher income per capita. This relationship seems intuitive to the extent that over-centralization limits the ability of a country to coordinate disparate information and adapt to changing conditions. However, it is important to note that the analysis does not explain causality of the relationship, which is likely to be complex. An additional regression was run removing Ireland, which is a centralized state and whose GDP per capita benefits from the practices of transfer pricing by multinational corporations arising from Ireland's low corporation tax rate. The removal of Ireland significantly improves the relationship between the two variables, with an R^2 of 0.32.

To constantly manufacture freedom and equality requires public power to be devolved, enabling local communities to develop their own built environment taking account of the natural world. These communities need to be supported by national contributory welfare programmes which include a universal safety net. This foundation also enables communities across countries to develop close links with other like-minded states and become members of supranational organizations.

While the dispersal of public power enables citizens to live a life of vitality, an ordoliberal political economy also requires power to be dispersed across labour and product markets. For product markets this requires a strong state to enforce competition and promote free trade, while labour markets must be able to adapt to changing conditions through constant skills development in order to remain at parity with capital.

8

Labour Markets: Continuous
Training and Flexibility

Mitbestimmung

Along the wall of the Ministry of Finance on Leipziger Strasse in Berlin, is an 18 m mural entitled *Aufbau der Republik*. The painting depicts a happy society with officials, tradesmen, farmers and engineers all working together for the construction of the classless East German Republic. The idea to base East German society on the equality of outcomes did not produce a sufficiently stable polity, although as George Orwell intimated in *Animal Farm*, party officials were more equal than others.

The ordoliberal focus was instead on achieving greater equality prior to voluntary exchange. With regards to the labour market, although Eucken argued in favour of freedom of contract, he also thought it had limits given it can lead to concentrations of power thereby curtailing freedom. Achieving a greater equality of initial conditions may therefore require some rebalancing of power between workers and managers which is why Eucken supported trade unions and worker representatives under certain conditions. Rüstow promoted the need for continuous training to address the dislocating effects of economic change, which he thought ought to be provided by the state to maintain the equality of starting conditions across the labour market. This chapter explores the effects of co-determination on the West German economy and the importance of continuous training. It relates these ideas to contemporary labour market debates including the changing returns to labour and capital and to what extent the European Commission's idea of flexicurity encapsulates the essence of ordoliberal ideology.

During the 19th century, the relationship between labour and capital became a focal point of class struggle and revolution. In response to poor working conditions and low pay, workers in factories began to group together to form unions in order to improve their bargaining position, particularly for more commoditized labour. Highly skilled labourers that were in demand had a more equal bargaining positioning which could be observed by the difference in wages.

By the late 19th century, the British Parliament recognized that trade unions played a key role in improving the balance of power which it acknowledged was also good for employers. This led to Gladstone passing the 1871 Trade Union Act which effectively decriminalized unions. While the trade union movement can be viewed as providing an impetus to equalize initial conditions in the labour market, liberalism has not always been sympathetic towards unions. Even within social liberalism that supported a collective approach to economic development in many areas, unions were often viewed as just another vested interest that had the potential to subvert the common good.

Indeed, Hobson noted that organized public service unions were able to use their power to advance their own interests rather than promoting the harmony and unity of the general will (Hobson, 1974:155). Such utopian ideals of the general will were of less interest to unions whose duty was to their members, and if that meant confronting the state or employers through striking to improve working conditions or pay, then confrontation was the right approach. Striking can therefore be partly understood as an indication of a persistent imbalance in power relations between workers and managers.

To achieve greater equality of initial conditions requires power to be dispersed across the labour market, which includes greater parity between workers and managers. The implication of this is that there are limits to the freedom of contract, particularly if contracts result in the abuse of economic power. Eucken was clear about the limits to freedom of contract which, although are a prerequisite for competition, can also eliminate competition and establish monopoly positions (Eucken, 1959: 170). Eucken saw a positive role for trade unions and co-determination to the extent that they could help reign in economic power and maintain a balance between partners in the economy. However, labour that gained excessive power in the market had to be avoided at all costs, hence the importance of maintaining competition (Eucken, 1959: 185).

Adenauer's 1947 Ahlener programme emphasized the principle of distributive power in the labour market and the need to redesign the relationship between employer and employee so there was no power concentration within firms (Rittershausen, 2007). Adenauer felt that distributive power equated to enabling employees to participate in running a business and participating in its success (Ahlener Programme, 1947). Müller-Armack's blueprint published in 1948 described the right for workers to have a say on working conditions. However, Böhm expressed reservations about diluting the decision-making powers of managers through worker involvement. Despite these reservations, there was a general agreement that workers had rights as well as duties, and this was a marked shift from classical liberalism (Nicholls, 1994: 339).

The introduction of *Mitbestimmung* or co-determination by Adenauer, where employees participate in the consultation and decision-making processes, did help bring about a balance of power between labour and capital. Forcing a consensus at board level helped eliminate confrontation and strikes while ensuring that workers' rights, particularly around training and investment, were safeguarded.[1]

Since the principle of co-determination was established at the board level in the coal, iron and steel industries in 1951, it has become central to the DNA of German industry. In 1952, co-determination was expanded for firms with more than 500 employees with workers having one third of the representation on the supervisory board. In 1976, this was expanded to parity for firms larger than 2,000 employees. And in 2004, co-determination was expanded to all private firms with more than 500 employees with a third representation on the supervisory board (Michel, 2007).

In addition to representation at board level, firms with more than five employees have the right to set up a works council which must be consulted on issues affecting employees, although rights are weak with regards to strategic planning. However, half of firms with less than 2,000 employees in the Western German service sector have not established a supervisory board, and therefore do not have co-determination at the enterprise level. As was noted in Chapter 4, German firms were able to benefit from co-determination as it forced workers to appreciate the relationship between profitability and investment in relation to wage bargaining. The broader empirical analysis also indicates that co-determination enhances productivity and wage growth. One study has shown that co-determination generates 36 per cent higher value added per employee; focusing on workers, including their training needs, raises both productivity and wages (Boneberg, 2010).

Other studies that have assessed the 1976 parity law have also shown that higher productivity growth results from co-determination in large firms. This highlights the concerns by some ordoliberals, including Böhm, that excessive employee participation might be damaging for corporate success has been overblown (FitzRoy & Kraft, 2004). Such concerns have often arisen in the US where heavy unionization has resulted in less innovation, which is particularly the case where unions remain focused on wage bargaining (Kraft, Stank & Dewenter, 2009). This raises a crucial distinction between the role of unions bargaining for higher wages versus worker representatives who are focused on the long-term success of the firm in which they are personally invested in. Hence, it is unsurprising that these two approaches can result in radically different outcomes. The British Labour Party in the 1970s thought that workers on boards was a good idea, but only if they were union representatives as recommended in the Bullock Report (Parkinson, Gamble & Kelly, 2000: 77). This, of course, misses the point of co-determination.

Another paper notes that co-determination in large firms leads to a slight improvement in innovation than in firms without co-determination. This is likely to be the result of a greater level of information sharing and processing, as well as an advisory board that is more encouraging of research and development and investment (Kraft, Stank & Dewenter, 2009). Indeed, co-determination does appear to help resolve information and co-ordination gaps between centralized managers and workers in decentralized production units. Organizations that are better able to process and adapt the information of time and place will be more successful, and co-determination is one way of helping resolve this issue. A survey of chairpersons of Swedish companies related to the informational benefits of having workers at board meetings showed 69 per cent described the impact as positive with only 5 per cent finding it negative (TUC, 2013).

An EU report written by the former CEO of Volvo in 1998 also encouraged a closer relationship within companies between their directors and employees. It noted that such a close relationship was sensible in ensuring an effective response in firms to economic and social change; however, the report did not argue in favour of compulsion to introduce such a reform (Parkinson, Gamble & Kelly, 2000: 103).

An analysis by the Hans Böckler Foundation on the financial crisis showed that firms with co-determination maintained jobs and investment while reducing hours and limiting wage increases and share buybacks. The result of this approach was that these firms recovered more quickly, subsequently registering higher profits (Rapp & Wolff, 2019). One important effect of firms registering higher productivity and wage growth is that it will tend to result in lower returns to capital.

One study has found that price-to-book ratios for firms with co-determination are 26 per cent lower; hence, the returns to capital are lower due to higher returns to labour (Gorton & Schmid, 2002). The general outperformance of the US stock market compared with Germany and the UK is also indicative of higher returns to capital. While the UK and Germany experienced a similar fall in returns to labour since the early 1990s, the US has experienced a much deeper decline in labour share (ILO & OECD, 2015).

This outcome has led some classical liberals to argue that co-determination is merely a wealth confiscation scheme (Alchian in Nutzinger & Backhaus, 1989: 277). This view assumes that the initial conditions prior to a trade are the natural outcome of the market. But economic relations are a function of legal relations; hence, there is nothing natural or spontaneous about initial conditions. If the equalization of initial conditions leads to a difference in outcomes, then these are justified morally by an adherence to an ordoliberal system that promotes freedom and equality.

This is not to argue that co-determination in Germany is without its faults. Some recent analysis indicates that firms with works councils are marginally less digitally equipped suggesting they might become laggards (Genz, Bellmann & Matthes, 2018). This may be one reason why some German firms are opting to set up *société européenne* (SE) structures to avoid some of the rules on co-determination. Other concerns have been raised as to what extent supervisory board members are sufficiently qualified to make decisions given the complexity of the global economy.

During the financial crisis the large number of bank failures, including in Germany, demonstrated that whether a bank had a single board or a dual structure with worker representatives made little difference. Evidence collected by INSEAD on the failures of the German banking sector suggested that the quality of the board had more of a bearing on corporate governance failures than institutional structures (Turecamo, 2010).

Despite some recent criticism by industry associations, who appear to be over-representing dissatisfied members, many German firms continue to value the system of co-determination. A paper that assessed this apparent contradiction noted that when the BDI president in 2004 called board-level co-determination an error of history, 'DaimlerChrysler CEO Jürgen Schrempp responded with ostentatious praise ... Schrempp, known otherwise as a staunch advocate of shareholder value orientation, pointed out that in his company he had positive experiences with board-level co-determination.' The paper noted other senior executives' willingness to endorse Schrempp's intervention. Allianz, the insurance group said that 'we do not challenge the principle of the [co-determined] supervisory board. Rather, the discussion should focus on questions of efficiency and professional competence' (Paster, 2012).

Many other senior managers were quoted in the paper on the importance of using board level co-determination to implement restructuring and jobs cuts. Hence, the most important aspect of *Mitbestimmung* is rather the development of a framework where capital and labour can come to an agreement about key decisions.

Since the mid-1980s, countries that have evolved co-determination between employers and employees, such as Germany and Austria, have lost hardly any working days due to strike activity. On average since the mid-1980s, less than five workdays were lost per 1,000 employees in Germany compared with close to 80 for the UK and nearly 500 for France (OECD, 2017). If striking is understood as a manifestation of a potential power imbalance between workers and managers, then it does suggest that countries that have introduced co-determination have been able to improve employer and employee relations at source.

In addition to the benefits of information sharing, ensuring that both labour and capital are signed up to a firm's strategic objectives appears to result in a form of de-proletarianization. It also provides a forum to seek a consensus on the appropriate rates of return to labour and capital given that both invest to ensure the longevity of the firm (Forcillo, 2017). To a certain extent tech firms have voluntarily followed a similar path with a flatter management structure to improve information flows, and employees provided with stock options to tie them into the long-term success of the business. While this works in smaller firms, such an approach becomes harder to sustain as they grow larger and become internationalized.

Despite the success of co-determination in having a positive effect on equalizing power between labour and capital, it hasn't prevented a broader shift in recent decades towards a declining labour share of income and a bifurcation within the labour market.

Falling labour share and bifurcation

The idea of constancy in the share of income flowing to capital and labour has been a highly influential assumption for decades largely down to the ubiquitous influence of Kaldor's growth model. Kaldor thought that the rates of increase of capital equipment and output per worker tended to be the same leaving the capital/output ratio virtually unchanged. Hence, he concluded that 'the share of wages and the share of profits in the national income has shown a remarkable constancy in developed capitalist economies of the United States and the United Kingdom since the second half of the nineteenth century' (Kaldor, 1957).

But such a conclusion is at odds with the data Kaldor himself cited. He noted that while the labour share of wages remained around 60 per cent up until 1929 in the US, it subsequently increased to 69 per cent during the post-war period. This can hardly be argued to be constant. As has been the case for many economic concepts, theory triumphed over empirical data. It wasn't until Piketty's *Capital in the 21st Century* was published that the idea of constancy has been largely discarded. However, Piketty's argument that OECD countries are now on an inevitable course of rising share to capital appears to be an attempt to justify his iron law of capitalism and inevitable U-shaped trajectory. Such a U-shape is largely dependent on when one decides to start the time series, which is arbitrary. Furthermore, Piketty forecast capital-to-income ratios out to the year 2100 to emphasize his U-shaped theory (Piketty, 2014: 196). Given that a central bank's one year GDP forecast can be unreliable, forecasting ahead 86 years is without any plausible empirical foundation and therefore should be ignored.

Piketty started his analysis in 1770 based on the availability of data. Marx thought that the most appropriate place for a starting point to analyse capitalism was 1846. In Chapter 25 (*General Law of Capitalist Accumulation*),

Figure 8.1: Capital vs labour split in Britain, 1840–2010

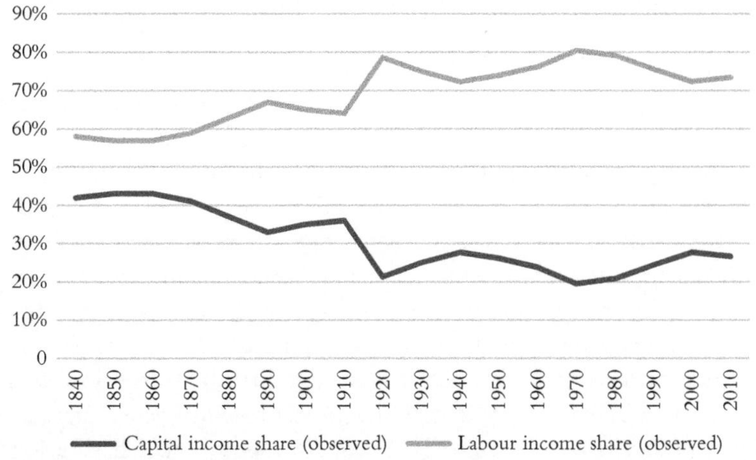

Capital income share (observed)   Labour income share (observed)

Source: Piketty, 2014

Marx argued that England between 1846 and 1866 was the best country to study the nature of capital due to the repeal of the Corn Laws in 1846 cutting off 'the last retreat of vulgar economics' (Marx, 1976: 802). The idea of assessing data sets within defined regimes is now commonplace within financial economics in order to account for structural changes to an economy (Hamilton, 1989).

The data from the mid-1840s to today for the UK indicates a general increase away from capital towards labour. Hence, industrial capitalism has been more beneficial for labour than it has for capital. But as the data series shows, it is not constant. Piketty's data in Figure 8.1 clearly shows that since the 1980s there has been an increase in the share flowing to capital.

However, there is nothing inevitable about the future direction of the shares flowing to labour and capital. As Larry Summers argued in his review of Piketty's book, 'rather than attributing the rising share of profits to the inexorable process of wealth accumulation, most economists would attribute both it and rising inequality to the working out of various forces associated with globalization and technological change' (Summers, 2014).

Research led by the economist David Autor indicates that the process of globalization has negatively impacted wages in the US. The analysis compares the rise in low-income country manufacturing imports from 1991 to 2007 which rose from 2.9 per cent to 11.7 per cent, of which China accounted for over 90 per cent. The effect of this shift in globalization resulted in rising unemployment, decreased labour force participation and crucially lower wages in local labour markets affected by the imported goods. The paper also found that exposure to Chinese import competition triggered a decline in wages outside the manufacturing sector, resulting in a fall in the average earnings of households (Autor, Dorn & Hanson, 2013).

When manufacturing jobs vanish through increased globalization and technological development, there has been a tendency in many countries for these jobs to be replaced in lower value-added services with lower wages rather than higher value-added sectors and higher wages, thereby decreasing the labour share (Haskel, Lawrence, Leamer & Slaughter, 2012; Elsby, Hobijn & Sahin, 2013). This tendency is part of a shift towards lower value-added jobs across the economy or the between effect which has muted productivity growth in many Western countries (Sainsbury, 2020). Another reason for these lower wages is the monopsony power of local employers given that labour is less willing to travel to work and will take what work is on offer locally (OECD, 2019d). In the US, this has been exacerbated by the licensing restrictions preventing cross-state labour mobility (Lindsey & Teles, 2017). Europe's single market has performed far better by eliminating these types of frictions, although cultural factors, of course, remain a significant barrier.

The entry of China, India and Eastern Europe into the global trading system from the early 1990s transformed global supply chains. As firms adjusted to these new opportunities with lower labour costs, it has placed increasing downward pressure on nominal wage growth, particularly for low- and medium-tech manufacturing where unions once had significant bargaining power. Research published by the Bank for International Settlements also indicates that inflation has been affected by globalization (Auer, Borio & Filardo, 2017). This effect can also be seen clearly in the changing slope of the Phillips Curve through time.

Bill Phillips in his seminal 1958 paper revealed a relationship between unemployment and wages stemming back to 1867 which appeared to show that as unemployment fell, there was a tendency for wages to rise. The central intuition was that if there was less slack in the labour market, then bargaining power for labour would increase. However, the aggregation of this long-run data set ignored the fact that the UK economy has transitioned through a number of very different economic regimes. Hence, an aggregated curve may do a poor job of explaining how it might behave in a specific regime.

While Phillips' intuition makes sense for a closed economy, in an open economy a fall in unemployment might not increase wages if production can be offshored to cheaper locations. Hence, one would expect the curve to be much flatter in an open economy. Such flatness was in fact noted by Phillips in his initial data set for the 1870s and 1880s, but he subsequently ignored the data noting that it was likely to be an anomaly. But this flatness was driven in part by falling import prices as the rest of Europe and North America began to industrialize driving prices down due to increased competition (Aubrey, 2012: 25–6). The gold standard may have also had some effect on

Table 8.1: UK Phillips Curve slope by regime

Period description	Period	Slope (log scale)	Trade openness
Pre-WW1 globalization	1873–1913	−0.8	55.3%
Interwar period	1919–1938	−1.1	46.1%
Post-WW2 to Bretton Woods collapse	1946–1971	No relationship	40.8%
From floating exchange rates to China WTO entry	1972–2001	−1.1	47.6%
From China entry into WTO	2002–2016	−0.8	56.0%

Source: Bank of England, Credit Capital Advisory

falling prices as gold production was unable to keep up with the increase in the demand for money as the global economy grew (Selgin, 2015).

The logic of this relationship is that the more open the economy, the flatter the Phillips Curve, as there would be a greater threat of offshoring tradeable goods and services. Research by Moretti indicates that the wages of local non-tradeable services tend to be correlated with the wages of local firms involved in tradeable goods and services. This is why Moretti finds that the wages of barbers are much higher in successful city-region economies, and much lower in areas of manufacturing decline (Moretti, 2013: 90).

Table 8.1 demonstrates that a higher level of trade openness corresponded to a flatter Phillips Curve during the first phase of globalization in the later 19th century.[2] This was followed by a steeper curve as trade contracted between the wars. From the post-war period to the breakdown of the Bretton Woods Agreement, the relationship between the two variables breaks down. This coincided with Friedman and Phelps arguing that the curve was vertical (Friedman, 1968; Phelps, 1968), implying that there was no trade-off between inflation and unemployment. Between 1972 and 2001, the level of trade openness was slightly above the interwar period but with a similar slope. The entry of China into the WTO resulted in a jump in trade openness and a fall in the slope back to the pre-1914 globalization period level.

While a flat Phillips Curve indicates downward pressure on nominal wage growth, there have been considerable benefits for firms that have been able to take advantage of greater trade openness. Globalization has enabled the most productive firms to become increasingly dominant with higher margins and a lower share of income flowing to labour. In addition to the fall in the relative price of investment goods, the ability of firms like Google and Amazon to exploit global network effects has enhanced this dominance. This has been supported, to a lesser extent, by a diminution of competition which is a combination of weaker antitrust enforcement and the difficulty of smaller firms to scale investment to be able to challenge these firms (Autor, Dorn, Katz, Patterson & Van Reenen, 2019).

It has been argued that this process is driven by the decline in the relative price of investment goods which induces firms to prioritize capital over labour, resulting in a decline of the labour share of income. This is particularly the case for firms investing in information and communication technologies (Karabarbounis & Neiman, 2013).

The decline in the relative price of investment goods has also given rise to predictions that robots are coming for everyone's jobs. Such concerns though are as old as the development of technology itself. The Abbot Johannes Trithemius in the 15th century wrote a tract in praise of scribes highlighting concern that the printing press would put monks out of the business of writing books. Such stark warnings make great headlines and provide work for commentators, but the reality is more mundane.

Despite the concerns raised by Trithemius, the scribal industry continued to prosper for decades, which was long enough for the existing scribes to make a living while enabling young apprentices to learn a new trade. Some scribes made a successful transition to become printers, while others found new jobs as type designers (Aubrey in Neufeind, O'Reilly & Ranft, 2018). According to the OECD, 'the net effects of major technological revolutions on employment have been positive and there are few signs of this trend changing' (OECD, 2019e: 44).

Further evidence demonstrates that automation has not been employment displacing although it has reduced labour's share in value added. While increasing total-factor productivity raises value added and lowers output prices, it does so by reducing the amount of labour required. However, this labour slack is taken up in customer industries, which is a classic shift of labour from progressive to stagnant industries, thereby reducing labour's share of value added (Autor & Salomons, 2018). But the shift towards lower value-added service roles is not always the case.

Although the displacement effect from automation tends to initially reduce the demand for labour and wages, demand rises for non-automated tasks. This is complemented by additional capital accumulation to improve existing processes which further increases the demand for higher-skilled workers to work with the new machines. These new tasks using capital deepening, result in labour having a comparative advantage relative to machines (Acemoglu & Restrepo, 2018).

This process was observed when banks opened ATMs to automate the process of cash withdrawals. This enabled banks to open more branches and bank tellers to specialize in more complex tasks. Research into industries associated with rapid technological and productivity growth including textiles, steel and the auto sectors shows that they all initially experienced strong employment growth (Bessen, 2019).

Another study has shown that the rise of e-commerce is creating better-paid jobs at faster rates than the traditional less well-paid jobs in the retail sector are being destroyed (Mandel, 2017). However, it is worth emphasizing that not all capital investments are equal in their outcomes. So called 'brilliant technologies' which displace tasks and drive up productivity thereby creating new roles perform differently to 'so-so technologies' which cause displacement without the productivity boost (Acemoglu & Restrepo, 2019).

OECD data shows that while overall employment is up in OECD countries between 1995 and 2015, it is dramatically lower in manufacturing with services taking up the slack (OECD, 2019e). This overall process has benefitted the top income earners, while those in middle-skill manufacturing jobs have lost out and with the less educated are now at a significant disadvantage (OECD, 2012).

This bifurcation in the labour market has resulted in lower-skilled workers experiencing a decline in real earnings since the 1970s, while those with higher levels of education have seen their wages grow. This is particularly the case for those with postgraduate degrees, while those with undergraduate degrees saw a much more modest increases in wages. This polarization is increasingly related to the nature of job tasks, with more complex job tasks being rewarded while simpler tasks are either automated or outsourced (Acemoglu & Autor, 2010). Hence, this has created greater unequal starting conditions depending on the skill set obtained by workers.

This evidence is clearly contrary to the narrative of a jobless future as proposed by Frey and Osborne. Their paper, which has since became one of the most cited reports, argued that as a result of computerization about 47 per cent of total US employment is at risk (Frey & Osborne, 2013). However, it appears that the authors have since retracted the implications of their research stating that 'we make no attempt to estimate how many jobs will actually be automated' (The Economist, 2019). In effect this media frenzy has largely been much ado about nothing.

Research by the consultancy McKinsey suggests that less than 5 per cent of all jobs are likely to become redundant as a result of new technology over the next few decades although just over half of tasks involved in data collection, processing and predictable physical work are expected to be automated (McKinsey Global Institute, 2017). However, even with these low estimates of redundancies, there is no necessity that even if the technology exists, businesses will actually decide to utilize it.

If the technology is too expensive, then there is no commercial reason to substitute it for labour. If it is cheaper, there may be cases where this results in lower demand for products. For example, cooking a meal is a relatively simple task to automate with a machine being able to make the same dish day-in day-out. While this might be the case for cheaper food, customers in a more expensive restaurant may prefer to spend money on a meal that has been cooked by a chef. The same goes for making coffee. Coffee–machine technology is widely used domestically, but coffee shops still employ baristas. The reality is that part of the customer experience of parting with US$3 for a cup of coffee is the human interaction with workers in coffee shops.

The importance of human interaction is also critical with regards to using artificial intelligence (AI). Where products or services are provided by AI, in the event that a client of the service wishes to query the output if it is an anomaly, the machine is unlikely to be able to explain why the machine has generated that specific result. Furthermore, it is unlikely that a human will fully understand why the machine has done what it has done because the machine learned to produce the output. Humans value interacting with other humans.[3]

This is not to argue that there are not substantial benefits from AI. It is plausible that AI will create some major productivity gains across the healthcare sector – which has tended to rise continuously in terms of its prices. AI may well lead to a diagnostics revolution facilitating faster and more accurate diagnosis – which is currently costly and time consuming. Once again it is unlikely to eliminate jobs, but rather enable medical staff to focus on other aspects of medical care (Wade, 2019).

The question for policymakers therefore is how best to deal with this bifurcation and power imbalance in the labour market given the rise of globalization and the fall in the relative price of investment goods. The idea that collective bargaining can restore this imbalance has been persistently advocated by many social liberals. For example, Jacob Hacker has argued that to restore the middle class means that workers must collectively negotiate for better terms of employment and a larger share of the rewards of growth (Hacker & Loewentheil, 2012).

Union power declined along with globalization from the mid-1980s in combination with the introduction of restrictive legislation to curb what was considered to be excessive power. It is unsurprising, therefore, that trade union density, which is the share of workers who are union members, has declined across OECD countries from 33 per cent in 1975 to just 16 per cent in 2018. This decline in density coincided with a decrease in the percentage of workers covered by a collective agreement across OECD countries falling from 45 per cent in 1985 to 32 per cent in 2017 (OECD, 2019d). The power of collective bargaining has also fallen due to a number of shifts in the nature of the labour market itself.

The introduction of national minimum wages in many countries has meant that the government has now taken on a role once monopolized by unions, particularly for low-paid services roles. The decline of large numbers of unskilled or semi-skilled workers in factories due to productivity improvements across the manufacturing sector have also played a role, as has the increase in the use of flexible forms of contracts.

Hence, the idea that a return to collective bargaining is the solution to rebalance the labour market does not appear to address the economic reality faced by developed economies. Furthermore, analysis by the OECD suggests that if such a policy were to be pursued it should avoid at all costs highly centralized bargaining systems. While these systems result in lower earnings dispersion, they are also associated with lower productivity growth. Centralized bargaining is also unable to deal with the required flexibility at the firm level which is needed to incentivize performance.

Where firm-level collective bargaining is coordinated it tends to deliver improved productivity outcomes and higher wages helping to remove any information asymmetry with employers (OECD, 2019d). This implies that some form of co-determination is more important than national wage bargaining. But co-determination, on its own, is not going to reverse the decline in the returns to labour. The challenge is therefore to not only disperse power between capital and labour but also within the labour market itself.

When Robert Solow published his study on growth accounting indicating that 80 per cent of the growth in output per worker was explained by what he called technical progress, it sparked an industry to try and explain this residual. One simple way of thinking about technical progress is that such growth is a function of how humans interacting with machines (both existing and new ones) can improve the production process in generating products and services that are in demand. More sophisticated machines require an increase in the capacity of humans to exploit them. In essence, capital intensity is a function of a more technically skilled workforce (Madsen, 2010).

Research by Goldin and Katz demonstrates that rising productivity in the US was driven by the ability of the US education system to improve human capital to exploit technology growth. They argue that 'the evolution of the wage structure reflects, at least in part, a race between the growth in the demand for skills driven by technological advances and the growth in the supply of skills driven by demographic change, educational investment choices and immigration' (Goldin & Katz, 2009: 91). However, since the 1970s, the US education system has not been able to keep up with the demand from technology which has also resulted in greater wage inequality as indicated by the large wage premium for college graduates. This raises the question where greater educational investment ought to be deployed.

In his book on information theory, the physicist Cesar Hidalgo argues that knowledge and know-how are the two key components of information. But as Hidalgo explains, 'the social nature of learning makes the accumulation of knowledge and knowhow geographically biased' (Hidalgo, 2015: 80). This learning process effectively places limits to the amount of knowledge and know-how an individual can acquire which is why networks are central to the production of information. Larger networks are able to embody large volumes of knowledge and know-how, but this is dependent on the costs of establishing those links (Hidalgo, 2015: 107).

More advanced economies have a greater advanced knowledge capacity; however, when low- and medium-tech manufacturing leaves a country, the need for this knowledge is reduced. If the only option for these workers is to take on lower-paid work requiring less specialized knowledge than they used to have, then their pay will fall. But this creates the bifurcation within the labour market where these workers now are at a distinct disadvantage. Without enabling displaced workers to accumulate new knowledge and contribute to higher value-added sectors, it is hard to see how power can be dispersed across the labour market.

Such an outcome may also result in lower aggregate demand and therefore potentially less investment. The lower share of income flowing to labour has depressed median wages much more than higher-paid workers who have seen robust earnings growth. Research by the ILO suggests that a 1 percentage point increase in income going to capital leads to a 0.4 per cent fall in global GDP due to lower aggregate demand (Onaran & Galanis, 2012).

Flexicurity

The research undertaken by Goldin and Katz indicates how a country can reduce power concentration across the labour market through human capital development by keeping up with technological developments. Indeed, until the early 1970s, the US education system had constantly been ahead of other countries which often followed a more elitist approach.

The US road to human capital development started with the widespread implementation of publicly funded elementary education in the early 19th century, followed by the implementation of secondary education for the masses in the early 20th century. This development complemented the increasing demand by employers for production workers to have a high-school education due to the rise in complexity of the machines that were being deployed. It was the same in offices which required workers with excellent written communication skills, maths and foreign languages. US educational institutions were also able to adapt more quickly with the explosion in science after the Second World War, which enabled the US to become the first country to pioneer mass higher education (Goldin & Katz, 2009: 174).

The authors suggest that the reasons behind the success story of the US system were due to the decentralized approach taken, the lack of discrimination of women and the fact that the system was publicly funded. The idea of public funding is close to Rüstow's concept of *Vitalpolitik* where members of the same community support public education to enhance social cohesion and improve the justice of initial conditions.

This decentralized approach is also fundamental with regards to increasing knowledge and know-how. Centralized bureaucratic organizations that are focused on administrative processes find it costly to establish new links to grow knowledge and know-how (Hidalgo, 2015: 102). This is why centralized states are less likely to be able develop policies that can enhance freedom and equality. Furthermore, when centralized organizations superimpose a new policy on to a complex localized system, there is almost no institutional knowledge or know-how of the existing system. This is why this centralized approach is more likely to fail and why the devolution of problem solving in many areas is more likely to be successful, with those closest to the knowledge of place and time being able to make decisions.

Since the 1970s, however, the US education system has not been able to keep up with the demand from technology which has also resulted in greater wage inequality as indicated by the large wage premium for college graduates. While some of this change has been due to low-skilled immigration, the largest driver has been from the native-born population. US high-school graduation rates now lag other countries. This leads the authors to ask the question how one might get the youth of America to make the right educational choices so they can earn the high wage premiums from the high-skilled jobs in demand that have insufficient supply (Goldin & Katz, 2009: 325).

But what choices should they make? The idea of merely pushing more students towards university does not necessarily chime with the facts. According to a recent study in the UK, over half of graduates with creative arts and mass communications degrees in 2012/13 earned less than £20,000 after more than ten years of experience (Institute for Fiscal Studies, 2016). In the US, a study by Georgetown University shows that half of all gradates in arts, education and psychology earn less than US$44,000 across the economy, which accounts for 23 per cent of all graduates (Carnevale, Strohl & Melton, 2015).

Following Hildago's idea on information theory, it appears that a greater return is likely to come from labour acquiring more specialist technical knowledge through vocational training. This would enable labour to reintegrate into local networks having acquired new knowledge instead of being ejected from existing knowledge networks. However, vocational training has not traditionally been a major focus in many Anglo-Saxon economies. Analysis on the UK suggests that over 300,000 core technical job vacancies were difficult to fill because of technical skills shortages with salaries of over £35,000 (Aubrey in Neufeind, O'Reilly & Ranft, 2018). Adjusted for inflation back to 2012, these salaries are 60 per cent higher than many graduate salaries after ten years published in the Institute for Fiscal Studies study.

Hence, it is crucial that workers can obtain the necessary skills to ensure they can get the good jobs that are in demand by employers. However, the process of reallocating labour to these new tasks is fraught with challenges. It needs to be clear to training providers and local officials what the skill sets are that are in demand, as well as a willingness for labour to retrain in these new skills.

This was one of the important agreements made between the CDU government and the West German Trade Union association in the 1950s to move towards a model of continuous education that was subsidized by the state (Giersch, Paque & Schmieding, 1992: 121). Without such a programme it is hard to for workers to adjust to the changing demand for skills in the workforce. In essence, continuous training is an essential component of equalizing power across the labour market. As Rüstow emphasized, no one should be denied access to training for financial reasons.

This training, however, must go hand in hand with increased employment opportunities through greater flexibility, as without such opportunities training will accomplish little. This approach of flexibility in the labour market and improved security through life-long learning has been central to the European's Commission's much debated policy of flexicurity.

In 2006, the European Commission stated its commitment to flexicurity arguing it was an appropriate response 'to the needs of both employers and workers in a rapidly changing labour market aimed at providing adequate bridges during periods of labour market transition' (European Commission, 2006: 39). The Commission highlighted four key areas including the flexibility of contractual arrangements, active labour market policies to support the return to work, credible lifelong learning systems and a social security system that supports workers during periods of absence.

These ideas were based on labour market reforms that were introduced in the Netherlands and Denmark in the 1990s that resulted in significant falls in unemployment. The Dutch model promoted the use of flexible types of employment that had similar rights for working conditions and social security as permanent employment. The Danish model of flexible standard employment with low-employment protection was built on by providing generous unemployment benefits in addition to pursuing active labour market policies aimed at upgrading key skills (Keune & Jepsen, 2007). It is the Danish model rather than the Dutch that is generally referred to as the benchmark for flexicurity – largely due to its active labour market policies.

The official aim of Danish labour market policy is to combat long-term unemployment by creating a well-functioning labour market with a continuous increase in the qualifications of the workforce, without imbalances between the supply and demand for labour. Despite Denmark being a small country in terms of size and population, this balance between the supply and demand for labour is tackled at a devolved or regional level. This results in a more flexible labour market policy that adapts to local needs and that works closely with social partners who have specific knowledge of local labour markets and can tailor programmes for unemployed individuals a well as those looking to leave a job and upskill (Madsen, 1999).

This is made possible because Denmark has developed the institutional capabilities through its localized public system of vocational education and training to continually upgrade the skill level of the work force. This system developed because the Danish private sector, which is dominated by small- and medium-sized enterprises, lacked the resources to train people beyond job-specific requirements. This resulted in the development of a vocational education system based on networks of local partners who have an understanding of the needs of firms and the capabilities of workers.

This is not to suggest that Danish firms don't invest in people. But firms expect the training system to provide the market with a sufficient number of core skills such as electricians or IT production engineers, who then receive more specific on-the-job training once they have been hired. Businesses could not function if they had to teach every occupation-specific skill on the job (Reed in Aubrey, 2017).

Switzerland has also achieved a reasonable balance of power across the labour market through its decentralized skills system. Again, each Canton has developed its own local institutional network to enable workers to be retrained and ensure that the unemployed can return to the workforce with new skills that are in demand from local employers. Like Denmark, the labour market is flexible in conjunction with a reasonably generous benefit system and high expenditure on active labour market programmes (Duell, Tergeist, Bazant & Cimper, 2010).

The institutional framework for skills in Austria is also devolved which has enabled local networks of training providers, employers and local government officials to develop. These networks adapt to changing market conditions much more quickly than centralized systems to ensure that the key skills demanded by employers can be met either through vocational schools or the system of apprenticeship training. Even where these local institutional networks have developed, it still requires a lot of effort and prioritization from local stakeholders to maintain these networks and ensure they function effectively.

Conversely, countries with more centralized skills systems such as the UK have struggled to adjust to changing market conditions. This should not be surprising given large, centralized organizations struggle to adapt, particularly due to the lack of local knowledge. A number of UK regional analyses have highlighted the potential effect on local economies due to specific skills mismatches. One area in the Midlands faced a potential annual undersupply of nearly 1,000 electricians, while at the same time there was an oversupply of fitness instructors by more than 1,000. A fast-growing technology-based region had a potential undersupply of nearly 1,500 non-graduate digital roles, which prevents firms from expanding. Another area in England, which still has a manufacturing base, had a shortfall of over 3,000 technical engineering and manufacturing roles. Despite this significant undersupply of personnel for advertised well-paid roles, there remains an oversupply of skills for sports and fitness instructors as well as beauticians (Aubrey in Neufeind, O'Reilly & Ranft, 2018).

Until the UK is able to develop local institutional frameworks that formally bring together employers, training providers and local government officials, the UK will struggle to reduce the power imbalance across the labour market. But even if there is a political desire to develop local institutions to ensure the balance between the supply and demand for skills, such programmes are expensive to run. In 2017, Denmark spent nearly 2 per cent of GDP on active labour market measures, with Austria, Germany and Switzerland all over 0.5 per cent of GDP compared with just 0.22 per cent on such programmes in Anglo-Saxon countries (Martin, 2015).

Hence, to drive up parity in the labour market requires a much more significant investment in human capital. When the Danish government decided to implement flexicurity it resulted in a shift from a budget surplus to a 5 per cent deficit (Jepsen in Bruegel Institute, 2017). This is why these kinds of labour market reforms without growth will not work and which is why flexible labour markets are needed. Just spending money on active labour programmes does not necessarily yield positive results. In recent years a burgeoning literature has developed to assess the performance of active labour market policies or ALMPs, indicating a mixed picture of success.

Where such programmes are successful, the impacts are generally seen after around three years after the completion of a programme with larger average gains for programmes that emphasize human capital accumulation and larger impacts for females and participants who enter from long-term unemployment (Card, Kluve & Weber, 2017). Direct employment programmes in the public sector tend to be less successful (Kluve, 2006).

Beyond developing local vocational institutions and ensuring that there is sufficient money for training programmes for jobs in demand by the private sector to improve job security, it is critical that the labour market is sufficiently flexible in the first place so jobs are created.

The UK reforms to the labour market in the 1980s have led to more jobs being created, although given the lack of training, these jobs have often been in lower value-added areas. Despite these issues, there were opportunities for people to work, whereas in countries such as France, stubbornly high unemployment rates effectively locked large numbers of workers out of the labour market.

In the early 2000s, Germany decided that its labour market was too rigid and in 2004 the Schröder government passed the Hartz reforms. The Hartz reforms were largely an attempt to improve flexibility in the labour market to reduce unemployment, particularly for temporary roles. To encourage marginal part-time work, individuals could earn up to €450 without having any tax or social security deductions. This was accompanied by cutting the duration of benefit payments. The reforms themselves while not having any impact on standard or permanent roles, led to a significant increase in temporary work and the end of mass unemployment. Crucially, these reforms also coincided with a growing demand for Germany's exports, particularly from Asia.

One negative effect of the reform was that it created a dual labour market with a significant wage gap for temporary workers who have limited chances of transitioning to permanent roles. Furthermore, there has been some evidence that employers are using this approach to fill tasks in sectors such as retail that previously would have been filled by permanent roles. In 2017, the government introduced new regulations for temporary workers that they should receive equal pay after 9 or 15 months depending on the sector and a maximum assignment of 18 months (Eichhorst in Bruegel Institute, 2017).

The Danish model on the flexibility side has come in for some criticism as a result of the financial crisis increasing unemployment. Analysis undertaken in 2011 indicated that the Danish system is far more likely to let employees go rather than keep them employed with fewer hours. Even the UK with its flexible labour market reduced hours rather than letting workers go (Andersen, Bosch, Deelen & Euwals, 2011). In Germany, agreements were negotiated to reduce hours worked, which in turn meant that there were fewer incentives to lay off workers (Burda & Hunt, 2011).

Flexibility also raises the question of immigration. As was highlighted by the Goldin and Katz study, low-skilled immigration impacts the ability of a country's education system to compete in the race against technological development, although it is important to note that this was not the most important factor. However, firms in tradeable sectors may prefer to pay low-skilled labour rather than investing in labour-enhancing capacity, thereby maintaining unequal power relations. This is often the case in lower value-added sectors such as agriculture where firms often remain wedded to maintaining a constant flow of lower-skilled immigration to fill the required relatively low-paid jobs.

For example, the Californian agriculture sector which produces more than a third of vegetables and two thirds of fruit and nuts in the US depends on immigrant labour (Duvall, 2019). In terms of value added per worker in agriculture, the US lies in ninth position at just under US$80 k of value added per worker according to the World Bank development indicators for 2017. This raises the question whether if this avenue were shut off it would result in more capital investment, innovation and fewer better-paid workers?

There is some evidence that for economies with flexible labour markets and a steady supply of low-cost workers, firms are less likely to invest in capital resulting in lower labour-productivity growth (Vergeer & Kleinknecht,

2014). Given that an ordoliberal approach aims at reducing the power imbalance between firms and workers, a free flow of lower-skilled workers into low value-added sectors that could benefit from incremental investment will not help disperse power. This is not to argue that there should be no lower-skilled immigration, but rather that the effects of such policies related to power imbalances should be understood rather than ignored. Non-tradeable sectors, however, are far less likely to be impacted by this issue.

Given the complexity and institutional nuances of skills policy, how one might measure the dispersion of power across the labour market will prove challenging. Whatever measure is used will not capture all the requisite factors; however, some high-level benchmarks can at least help to estimate elements of the dispersion of power.[4]

First, an economy needs to create as many jobs as possible to provide individuals with an income in order to participate in *Vitalpolitik*. The employment participation rate can be seen as a measure of ensuring equal access to the labour market, with high rates less likely to result in long-term unemployment. Second, according to the OECD, an upper-secondary education is the minimum credential required for successful entry into the labour market across knowledge-intensive OECD countries (OECD, 2013). Hence, the percentage of citizens with an upper-secondary education provides another metric of the dispersion of power across labour markets.

These measures, however, do not take into account how a skills system enables workers to retrain and regain access to new knowledge networks. Hence, workers need to have access to the necessary technical training and reskilling opportunities to obtain the well-paid specialist technical and professional roles, which are generally delivered through vocational programmes (OECD, 2010). Countries with well-developed vocational education systems are therefore more likely to reduce the inequality in skills at the post- and upper-secondary level. The quality of a vocational system is indirectly measured by the level of participation, which reflects its greater attractiveness (Green & Pensiero, 2016). In addition to this training, individuals need to be directly supported in regaining access to the labour market which can be achieved through active labour market programmes. The third factor is therefore estimated as the product of the percentage of post- and upper-secondary vocational education and spending on active labour market policies as a percentage of GDP. Combining these two measures provides greater certainty that vocational education will have a more direct effect on the job market by ensuring a match between the demand and supply of skills. The aggregation of these three factors, which is aligned with a considerable amount of labour market research, provides a simple metric of the dispersal power across labour markets.

Nordic and central European countries with high employment participation rates along with strong vocational training and active labour market policies score well on the labour market measure indicating a greater dispersion of power. Conversely, Britain, Canada and the US perform less well largely due to a deprioritization of vocational training as highlighted by Table 8.2.

With regards to the Nordic countries, the emphasis on the efficiency and delivery of public services by institutions that were closest to social issues was complemented by a prioritization of work, hence the development of active labour market policies. Denmark's flexicurity system developed in the 1990s through slowly reducing the duration of unemployment benefits, while boosting investment in careers advice, job searching, as well as education and job training in addition to a shift towards decentralized wage bargaining. The political consensus during the breakdown of the corporatist model that emerged was that while the neoliberal diagnosis of the problem was correct, it was thought that the market had little chance of resolving the issue on its own (Larsen & Andersen, 2009).

The Nordic model today can largely be characterized as one with contributory and universal benefits for healthcare, and pensions coupled with active labour market policies to increase labour force participation. This includes flexible labour markets, lifelong training with generous family and social security support which not only provide a collective risk-sharing mechanism but has also enhanced a favourable attitude towards globalization and competition.

While the driving force behind the Nordic model appears to have been based on practical policies rather than any ideological approach (Veggeland, 2016), it has been argued that institutions have adapted through time based on ideas of equal concern for citizens (Rothstein, 1998: 180). Historically, most of the Nordic countries were not faced with the huge inequalities of landownership that were created by the feudal system. Hence, the starting point for voluntary exchange was already more equal, although the countries were relatively poorer than other parts of Western Europe. In addition, gender equality appears to have been an important characteristic although this may have been an unintended consequence of the need to increase the supply of labour which was increasingly provided by women (Bergh, 2011). A comparison of income inequality across Sweden, Canada, France, Netherlands and the US shows that by 1920, Sweden had comparatively lower levels of inequality prior to the existence of a redistributive welfare state (Sanandaji, 2015: 56). The fact that Scandinavian countries were highly literate societies is also likely to have been a factor why inequality levels were low (Olsson, 1990: 43).

The analysis in Figure 8.2 shows a positive relationship between power dispersal across the labour market and GDP per capita. Although the relationship is weaker than for the dispersal of public power, it is still positive indicating support for *Vitalpolitik*. Wealthier countries, therefore, tend to

Table 8.2: Comparison of power dispersion across OECD countries (labour market)

Country	Labour market power dispersal 2018 (%)	Rank order
Finland	76.29	1
Denmark	75.43	2
Austria	66.75	3
Belgium	62.91	4
Switzerland	62.06	5
Sweden	61.88	6
Germany	60.97	7
Netherlands	59.06	8
Hungary	54.19	9
Czech Republic	53.44	10
Estonia	52.83	11
France	52.61	12
Poland	51.35	13
Norway	50.74	14
Slovak Republic	49.39	15
Slovenia	48.95	16
Lithuania	48.29	17
Australia	46.84	18
Spain	46.80	19
Ireland	46.47	20
Latvia	45.22	21
New Zealand	44.54	22
UK	44.45	23
Canada	43.37	24
Italy	43.10	25
Israel	42.74	26
Korea	42.53	27
United States	41.56	28
Japan	41.37	29
Iceland	40.47	30
Greece	40.05	31
Portugal	38.11	32
Mexico	25.89	33

Source: OECD

Figure 8.2: Labour market power dispersal metric vs GDP per capita

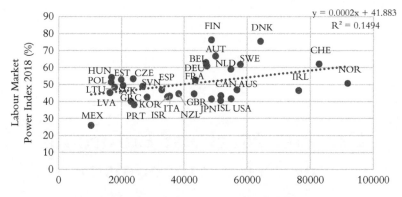

2018 GDP per capita in 2010 constant US$ (World Bank)

Source: OECD, World Bank

have a greater level of power dispersion across labour markets, although this does not provide much insight into causation.

In order to constantly manufacture freedom, power needs to be continually dispersed across labour markets. Where labour and capital work in tandem, the evidence suggests that productivity growth increases which in turn benefits labour. However, moves towards greater equalization of this relationship does not address the increasing bifurcation of the labour market. This requires labour markets to be flexible to create jobs, and workers to have at least an upper-secondary education. In addition, local institutions need to provide continuous vocational training to improve skill levels for jobs that are in demand, which requires significant investment in active labour market programmes.

For power dispersal across labour markets to have a greater effect, the cost of living must also fall relative to wages. Hence, the dispersal of power also needs to take place across product markets.

9

Product Markets: Enforcing the Price Mechanism

In performance competition we trust

In March 2014, the public caught a rare glimpse of a Wilhelm Schreuer painting at an auction in Cologne entitled 'The Council Meeting of the Hanseatic League'. The painting depicts well-to-do merchants discussing their plans around the table with smiles on their faces. Adam Smith's comment that when people of the same trade meet, the conversation ends in a conspiracy against the public is perhaps an apt description of Schreuer's work. The Hanseatic League was, after all, one of the world's earliest examples of an international cartel.

The central tenet of ordoliberal ideology was for the state to enforce competition. This was required to remove distortions from the price mechanism, thereby protecting individual economic freedom of action. Böhm did not believe in a utilitarian maximization of welfare but instead proposed that the dispersal of economic power should be the goal of antitrust policy based on performance competition. This enabled firms to reap the rewards of innovation through temporary monopolies, but placed significant constraints on firm behaviour from distorting the market. To complement performance competition, the free trade of goods and services was promoted to further reduce the power of domestic vested interests. Röpke, however, was careful to recognize the downside to free trade which had to be managed through policy intervention.

This chapter explores the development of performance competition and how it influenced both German and EU law. It highlights the distinction between consumer welfare as promoted by the US, and the ordo notion of dispersing power in relation to current competition law debates. Ordo ideas on free trade remain prescient to contemporary discussions on the multilateral trading system, which promote trade between like-minded states. This is particularly relevant to the ongoing dispute between liberal democracies and China, which has been able to maintain unequal conditions prior to trade through state subsidies. Although the freedom of movement of capital was not a major topic of discussion, addressing capital flows from authoritarian countries remains a central issue to stabilize the currency and sustain a liberal order.

Competition was understood as an instrument to neutralize power, which required the state to constantly intervene to prevent such build-ups. All abuse of private power was incompatible with the public interest. Perfect competition is, however, an unrealistic scenario, which Eucken had initially proposed. Furthermore, if it is not possible for firms to benefit from new technologies thereby creating temporary monopolies, it reduces the incentive to innovate. The alternative was to focus on a dynamic concept of competition which rejected the static idea of perfect competition (Behrens, 2014). This is a vitally important distinction and one which post-war ordoliberals have argued was likely to be more effective in driving innovation. Friedrich Lutz, who was Eucken's assistant at Freiburg, argued that in a dynamic process firms are like soap bubbles rising to the surface of water, lasting for a while before bursting under the pressure of more competition (Lutz in Peacock & Willgerodt, 1989a: 161). In that sense dominant firms are not an issue per se; what matters is if dominant firms behave in a way that actively hinders competition.

This issue at the policy level was addressed by the Josten Report commissioned by Erhard and published in 1949. The report set out a draft law which would provide the rules to frame desired market behaviour. These rules would be monitored by an independent body to safeguard the rules and the price mechanism, with case law subject to judicial review to ensure impartiality.

The report, which was under the guiding influence of Böhm who was a member of the expert committee, argued that the legal system must be aligned to the social market economy and, in particular, performance competition or *Leistungswettbewerb*. Performance competition is central in enforcing and protecting the market from the formation and exercise of economic power by individuals, firms and the state itself.

Economic power was defined where businesses were able to influence market prices and general conditions without taking competitors into account. However, if a firm is able to achieve market power by meeting a new need or an existing need in a new way then this definition does not apply. This is the crux of performance competition which encourages firms to innovate, who in turn benefit from short-term monopolies. The report makes it clear that this kind of market power is only temporary in nature which acts as an incentive to technical progress to improve the quality of goods and services on offer, thereby benefitting society (Josten, 1949: 38).

While the report was encouraging of performance competition, firms that gain market power through cartels or cartel-like agreements or buying market share through mergers were to be subject to quite onerous measures. These included a complete prohibition of cartels unless specifically granted by the proposed independent Cartel Office for specific reasons. Firms and potential mergers identified as having or creating market power were to be subject to decartelization and de-concentration through the unbundling of conglomerates (*Entschachtelung*) and the carving up of individual firms (*Aufgliederung*), or preventing mergers from progressing.

The independent Cartel Office was to be empowered to use all necessary measures to eliminate the identified market power. However, the office was expected to undertake such measures using the least interfering means possible in order to promote the ongoing success of targeted firms. More draconian measures were only to be taken if firms did not cooperate by taking the appropriate actions to eliminate economic power.

One of the most innovative recommendations with regards to enforcement was the 'as if' clause, which placed restrictions on dominant firms to take decisions as if they were exposed to competition. This followed on from Böhm's earlier work that aimed to prevent individual agents from gaining excess power by influencing their behaviour to stop this from occurring in the first place. The idea was to engender a change in market conduct in order to prevent cases coming to the Cartel Office through actively promoting the prohibition of the abuse of market power (Josten, 1949: 49). To support this kind of improved behaviour, rules required holders of economic power to do business with all persons who are in demand for their goods and commercial services on the usual terms and conditions in accordance with the principle of equal treatment. The draft proposed to amend company law where consolidation had been favoured, and also recommended pro-competitive measures which included, among other things, the overruling of patents under certain conditions. Finally, strong criminal sanctions were recommended for violations of the law.

German industry thought that the proposed rules would be extremely damaging for them and they put their weight behind Curt Fischer's minority report which criticized the proposals (Günther in Sauermann & Mestmäcker, 1975). Firms like competition in theory but not in practice. Innovation is hard to get right, hence managers of firms will generally take the easiest route to making money, which if they are permitted, will be to buy market power.

As argued in Chapter 4, the introduction of the 1957 Law was a major setback for the ordoliberals, which merely introduced a ban on cartels or horizontal restrictive agreements in addition to vertical restrictive agreements relating to resale prices. By 1973 though, German competition law did begin to look distinctly more ordoliberal with a new Act enabling antitrust authorities to prohibit mergers that would result in a dominant market position. In addition, specific criteria were introduced to prevent market domination as well as measures to support smaller enterprises. The idea of these amendments was to superimpose a system of conduct and to force firms to restrain their behaviour (Markert, 1975).

The 1973 Act also demonstrated its support for economic freedom by providing SMEs with tools to shield themselves against aggressive competition, and even allowing SMEs to combine and cooperate with each other. German antitrust law also requires publicly owned organizations to comply with the law, with a number of publicly owned entities becoming targets of enforcement actions (OECD, 2004).

Although it took time for these ordoliberal principles to develop and influence German antitrust law, once they were in place, Germany has developed one of the most active programmes of merger control across Europe. One recent example includes the *Bundeskartelamt* acting extra-territorially by prohibiting a merger between a Danish and a Swiss firm which would have consolidated the international market for hearing aids, despite the fact that turnover in Germany was less than 10 per cent of their total turnover (DFEACC, 2016).

While the ordoliberals failed to influence German competition law in the 1950s, they were far more successful in influencing the development of EU competition law. Erhard requested Müller-Armack to lead the German delegation at the 1956 Brussels Conference along with Hans von der Groeben, who subsequently became chair of the committee responsible for the common market (Behrens, 2015a).

Article 85 of the EC Treaty (101 TFEU) places a priority on the functioning of the common market and can be understood as an anti-cartel rule. This prohibits agreements, decisions and practices which may affect trade between member states which have as their objective the prevention, restriction or disruption of competition. It has been argued that this was substantially influenced by American antitrust law (Akman, 2012).

Article 86 of the EC Treaty (102 TFEU) is related to market abuse which states that market abuse is incompatible with the common market referencing unfair pricing and trading conditions, limiting production, price discrimination or discriminatory contracts. The prevention of market abuse raises the idea that dominant firms have a special responsibility to behave no differently than they would have done in a competitive situation (Behrens, 2015b). This places a greater emphasis on the need to maintain competition as an end in itself rather than to just achieve efficiency, which has a distinct ordoliberal outlook. Furthermore, Article 86 does not prevent firms succeeding on the basis of superior performance, indicating a greater understanding of the importance of innovation.

At an international cartel conference in Frankfurt in 1960, the concept of economic freedom was discussed in relation to the new supranational community. Groeben, who was the commissioner responsible for antitrust policies noted that 'there are probably few supranational economic arrangements in which the principle of competition has been given such prominence. That it should be so in this case is not fortuitous ... it is impossible to coordinate economic activity by intervention on the part of the central administration' (Groeben in Müller, 1961: 66). In essence, the price mechanism was deemed to be the way in which the competitive system was to be ordered to generate freedom.

Böhm also spoke at the conference noting that not only should no effort be spared to prevent the rise of economic power given the free market is incapable of eliminating such power once it has been established, but also that private power does not in any way fit into a constitutional democracy (Böhm in Müller, 1961: 25, 27, 33).

The tension between the ordoliberal focus on market abuse embedded in Article 86 and Article 85 which is focused on consumer welfare has resulted in a long-standing debate on the potential conflict between economic freedom and consumer welfare (Zimmer, 2012: 66–7).

According to the *Bundeskartellamt*, the model of economic freedom 'is based on the belief that in the long run both goals [economic freedom and consumer welfare] are not in conflict, as safeguarding of a vivid competition process will enhance consumer welfare' (Gormsen, 2007). Protecting economic freedom, therefore, improves the outlook for consumers in the long run indirectly, but economic freedom takes precedent as the moral foundation of a commercial society.

The ECJ followed a similar train of thought, ruling in the 1973 *Continental Can* case, that its interpretation of Article 86 (TFEU 102) set a higher value on economic freedom. This judgment was foreshadowed by the ordoliberal jurist Mestmäcker who argued that the principle of economic liberty could not be reduced to a price model. Hence, welfarism cannot become a normative foundation of competition policy, which is why he opposed the view that Article 86 was merely concerned with the protection of consumers (Zimmer, 2012: 174–5).

The ECJ argued in *Continental Can* that to prevent market abuse requires that Article 86 should not only be applied to exploitative cases but also to exclusionary cases, thus suggesting that competition in and of itself has some ultimate value (Behrens, 2014). Hence, in law the notion was to make it clear to dominant firms that any attempt to hinder competitors, in addition to exploitation, would be seen as a violation of antitrust laws (Gerber, 1987).

The ECJ in *Continental Can* interpreted Article 86 as establishing a system to ensure that competition in the internal market is not distorted, and that dominant firms must refrain from engaging in conduct that would not be possible under competitive conditions (Behrens, 2015b). Hence, to support economic freedom, consumers might lose out in the short run if competition is enforced and competitors are not as efficient as the dominant firm. The exclusion of smaller firms which lack economies of scale to guarantee lower prices would provide potential short-term consumer welfare benefits, but at the expense of economic freedom (Gormsen, 2007).

This pro-active approach to market abuse largely explains the divergence between EU and US competition law and is why the ECJ continues to be reluctant to follow a strict welfarist approach (Deutscher & Makris, 2016). Despite the ordoliberal drift of the ECJ, the European Commission in 2004 has continued to emphasize a US-style consumer welfare stance describing the objective of Article 85 as protecting competition 'as a means of enhancing consumer welfare and of ensuring an efficient allocation of resources' (European Commission, 2004).

This notion was reiterated by Commissioner Verstager noting that 'competition is not an end in itself. It contributes to an efficient use of society's scarce resources, technological development and innovation, a better choice of products and services, lower prices, higher quality and greater productivity in the economy as a whole' (European Commission, 2016a). It is unclear why the Commission has decided to move in this direction, although it is possible because consumer welfare, in theory, is a clearer quantitative measure than more abstract notions of economic freedom.

Despite this shift within the Commission, it is generally accepted that the abuse-of-dominance standard in Europe is stricter and reaches further than American rules on exclusionary conduct (Ohlhausen, 2016), which is why it is easier to prove a case of market abuse in the EU. This debate is worth exploring in more detail, particularly as the data indicate EU antitrust law is doing a better job than the US in terms of limiting the concentration of market power.

The failure of consumer welfare?

A recent report on competition, which cited excess profits as a measure of concentration, noted that 72 per cent of global excess profit flows to US firms whereas only 26 per cent flows to European firms (The Economist, 2018b). This suggests that competition is far greater in Europe. This rise in excess profits has also affected the distribution of income with better-educated well-paid workers congregating in more profitable firms. In essence, the growing inequality in profitability between firms is affecting the inequality of incomes as well (Rajan, 2019: 203).

Thomas Philippon noted in *The Great Reversal* that since 2000, the profit rate and concentration ratio has increased in the US by 8 per cent more than in Europe despite similar productivity growth. This indicates that many European markets are now more competitive, leading to lower prices, lower profits and lower concentration (Philippon, 2019: 124). The effects of increasing market power and the extraction of economic rent can be increasingly observed in the US, particularly in the telecoms, healthcare and airlines sectors (Khan & Vaheesan, 2017).

The US invented antitrust policy as a reaction to the ongoing consolidation across many sectors of the American economy, which was often accompanied by business practices that were deemed as being unfair. The Sherman Act of 1890 introduced the idea that any unreasonable restraint of trade should be declared illegal and that any attempt to monopolize any part of trade shall be deemed guilty of a felony. The Clayton Act of 1914 introduced the concept of price discrimination between different purchasers which may lessen competition or create a monopoly. It also placed additional restraints on firms if mergers substantially reduced competition.

Despite this first mover advantage, the US appears to be suffering from the refeudalization of its economy with lobbying by incumbent players playing a greater role in its political economy. This has led to what the economist Luis Zingales calls the 'diabolical loop between economic power and political power' (Philippon, 2019: 202). This is precisely the issue raised by the ordoliberals where the state fails because it is seen as prey by dominant commercial players. The result of this lobbying can result in increasing restrictions which raise barriers to entry, as well as the acceptance of large-scale mergers to increase market power and quash competition. This strategy has been particularly prevalent in the pharmaceutical industry where dominant firms target companies who have the potential to compete against them in specific drugs, thereby reducing potential competition (Philippon, 2019: 82).

The relative fall in competition in the US compared with the EU was preceded by a shift in antitrust policy from the 1980s which narrowed the range of conduct to which large firms are subject to. This shift has resulted in dominant firms being exposed to far fewer risks of liability for the offenses of monopolization and attempted monopolization. Kovacic argues that this shift was initially introduced by two Harvard School scholars, Phillip Areeda and Donald Turner, who in 1975 stated that a dominant firm 'can ordinarily be presumed to be acting legally under the antitrust laws when it sets its prices at or above its average variable costs' (Kovacic, 2007). While this began to have practical implications, Bork's *Antitrust Paradox* provided a broader ideological framework within which this shift took place.

Bork's arguments focused on the intrusiveness of prior court judgments questioning whether they really had made a difference to competition or critically for him for consumer welfare, which was really a rebranding of total welfare (Crane, 2014). Bork argued that the objective of the Sherman Act could be reduced to consumer welfare. But he also noted that intervention requires the courts to be clear that such an intervention would indeed improve consumer welfare, as otherwise it might cause greater harm. This subsequently raised the knowledge question and to what extent the courts could ensure that such intervention would indeed improve welfare.

A number of scholars focused on innovation have also argued that excessive intrusiveness in antitrust enforcement is negative for the economy, acting as a constraint on innovation. Too often, claims are made by lagging firms attempting to use antitrust law to prevent innovative firms from forging further ahead. Teece and Jorde argue that the best guarantor of dynamic or performance competition, which is driven by innovation, is an open international system combined with policies that facilitate innovation. This creates market rivalry, driving firms to try and surpass prior innovations. Hence, they argue that antitrust laws based on static price competition are not supportive of this approach given the dynamic nature of competition (Teece & Jorde, 1991).

The move away from more intrusive investigations into dominant firms has led to a significant fall in cases (Blumenthal & Wu, 2019). Another potential reason for the fall is the complexity of cases including the fact that dominant tech firms also provide consumers with benefits. For example, Microsoft users found it useful to have explorer bundled with its Windows operating system; however, Judge Jackson in 2000 found Microsoft in violation of §1 of the Sherman Act by unlawfully tying its web browser to its operating system. In addition, the court concluded Microsoft was in violation of §2 through maintaining its monopoly power by anticompetitive means and attempting to monopolize the web browser market.

While the shift towards consumer welfare does provide a clearer goal of whether firms are in breach of market abuse along pure utilitarian lines, the question is whether such an outcome is compatible with the underlying liberal principles of freedom and equality. As noted by Röpke in Chapter 4, if price is the only issue that matters, then monopolizing news would be acceptable given that such a service could be provided for free.

In the US, the rise of a handful of dominant tech firms has caused a reaction in antitrust thinking. According to a former member of Obama's National Economic Council, Tim Wu, the US has returned to the gilded age of the late 19th century and the culture of monopoly. Wu laments the US court's shift away from its previously more interventionist approach and urges a return to the 'Big Case' tradition such as the divestiture of AT&T initiated by the Department of Justice in 1974. Wu suggests that consumer welfare could be replaced by the notion of protecting the competitive process as a means of promoting economic efficiency (Wu, 2018: 138). A similar view is taken by Lina Khan in her attack on Amazon. She argues by measures of consumer welfare, Amazon has excelled in reducing prices for consumers. But she remains concerned about Amazon's market power arguing that the goal of antitrust policy ought to focus on the competitive process itself (Khan, 2017).

Khan argues that prior to Bork's intervention antitrust policy was to promote anticompetitive forms of conduct based on the idea that concentrated market structures define the extent of the competitive process. However, such a reversal to a 'Big Case' tradition ignores the need to promote innovation and does little to counter Bork's argument that such an approach creates uncertainty and potentially arbitrary decisions. Indeed, there is potentially an argument that Bork's influence has led to greater innovation although the causality of this shift in jurisprudence is difficult to prove with any degree of certainty.

The challenge with the focus on the competitive process leading to market efficiency is that these two concepts might well be in direct conflict with each other with more competition leading to less economic efficiency. Indeed, as soon as the concept of economic efficiency is referenced, the topic of consumer welfare is not far behind.

A former director at the FTC has argued that antitrust policy ought to be far more wary of horizontal mergers, price coordination, exclusion as well as supplier relationships. This is particularly the case for big tech firms whom he argues are abusing their platform power when it comes to removing competitor R&D capabilities through acquisitions. But Baker does appear to recognize the tension created by potential uncertainty and hence argues that trade-offs must be analysed using the existing economic welfare framework to provide more certainty to firms (Baker, 2019: 157, 208).

It is not obvious that a more balanced approach to welfarism will provide any more clarity for firms given the complexity of the topic and the, sometimes, heroic assumptions involved. Hence, it does little to address the limits to our knowledge of the welfare effects of mergers. It is plausible that the focus on remaining within the constraints of welfare economics is related to a jurisprudential tradition of subsuming law to economics. Posner's view of law is one of rational and efficient rules based on a Pareto optimization process where 'human satisfaction as measured by aggregate consumer willingness to pay for goods and services-is maximized' (Minda, 1978). Such an approach though is at odds with the concept of freedom, which the ordoliberals argued ought to be the end goal of public policy.

Besides the ever-increasing complexity and scale of such investigations, a more interventionist approach to antitrust enforcement does not appear to recognize the need to encourage innovation and performance competition. This means antitrust law must actively welcome transient monopolists. For example, Google has close to 90 per cent of global market share of internet searches.[1] To encourage innovation, this market dominance ought to be welcomed, as it will hopefully encourage firms to build a better search engine. Indeed, there remain many drawbacks with the current approach to search leading to some fundamental challenges related to epistemology (Bhatt & McKenzie, 2019). To an increasing extent, the internet has become a bias amplification system with users generally directed towards more popular sites that merely reinforce tribal views.[2] Furthermore, the idea of a one-stop shop for any service is contrary to the concept of increasing specialization inherent in complex societies. Hence, in time, new competitors may emerge with perhaps an improved but more specialist understanding of searching information across specific areas such as academic journals or shopping.

While innovation should be rewarded, dominant firms should not be allowed to abuse their market power such as discriminating between suppliers and their own goods. In 2017, the European Commission fined Google €2.42 bn by abusing its market dominance for search for advantaging Google's comparison shopping service. This was followed by another European Commission fine in 2019 of €1.49 bn for abusing its market dominance for imposing a number of restrictive clauses in contracts with third-party websites which prevented Google's rivals from placing their search adverts on these websites.[3]

The Department of Justice is currently pursuing a case against Google based on section 2 of the Sherman Act for paying Apple US$8–12 bn in advertising revenue each year to make Google's search engine the default for Safari.[4] It is difficult to understand how such a contract would be in keeping with the ordoliberal 'as if' policy as set out in *Continental Can* as if Google were not such a dominant player it would not behave in such a manner.

While it is feasible that the influence of Bork's light-touch intervention has led to more innovation, this appears to have come at the expense of increasing market abuse. A recent report on competition in digital markets by the Congressional Subcommittee on Antitrust, Commercial and Administrative Law highlighted an increasing tendency towards greater concentration and less competition. The report explicitly criticizes the adoption of 'a narrow construction of consumer welfare as the sole goal of the antitrust laws', suggesting that the focus primarily on price and output rather than the competitive process contravenes legislative intent. (Antitrust Subcommittee, 2020: 390).

The report attacked Google for systematically ranking its own content above third-party content, even when its content was inferior or less relevant for users. It honed in on Amazon's asymmetric access to, and use of, third-party seller data creating the potential for Amazon to abuse its platform privilege to compete more effectively with its sellers. Apple's App Store rules were heavily criticized for demanding 30 per cent commission for transactions. Facebook was criticized for acquiring competitors such as Instagram and Whatsapp to shore up its dominant position. Indeed, the report noted that not only have the four tech giants acquired more than 500 companies since 1998, research has found that this has led to a significant fall in investment in start-ups.

Such outcomes indicate an ongoing abuse of market power and a restriction of economic freedom, which would not be tolerated under ordoliberal jurisprudence. The debate between consumer welfare and economic freedom will no doubt continue. For ordoliberals though, enforcing competition was not enough; it had to be accompanied by free trade. After the protectionist period of the 1930s, openness to trade was conceived as being not only central to maintaining freedom but also to act as a driver of competition and innovation.

The benefits and limitations of free trade

The freedom to trade in domestic and international markets has long been central to the liberal idea since the enlightenment. Thomas Paine thought that if individuals were able to pursue their commercial lives freely, this would transform society for the better. Indeed, he went so far as to argue that 'if commerce were permitted to act to the universal extent it is capable, it would extirpate the system of war, and produce a revolution in the uncivilized state of governments' (Paine, 1894: Vol II, 289).

The ordoliberals argued that free trade was an essential component of maintaining open markets. Eucken thought free trade could help break the economic power of domestic private interest groups and hence reduce their ability to distort the price mechanism. By focusing on promoting free trade to help eliminate domestic distortions to the price mechanism, it also avoided the challenge of trying to optimize welfare and whether such outcomes could be considered equitable.

The economist Ian Little was dismissive of the argument that free trade maximizes world welfare which, 'not only presupposes optimum conditions of production and exchange within all countries and full employment but also ignores the distribution of real income between countries' (Little, 1973: 250). The trade economist Paul Krugman concludes that 'free trade would be fine in an ideal world of perfectly competitive markets ... but we all know that markets are hardly ever perfect, and thus free trade is hardly ever the best policy' (Krugman, 2019).

During the post-war reconstruction period there was limited interest in free trade; hence, it should not have been surprising that the idea of creating an International Trade Organization was quickly quashed. A temporary solution was drawn up in 1947 known as the General Agreement on Tariffs and Trade (GATT) for goods, which was signed by 23 countries. The broad intent was for these countries to move towards freer trade from one of protectionism, subsidies and tariffs which would have a positive rather than a negative effect, particularly given the high level of protection. Hence, GATT included rules on minimizing state subsidies (Article XVI) and also anti-dumping rules (Article VI).

Against this backdrop, Röpke argued that countries ought to embrace free trade if they were to have their own interests at heart. But he also recognized it raised critical issues that were difficult to solve and which required a level of state regulation. Röpke noted the benefits of rising productivity came at a price in terms of possible economic, social and cultural disadvantages. Indeed, he thought that while the importation of cheap goods was generally advantageous it 'can have a paralyzing influence on the future development of domestic production or can lead to costly dislocations to which it would be undesirable to see the domestic economy exposed' (Röpke, 1963: 172). However, he cautioned that those who seek to exploit these concerns often do so to further their own economic interests.

Managing this potential social dislocation was recognized by Adam Smith who highlighted that if free importation were permitted, domestic firms would suffer forcing workers to seek other employment. Smith thought that to counter the displacement of workers, labour markets would need to be flexible enabling workers to find new jobs, hence Smith's attack on labour market restrictions. Smith also raised concerns that removing restrictions on trade should never be introduced suddenly, but slowly and gradually after a very long warning. Otherwise manufactures and workers may suffer considerably (Smith, 1904: Vol I, 377).

Despite these concerns, Smith was still a strong advocate for free trade urging Ireland to form a closer union with Britain so it would benefit economically. However, within 30 years of the Act of Union, the Irish cotton and wool industry had collapsed. Although demand for linen and agricultural products did rise, there was insufficient labour demand to compensate for those jobs lost in textiles which led to a substantial rise in emigration during the 1820s and 1830s (O'Malley, 1981). The devastation wrought on Irish firms and workers has often been ignored by free trade purists. Ricardo's theory merely assumed that labour would seamlessly move towards those industries with a comparative advantage, but this ignored whether there would be sufficient demand to absorb displaced workers while assuming all skills were interchangeable.

Jacob Viner countered the fundamentalist free trade argument in the 1920s noting it was important to distinguish between permanently low imports due to higher levels of productivity of a foreign producer compared with temporary prices whose aim was anticompetitive. He argued that

> there is a sound case ... for the restriction of imports of dumped commodities, not because such imports are cheap in price, nor because their prices are lower than those prevailing in their home markets, but because dumping prices are presumptive evidence of abnormal and temporary cheapness. There is even a stronger theoretical case for the restriction of imports sold at a price less than their cost of production. (Viner, 1923: 147)

In addition, the increasing returns from trade as liberalization proceeded led to a surge in government support for individual firms. From an ordoliberal perspective this merely results in vested interests attempting to influence policy for their own benefit, such as the EEC contemplating setting up a European company to compete with IBM. The trade theorist Max Corden was highly sceptical of the value of such bureaucratically determined industrial policy. This led to a shift in thinking about industrial policy towards creating the right conditions for success such as improving infrastructure, investing in innovation to solve real-world problems and ensuring a sufficient level of training and human capital development. This is much closer to an ordoliberal approach as described by Rüstow.

Post-war trade theorists were also aware of the hollowing-out concerns and argued that trade should not result in absolute reductions in real income for any section of the community. This was termed by Max Corden as a conservative social welfare function, who noted that where there are dislocations, governments should intervene to provide adjustment programmes, particularly if the industry losing out from trade was geographically concentrated (Corden, 1997: 77–8).

One example from West Germany was the realization that oil was going to lower demand for German coal. The government in order to prepare for the inevitable shift out of mining employment levied a tax on oil imports which was used to retrain mine workers (Nicholls, 1994: 356–7).

The pace of freeing up trade between countries, therefore, has some natural limit in relation to the ability of displaced workers to gain employment at higher value-added levels, which in turn depends on factors such as innovation and training. The wages of workers in non-tradeable services tend to be linked to those in tradable goods and services (Moretti, 2013: 58–9). Hence, if workers are only able to find work in lower value-added jobs, it would negatively affect an individual's economic freedom. Meade also noted that the pace of change is dictated by the initial starting conditions for trade between countries. Indeed, Meade concluded that positive outcomes for free trade among a group of countries requires them to 'adopt reasonably similar objectives for their domestic policies and employ reasonably similar price mechanism instruments for their attainment' (Meade, 1966: 570–1).

Such a conclusion was in complete alignment with an ordoliberal outlook. Röpke argued that trade must be carried out between countries with similar value systems using freely convertible currencies, which had to be accompanied by a corresponding non-economic social integration (Röpke, 1959). For a domestic competitive market to function requires individuals to restrain the passions in order to reduce the level of selfishness that is acceptable to other selfish agents (Hont, 2015: 37). Rüstow argued that this reciprocity does not scale internationally; hence, for international trade to function there has to be order at the national level between similar countries given there is no single international body to enforce a liberal economic order.

International transactions, therefore, take place with greater uncertainty and hence are fragile in nature (Curzon in Peacock & Willgerodt, 1989b: 180).

This is one reason why the development of global free trade has often been associated with a liberal hegemon. If the power of the hegemon erodes, then the liberal order is expected to unravel with a shift towards mercantilist arrangements. This theory was used to explain the international economy's shift towards protectionism due to Britain's decline from 1919, and the subsequent revival of trade by the US after World War Two. To what extent this narrative also explains the current disruption to the global trading system and relative decline of US power remains to be seen. Ruggie though, thought that a liberal system did not require a hegemon and instead could depend on embedded liberalism within individual states which can 'devise a form of multilateralism that is compatible with the requirements of domestic stability' (Ruggie, 1982). This chimes closely with Ropke's view of trade between like-minded countries who are able to enforce a liberal order on their domestic markets.

The growth of trade between Europe, North America and Japan during the post-war era was between countries that were quite similar, and who had similar starting conditions prior to trading. While this did create winners and losers, on the whole those who lost their jobs due to comparative advantage found new work without seeing a significant fall in their standard of living.

After the fall of the Berlin Wall, it seemed natural to turbocharge GATT given its relative success via the newly formed WTO in 1995. This phase of globalization has been transformational for many developing countries. According to Paul Krugman, 'the rise of manufacturing exports from developing countries has been probably responsible for more human progress than anything else that has happened in world history' (Krugman, 2019).

However, this phase of globalization appears to have accelerated much faster than developed economies were able to absorb new jobs at higher value-added levels. Hence, it is unsurprising that voters have become less interested in supporting free trade. What adjustment mechanisms that were put in place have not performed well; hence, compensation has not worked as the theory suggested it should. As a result, the winners have surged further ahead while the losers lag further behind.

Bhagwati notes that workers and citizens appear to be accepting if jobs are lost due to domestic competition; however, this is not the case if firms are allowed to go to the wall due to foreign competition (Bhagwati, 2004: 234). Bhagwati argued that 'if you are importing labour intensive goods and their relative price falls ... the real wage of labour will fall' (Bhagwati, 2002: 82). While job losses from automation have in the long run been much higher, such losses do not generally result in large layoffs that affect an entire region which is ominous for the living standard of less-skilled workers. This is why Philippon stated that 'domestic competition is much stronger than the argument for free trade because the benefits from free trade are more difficult to share among citizens. When trade shifts production overseas the jobs are literally gone' (Philippon, 2019: 24).

Dani Rodrik cites both Paul Krugman and Larry Summers who in the 1990s were in the vanguard of promoting globalization but have since shifted their views as the facts have changed. Summers accepts that there is a 'growing recognition by workers that what is good for the global economy and its business champions [is] not necessarily good for them ... Greater global integration places more competitive pressure on an individual economy [and] workers are likely disproportionately to bear the brunt of this pressure' (Rodrik, 2011: 84–6).

David Autor's analysis of the China shock on the US economy indicates that economic integration extended to a far greater extent than Röpke's concept of social integration. China's initial comparative advantage in labour made it the default location for all kinds of labour-intensive production. This was particularly the case for the manufacturing of apparel and furniture (Autor, Dorn & Hanson, 2016). Due to the geographical concentration of these sectors in the US, local labour markets were unable to absorb workers leaving these sectors. According to one study, the China shock resulted in 'net job losses of 2.0 to 2.4 million stemming from the rise in import competition from China over the period 1999 to 2011' (Acemoglu, Autor, Dorn, Hanson & Price, 2014). The employment effects in localized labour markets can be large in magnitude as demonstrated by the devastated areas of Tennessee and the Carolinas as Chinese manufacturing ramped up.

With little chance of good jobs, workers from the 40th percentile and below end up in lower-paid service jobs or dependent on the social security system and often exiting the workforce. Many ended up suffering from alcohol or drug abuse with high rates of suicide (Autor, 2017). The lack of relevant skills prevents these workers from maintaining their living standards derived from their once stable employment in manufacturing. The US economy is also demonstrating less labour mobility with cost of living differences between areas, particularly for housing, becoming an obstacle.

One effect of this has been the polarization of politics with data from the Pew Research Center showing that both Democrats and Republicans have increasingly moved away from support for globalization. Although as noted by Adam Posen the absolute impact to the US economy of the China shock is small (Posen, 2021), its psychological effect due its concentration has clearly had a substantial impact. To a lesser extent the same can be seen throughout Europe with increasing support for more nationalist or socialist political parties. If liberalism has failed in its attempt to provide a good life for some of its citizens, it should not be surprising voters are deserting it as a cause.

Rodrik has argued that it is not possible to have globalization, sovereignty and democracy at the same time. According to Rodrik, hyper-globalization restricts democracy; hence, to increase democratic legitimacy, globalization has to be limited. An alternative is to globalize democracy, but this in turn eliminates national sovereignty. The logic of Rodrik's trilemma is that it is not feasible to purse all three policies. At least one of them has to give (Rodrik, 2011: 200).

This has been exacerbated by the fact that since China joined the WTO it has not only become an economic powerhouse with new comparative advantages in manufacturing, but it also has a political system that is firmly opposed to liberal values. This further raises the question of the sustainability of the current global trading system. Röpke advocated that such a relationship between illiberal countries was not only unsustainable, but that it would only serve to undermine freedom. This is why the GATT was predicated on a liberal understanding of an economy in order to protect the equality of competitive conditions (Mavroidis & Sapir, 2021: 11, 164).

The Marrakesh Declaration of 15 April 1994 makes it clear that the WTO was to be based upon open, market-oriented policies. But as Mark Wu has argued, 'China's economy is structured differently from any other major economy and is different in ways that were not anticipated by WTO negotiators' (Hillman, 2018). Wu describes the Chinese economy as a 'complex web of overlapping networks and relationships—some formal and others informal—between the state, Party, SOEs, private enterprises, financial institutions, investment vehicles, trade associations, and so on' (Wu, 2016). The ability of the Communist Party, which runs the economy, to place its officials in key roles and create the linkages between the public and private sector not only makes China's economy unique, but also hard for WTO rules to deal with (Hillman, 2018).

This view was echoed by the former US trade representative Robert Lighthizer who stated that the WTO settlement system was not designed to deal with a legal and political system so at odds with the basic premises on which the WTO was founded. Lighthizer argued that US supporters of China's WTO accession assumed that WTO membership would lead Beijing to adopt a Western political economic and legal model (Blustein, 2019: 143, 228). But freedom is not a teleological function of economic development. It requires people who believe in freedom to make the case for it and to constantly manufacture it.

In 2019, China pulled its WTO suit over the claim that it is a market economy, probably to avoid the ruling that would make it clear that China is still a non-market economy (Hosman, 2021). This raises the spectre of a non-market economy dominating a global trading system of market economies. China has benefitted substantially from its membership of the WTO, and is generally considered to adhere to the rules, but this is because its economic model is largely outside the scope of the rules. This is particularly the case for preferential state procurement and its ability, at least in its first few years of membership, to maintain downward pressure on its exchange rate to maintain international competitiveness. Countries who depress their currencies to artificially maintain their export sectors are practicing unfair competition, akin to dumping. Corden criticized both Japan and Taiwan for such practices in the past.

In addition, forced technology transfer has been an issue for international firms operating in the Chinese market. According to one report, 90 per cent of the intellectual property of China's high-speed rail sector that is owned by Chinese firms was derived from international firms. Transport manufacturing companies were required to handover proprietary technology in order to gain access to the market. Furthermore, the theft of intellectual property has also been an issue with the identification of the corporate hackers, APT1, as being linked to the People's Liberation Army. This led to the Xi-Obama non-aggression pact in 2016 (Blustein, 2019: 120–1, 196, 199).

Since 2010, China has ramped up intervention, with state-owned enterprises (SOEs) directed to obtain know-how from foreign partners, which contravenes the WTO agreement. The so-called 2025 Made in China strategy aims for 70 per cent self-sufficiency also suggests an element of autarky. Chinese officials claim that this is not a government policy but one proposed by academics and industry experts. However, it is thought that hundreds of billions of dollars in subsidies are involved with the share of loans going to state firms rising from 28 per cent to 65 per cent between 2011 and 2015. Although under WTO rules subsidies from governments are carefully scrutinized, China won an important case at the WTO Appellate Court which argued that SOEs are not government bodies as they have their own legal personality. As such there is no breach under WTO rules, potentially legitimating countrywide subsidies and the ability to manipulate markets to gain market share (Blustein, 2019: 118, 157, 188).

The use of state power to nurture corporate national champions is precisely the reason why ordoliberalism arose as an ideology in the first place to advocate for a dispersal of power. Hence, it is not surprising that the liberal world trading system is floundering with very little reciprocity taking place between the major trading blocs and an increasing drift towards the concentration of power.

This raises the question as to whether the WTO has a future given this impasse between China and its liberal members. Hillman, a former judge on the WTO appellate board, has argued that it is important to save a market-based world trade system and the way to do this would be to bring a comprehensive case backed by multiple members based on the non-violation nullification and impairment clause. Hillman writes:

The United States and all other WTO members had legitimate expectations that China would increasingly behave as a market economy—that it would achieve a discernable separation between its government and its private sector, that private property rights and an understanding of who controls and makes decisions in major enterprises would be clear, that subsidies would be curtailed, that theft of IP rights would be punished and diminished in amount, that SOEs would make purchases based on commercial considerations, that the Communist Party would not, by fiat, occupy critical seats within major 'private' enterprises and that standards and regulations would be published for all to see. (Hillman, 2018)

As such, it has been argued that it is not new rules that are needed, but rather enforcing the existing ones (Zhou, Gao & Bai, 2019). This is not to argue that the WTO system prior to China's entry was by any means perfect. The ongoing protection of low value-added sectors such as agriculture by developed countries has almost certainly hindered the prospects of developing economies. However, it is clearly preferable for developed and developing countries to have access to a functioning multilateral trade regime given that bilateral solutions will be less effective. Such a mechanism enables governments to agree on rules for trade policy including tariffs and treating foreign products in a non-discriminatory manner.

Hillman's recommendation, however, has been criticized on the grounds that non-violation clauses (NVCs) are associated with a high burden of proof, and any success with a NVC does not lead to an obligation to remove the challenged measure. Mavroidis and Sapir instead recommend that the major liberal trading blocs should bring China to the negotiation table to reach a new agreement that addresses forced technology transfer and the issue of SOEs. This latter issue has become more complicated since the WTO appellate ruled that private firms can also be considered SOEs if links between the company and the government can be established (Mavroidis & Sapir, 2021: 156–7, 183, 207).

It is certainly plausible that the Communist Party might agree to an amendment on forced technology transfer as set out in the Comprehensive and Progressive Agreement for Trans-Pacific Partnership (CPTPP). China has been incredibly successful to date in capturing technology, which may be why it is now confident enough to pursue its China 2025 agenda and shift towards a more autarkic economy. Hence, the next stage of technology development is more likely to be indigenous, although whether Communist Party-sponsored hacking will stop remains to be seen. Moreover, international firms are likely to be much more careful in handing over their entire IP given that it might result in Chinese firms out-competing them in other markets.

With regards to SOEs, such an agreement appears highly unlikely given that the Communist Party is increasing rather than decreasing its grip across the Chinese economy. Hence, many public and private firms would remain classified as SOEs as they do not behave in accordance with commercial considerations, are discriminatory and limit competition. This leaves liberals with a major challenge given that the global trading system contains a fundamental power imbalance, where the dominant player is also an illiberal one, thereby wrecking the underlying liberal principles of GATT.

The COVID-19 pandemic has further highlighted this power imbalance. According to *The Economist*, China supplied 42 per cent of the world's exports of personal protective equipment, almost three-quarters of Italy's blood thinners and 60 per cent of the ingredients for antibiotics imported by Japan. 'Such dependence on any country seems unwise. Such dependence on China, which has been known to abuse its market dominance, seems idiotic' (The Economist, 2020b).

This dominance has led to a rise in protectionist sentiment within liberal democracies, which also poses a significant threat to freedom and equality. One approach for liberal countries is to instead encourage a diversity of supply as noted by the writer Martin Wolf, rather than a shift towards less competition and autarky (Wolf, 2020). Hence, liberal democracies should be articulating the benefits of power dispersal and encouraging trade with countries in Africa, South America and Asia that are sympathetic to liberal values.

Such an approach would also need to focus on the equalization of the terms of trade in non-tariff areas such as environmental factors including reducing plastic pollution and CO_2 emissions. Rodrik in the Macron Commission also argued that the violation of worker rights ought to be taken into account, proceeding via an anti-social dumping procedure when trade practices violate such laws. This would be analogous to import tariffs on carbon-intensive products when domestic carbon policies are stricter than those in trade partners. Rodrik suggested that this could be aligned with existing antidumping procedures within the WTO which allows countries to impose anti-dumping duties when imported goods are being sold below cost (Blanchard & Tirole, 2021).

The implication of Rodrik's proposal is that countries that have no desire to cooperate in areas such as reducing coal-fired power stations or eliminating slave labour would be taxed out of participating in international trade. However, this also might result in discrimination against poorer countries who do not have the institutional infrastructure in place nor the ability to afford to implement such policies. Such an approach would not only lead to an increase in the concentration of power, but it would also detract from the poverty alleviation effects of trade, which as Krugman has argued have been considerable. This proposal also raises the question as to why authoritarian countries would sign up to such a treaty change at the WTO, given that it is not in their economic interest.

This impasse between authoritarian and liberal countries is likely to render the WTO powerless to make any substantive changes, which finds itself caught between authoritarian countries who benefit from the current rules and liberal countries who are struggling to articulate the benefits of free trade to their citizens. One option suggested by Wu is that if liberal trading blocs are unable to make China move on the SOE issue at the negotiating table, then they should look to use the CPTPP as the foundation for new rules. In essence, liberal trading blocs would remove themselves from the WTO and create a parallel trading system via the CPTPP framework. As President Obama remarked, '[W]e can't let countries like China write the rules of the global economy' (Wu, 2016). However, the decision by the Trump Administration to withdraw from the agreement in 2017 has diminished the possibility of following this path.

The sustainability of an ordoliberal global trading system requires trading blocs containing liberal democracies to be able to articulate to its citizens the benefits of trade. How these trading blocs might ultimately decide to manage the international legal order will be down to the outcome of these discussions and negotiations. However, it seems unlikely that the WTO can play a central role unless the Communist Party decides to abandon its control of the Chinese economy. Whatever the outcome of rethinking the multilateral trading system to promote a liberal order, support for the freedom of movement of capital is unlikely to be a focus.

The movement and parking of capital

Supporters of hyper-globalization such as Bhagwati have been negative about the freedom of movement of capital due to investor herding and the subsequent instability that was demonstrated during the Asian financial crisis (Bhagwati, 2004: 202). *The Economist* magazine, which was founded on the idea of free trade, has also argued in favour of capital controls for developing countries (The Economist, 2003). More recently Raghuram Rajan the former chief economist at the International Monetary Fund (IMF) has argued more broadly that 'capital flows into a country are not an unmitigated blessing' (Rajan, 2019: 353).

There are also good reasons for capital controls to be put in place for developed countries as excessive inflows can increase the value of a currency (Dornbusch & Fischer, 1980; Mussa, 1984; IMF, 2011), causing a loss of competitiveness and a shift from higher to lower value-added jobs (Corden, 1997: 268–9). Indeed, there is some evidence that the overvaluation of sterling between 1997 and 2007 was sustained by large net inbound capital flows (Aubrey & Reed, 2016). In addition, further controls would also help reduce money laundering which currently only serves to strengthen organizations that have no vested interest in freedom and equality.

One of the consequences of an economic system founded on private property and liberal values is that it is attractive for individuals and firms from illiberal countries to park this capital knowing that it will be protected. This capital would not receive the same level of protection from its country of origin either because the money is illegally derived, the state is unstable or because the country is authoritarian.

Capital moves into liberal countries via a number of different paths, including: debt and equity portfolios which account for less than 10 per cent of the ownership of firms or financial instruments; foreign direct investment (FDI) which includes the acquisition of firms, property and to a lesser extent investment in physical plant; and the outright acquisition of debt instruments.

The question for liberal countries is to what extent should further capital controls be applied to protect liberal values and prevent distortions to the exchange rate? There remain strong arguments to permit free capital flows into debt and equity portfolios from illiberal countries given that ownership remains at less than 10 per cent and this demand has benefits for domestic firms given it will reduce the cost of equity and debt. There are also positive arguments for permitting the acquisition of debt securities, although a number of concerns have been raised by the acquisition of US Treasuries by Chinese institutions might result in greater volatility. However, evidence for such concerns appears scant.

Capital controls already exist related to FDI where most countries have a regime in place to prevent the acquisition of firms by foreign agents in sensitive sectors such as defence and the media. However, there are strong arguments to strengthen certain kinds of FDI controls, such as preventing the acquisitions of domestic firms that are likely to reduce global competition as is already conducted by the *Bundeskartelamt* with its extraterritorial rulings.

In 2017, Germany introduced controls which effectively targeted Chinese firms acquiring companies operating in critical infrastructure. In 2020, the European Commission adopted a white paper to address subsidies by non-EU countries from distorting competition in the single market. The acquisition of European firms involved in critical sectors by companies from countries that are fundamentally opposed to freedom seems to be hard to justify, particularly if the European firms have benefitted from taxpayer funds. In 2020, the US Treasury also tightened its provisions pertaining to investments by Foreign Persons in critical technologies.

In addition, many countries have introduced restrictions on the foreign acquisition of residential property including Canada, Switzerland, Australia, New Zealand and Singapore. Rules on property acquisition have generally been introduced in an attempt to reduce demand, given that excess demand relative to supply can causes price to rise, exacerbating affordability issues.

A number of studies have investigated the effect of these inflows on localized house prices, including the global super rich's purchasing power forcing the indigenous wealthy population out of the most exclusive areas of West London (Glucksberg, 2016). Another has demonstrated the effects of inbound Chinese capital on increasing US house prices in areas with high foreign-born Chinese populations after 2011 (Gorback & Keys, 2020). However, there is not much evidence that these flows have an effect at the national level.

A far greater issue for urban conurbations of developed economies is that they have become prime targets for illicit capital as part of the money laundering process. According to the United Nations, this costs the global economy as much as between 2–5 per cent of GDP per annum (United Nations, 2011). Estimates by the UK Treasury Select Committee suggest that the amount of illicit capital laundered annually probably runs in to hundreds of billions of pounds, (Treasury Committee, 2019) and significantly distorts the price mechanism for housing assets as well as potentially the exchange rate. Hence, liberal countries that decide to accept illicit capital flows are therefore likely to experience upward pressure on the exchange rate, potentially localized higher housing costs due to higher demand, as well as supporting regimes or individuals that are fundamentally opposed to freedom.

The other issue with capital flows is the ability of citizens of liberal countries to park their own capital offshore, thereby avoiding the liabilities that all citizens of free societies are obliged to pay through taxes. This touches on one of the fundamental ideas of ordoliberalism, which is the equality of initial conditions. There is nothing equal between law-abiding citizens who pay their taxes and those who choose to earn their money illicitly or avoid paying their tax liabilities.

During an interview with a Swedish TV firm in 2016, the Icelandic prime minister was asked what he thought about people or companies that use tax havens to hide assets. He replied that this was cheating the rest of society which is why it is taken very seriously. Unfortunately for the prime minister, the Panama Papers which were leaked from the law firm Mossack Fonseca, indicated that his wife owned the offshore firm Wintris which was a creditor to the failed Icelandic banks, ultimately leading to his resignation.

According to the economist Gabriel Zucman, around 8 per cent of global financial wealth is held in tax havens which amounts to around US$7.6 trillion, which he estimates is around US$200 bn in lost tax revenues. In recent years there have been attempts by the US to change this, including the Foreign Account Tax Compliance Act 2010 which mandated the automatic exchange of data with a number of countries including Switzerland. However, many countries are still outside the Act and hence avoid the threat of a 30 per cent withholding tax on all dividends and income. Zucman was particularly disparaging about the EU for refusing to overrule Luxembourg's tax loopholes that he reckons has inflated Luxembourg's GDP by around 30 per cent. He has argued that there is no place in the EU for a country that reduces the ability of the EU to collect tax that is owed (Zucman, 2015: 35, 47, 64, 89, 91). Unsurprisingly, Luxembourg takes a different view, given that a fall of GDP of 30 per cent is unlikely to be a vote winner.

Some restrictions on capital flows are therefore a prerequisite for an ordoliberal global trading system: a system which prevents currencies from being misvalued, stops agents from authoritarian countries acquiring strategic assets, eliminates money laundering and ensures that citizens of liberal countries pay their fair share of taxes.

Attempting to come up with a simple metric that indicates a dispersion of power across product markets is clearly challenging. One important factor for citizens is that there needs to be a relative downward pressure on prices to improve living standards through innovation, competition and international trade, given that wages need to be stabilized by the central bank. In conjunction with lower prices, nominal wages must not fall as a result of a shift in employment towards lower value-added sectors. One simple measure of the success of an ordoliberal product market is to look at the long-run growth rate in real wages across the income distribution over two electoral cycles. This provides a sufficient period of time for policies to have an effect and that can be considered sustainable.

To run a comparison across the income distribution for all OECD countries presents a number of significant data issues, although if the median were available for all OECD countries it would be a reasonable proxy.[5] Due to data issues, the real growth of mean wages are used as a proxy to measure the extent of the ordoliberal function for product markets, although this will be skewed to a certain extent by the upper quintile.[6]

According to Table 9.1, real wage growth has remained strong in parts of Eastern Europe. This is largely a function of starting from lower wage levels combined with access to the single market of the EU, although as these economies converge such growth is unlikely to be sustained. Sweden has also performed well on this measure indicating a reasonable dispersal of power across product markets. Conversely, Greece, Italy, Spain and Portugal have all performed poorly in terms of the ordoliberal function, partly reflecting their eurozone membership which limited their ability to implement targeted monetary and fiscal policy to deal with the financial crisis.

One point of interest for the Scandinavian economies is that due to their small scale it forced them to be relatively open as they began to develop (Hilson, 2008: 57), resulting in a greater acceptance of globalization and competition. Moreover, during the corporatist period there was no great nationalization programme as had been the case in post-war Britain. Indeed, Sweden retained the idea that business played a positive role in raising living

Table 9.1: Comparison of power dispersion across OECD countries (product markets)

Country	Product market power dispersal 2018 (%)	Rank order
Estonia	26.70%	1
Poland	24.50%	2
Slovak Republic	21.53%	3
Czech Republic	20.93%	4
Iceland	20.30%	5
Sweden	17.14%	6
Korea	15.77%	7
Latvia	15.68%	8
Germany	13.42%	9
Israel	11.22%	10
Norway	10.19%	11
New Zealand	9.18%	12
Slovenia	8.95%	13
Denmark	8.44%	14
Finland	7.79%	15
France	7.56%	16
US	7.34%	17
Hungary	6.83%	18
Ireland	5.60%	19
Canada	5.49%	20
Austria	4.10%	21
Australia	3.68%	22
Switzerland	3.15%	23
Lithuania	1.72%	24
Belgium	1.07%	25
Netherlands	−0.41%	26
Mexico	−2.21%	27
Portugal	−2.60%	28
Spain	−2.84%	29
UK	−2.89%	30
Italy	−3.15%	31
Japan	−4.34%	32
Greece	−25.31%	33

Source: OECD

Figure 9.1: Growth in real mean wages vs growth in GDP per capita

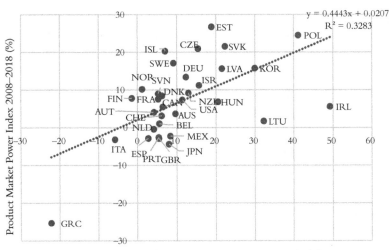

GDP per capita growth 2008–2018 in constant 2010 US$ (%)

Source: OECD, World Bank

standards and remained business friendly with low marginal tax rates (Blyth, 2002: 113). As these economies moved away from the corporatist model in the 1980s, greater deregulation in previously regulated sectors such as energy and communication was introduced to stimulate competition (Andersen et al, 2007).

An interesting case study related to the open nature of this model is that Saab, despite no longer manufacturing cars, has maintained 80 per cent of its 17,000-strong global workforce in Sweden by morphing into a high-tech company active in aeronautics, surveillance and a range of related services, upskilling its workers along the way (Brende, 2020). In essence, it has been able to manage the process of globalization better due to its focus on empowering labour through retraining.

Figure 9.1 indicates a positive relationship between an ordoliberal product market function using rising real mean wages and the utilitarian measure of changes in GDP per capita, although this does not imply causality. Once again, this suggests that such an approach to dispersing power across product markets coincides with positive growth and hence supports *Vitalpolitik*.

In summary, an ordoliberal economic system for product markets is one that is based on performance competition and supports the freedom of trade between liberal legal orders to help disperse economic power. The pace and extent of free trade should, however, not exceed the ability of countries to invest in innovation and training to support an adjustment process. Such an economic system must also prevent capital flows from distorting the exchange rate, and eliminate illicit money flowing in and out of liberal countries.

10

Confronting Liberalism's Fatal Flaw

Ideas matter

In Oosterbeek cemetery in the Dutch town of Arnhem lie the bodies of Dutch civilians and servicemen from the UK, Poland, Canada, the Netherlands, Australia and New Zealand. A few miles to the south near Nijmegen, the bodies of American servicemen were laid to rest at the Molenhoek cemetery before being removed in 1947 to the American cemetery near Maastricht. Operation Market Garden, as the Allied attack on the Dutch bridges in September 1944 was codenamed, failed to achieve its objectives and resulted in a casualty rate of nearly 75 per cent for the British Paratroop regiment dropped into Arnhem.

Military historians generally regard the operation as flawed from the start. It was poorly planned by people who had little understanding of conditions on the ground and who chose to ignore local information that was provided. Moreover, no attempt was made to adapt the plan to changing conditions on the ground (Beevor, 2018). Despite the level of incompetence of senior generals who remained far from danger, the accounts of the battle are extraordinary with five Victoria Crosses awarded, four of them posthumously (Frost, 1984).

Historians today rightly caution against assumptions as to what drove individual civilians and soldiers on to acts of heroism, beyond an element of professionalism and to protect or sometimes seek revenge for the death of close friends. However, the idea that individuals were also fighting against what they thought was a terrible tyranny is not easy to dispel entirely. Every year liberal democracies remember those who died in battle defending freedom through remembrance services. One question that ought to be raised at such services is whether the legacy of the commemorated acts of heroism has actually resulted in the pursuit of freedom?

Ideas matter. As Fukuyama argued in the *End of History and the Last Man*, there can be no democracy without democrats. It is the same for liberalism. If there is no one to make the case for the foundational ideas of freedom and equality, there is no reason to expect that a society would decide to follow such a route. There are, after all, alternatives.

Neither classical nor social liberalism has succeeded in sustaining a liberal society. One common factor behind this failure is the utilitarian ethical foundation of both versions of liberalism. While utilitarianism has provided an incredibly useful framework for public policy, it has paradoxically resulted in the decline of freedom and equality due to the entrenchment of vested interests and the inequality of power relations prior to voluntary exchange.

During the 1930s, an alternative strand of liberal thought developed to counter the arguments of classical and social liberalism. This formulation in the US and Germany was not only sceptical of relying on market outcomes to improve liberty but also sceptical that continual state intervention would resolve underlying social and economic issues. The ordoliberals argued that an alternative approach to liberalism could be based on rule formulation which minimized the concentration of power. This primarily required the state to be strong enough to prevent concentrations of private power, but also that the state's own power had to be dispersed to prevent a leviathan from arising and destroying liberty. The outcome of a society that focuses on the dispersion of public and private power appears closer to the original ideals of liberalism, where each individual is able to pursue freedom while participating as an equal member of that society.

Although this short-lived movement was somewhat influential in the foundation of West Germany and in some elements of post–war European reconstruction such as competition law and the welfare state, its influence has been hindered by its lack of a quantitative approach. The framework proposed in this book is an attempt to demonstrate how the notion of the dispersal of power could potentially replace Bentham's utilitarian outlook as an ethical foundation for public policy and therefore contribute to the current public policy debate. This book has also suggested how this ethical foundation might be measured and benchmarked enabling public policy professionals to improve on outcomes.

While no attempt has been made to measure the extent of the discrete variables mainly due to their binary nature, monetary policy remains a highly relevant issue. And not just for those countries in the eurozone that no longer have control over monetary policy, but also because inflation targeting can negatively affect freedom and equality due to productivity gains not flowing through to workers' pay. With regards to the policy of making directors liable for their actions through the public enforcement of director duties and increasing scale in pension funds to provide corporate governance oversight, this has been introduced in some countries but remains lacking in many others. Furthermore, although all OECD countries base their economies on the ownership of private property, Anglo-Saxon countries, in particular, continue to ignore fundamental liberal property rights and promote neo-feudal policies that support the extraction of economic rent from the land market. In addition, intellectual property rights are increasingly supporting greater levels of rent extraction, which appears to be having a negative impact on innovation. Property rights are contingent on providing society with some benefit, hence these rights need to be recast.

With regards to the proposed quantitative continuous measures, this is not to argue that the chosen variables are necessarily the most appropriate to measure power dispersion, but rather that they provide an example of how one might proceed. No doubt through time, considerable improvements can be made as to how one might measure the dispersion of public and private power. The data analysed in the individual chapters indicates that a country doesn't have to be wealthy in absolute terms to be considered a successful liberal society. This seems more intuitive for a political philosophy that it is focused on how one might continue to manufacture freedom. Conversely, although a society might be wealthy, this wealth may have come at the expense of an increase in the concentration of power which would contradict an ordoliberal ethical foundation.

The success of Nordic countries based on the derived measures of power dispersion may well have been supported by a stronger embedded notion of the liberal idea of equality, given the region at the outset of industrialization had largely avoided the polarizing effects of feudalism. Furthermore, the centrality of work and embrace of globalization across the Nordic region forced a policy rethink in terms of how it might be possible to increase the power of labour prior to voluntary exchange through devolved active labour market programmes and increased competition.

Ordoliberalism and the future of liberalism

If ordoliberalism has a future as an alternative strand of liberal thinking, the writings of its four key thinkers need to be better known to both academics and policymakers. The fact that this body of thought developed when liberalism was last in serious trouble makes the current need to reconsider their ideas all the more prescient. Particularly as the increasing divide between individuals who have access to legal and political rights and can pursue their idea of freedom, and individuals who do not is eroding faith in liberalism as an ideology. Furthermore, the rise of illiberal political parties that use the will of the people to override the rules and institutions that have maintained liberal democracies with a focus on mythmaking to sustain their legitimacy highlights the precarious nature of freedom and equality.

While there is increasing recognition of the failure of promoting market-based outcomes as supported by contemporary neoliberalism, there appears little reflection as to whether the state can merely solve these issues through more redistribution due the knowledge question. Moreover, as contemporary social liberals explore well-being, too little attention has been paid to how one might systematically prioritize between competing policies.

Liberalism is coming under increasing pressure from a potential resurgence of global conflict with authoritarian regimes, exogenous shocks such as pandemics, climate change and a loss of bio-diversity, the ageing of its societies, entrenched inequality and a perceived loss of freedom. If these issues are not adequately addressed, it may result in a further decline in support for liberal values.

Any attempt to reinvigorate liberalism must address the widespread concern of electorates that liberal democracies have merely become vehicles to benefit those with access to power. A reinvigorated liberal order must therefore seek to increase the trust of its citizens, which is why the idea of eliminating power concentrations may chime with electorates. The liberal movement has a long history of fighting abuses of power, but as was highlighted at the Lippmann Colloquium, it has fallen into a doctrine of passivity.

An ordoliberal public policy programme that is aimed at dispersing power has the potential to reverse this passivity by addressing many of the current policy challenges facing liberal democracies. However, such a programme is likely to be strongly resisted by those who have built up concentrations of power and is one reason why ordoliberalism can be considered to have ultimately failed in West Germany. But this is precisely why both classical and social liberals ought to re-engage with the fundamental building blocks of freedom and equality. Simply clinging on to a utilitarian outlook that appears to erode the fundamental building blocks of liberalism is surely counterproductive.

If liberalism is to have a future, it will require those who believe in liberal values to make the case for an alternative ethical foundation; one where freedom and equality can be constantly manufactured by the continuous dispersal of public and private power. If liberals are not able to win the hearts and minds of citizens by promoting a framework that can enhance freedom and equality, ideologies that are opposed to liberal values may well take its place much sooner than envisaged.

APPENDIX

Methodology Used for Measuring the Dispersal of Public and Private Power by Policy Field

To ensure consistency of data across policy fields, 2018 data are used which is the latest available information for active labour market programmes.

(i) Dispersion of public power within the structure of the state (D): This is approximated by assessing the percentage of revenue and expenditure that is centralized or devolved.

$$D = (a_1 + a_2)/2$$

Where a_1 = Taxation collected at the state and local level as a per cent of general government expenditure

And a_2 = Revenue spent at the state and local level as a per cent of general government revenue

(Social security is considered to be centralized rather than devolved)

Source: OECD Government at a Glance 2021 database (www.oecd.org/gov/government-at-a-glance-2021-database.htm). No data issues identified for 2018.

(ii) Dispersion of private power in labour markets (L): Maximize labour force participation and ability to compete in the labour market through upper-secondary education, vocational training and active labour market schemes.

$$L = (b_1 + b_2 + b_3)/3$$

Where b_1 = Labour force participation rate in per cent

And b_2 = Population with at least an upper-secondary education in per cent

And b_3 = per cent of upper-secondary education undertaking vocational training × per cent GDP spent on ALMP

Sources: Employment – Labour force participation rate – OECD Data (https://data.oecd.org/emp/labour-force-participation-rate.htm). No data issues identified for 2018.

Education attainment – Adult education level – OECD Data (https://data.oecd.org/eduatt/adult-education-level.htm). Data for Japan taken from (OECD, 2015) hence it is stale although is unlikely to have changed significantly.

Enrolment by type of institution (https://stats.oecd.org/Index.aspx?DataSetCode=EDU_ENRL_INST). No data issues identified for 2018.

OECD iLibrary – Labour market programmes: expenditure and participants (www.oecd-ilibrary.org/employment/data/oecd-employment-and-labour-market-statistics/labour-market-programmes-expenditure-and-participants_data-00312-en). Data for Greece taken from (Martin, 2015), UK padded forward from 2011 and Iceland is estimated from publicly available information. Hence, UK and Greece data is stale but are the best available estimates.

(iii) Dispersion of private power in product markets (W): Mean real wage growth over a ten-year period (median wage growth would be a more appropriate measure due to faster rise in wages of top decile but due to data limitations the mean is used).

$W = (r_{2018} - r_{2008})/r_{2008}$ where r_i (real wages) are indexed at 2008 = 100
r_i = Nominal wage growth$_i$ – CPI$_i$

Sources: Average annual wages (https://stats.oecd.org/Index.aspx?DataSetCode=AV_AN_WAGE). No data issues identified for 2018 Prices – Inflation (CPI) – OECD Data (https://data.oecd.org/price/inflation-cpi.htm). No data issues identified for 2018.

(iv) In order to ascertain whether the three power indices are linked to positive growth or higher levels of wealth, GDP per capita in constant 2010 US$ is used 2008–2018.

Source: World Bank Open Data (https://data.worldbank.org/)

Notes

Introduction

[1] A poll conducted by Populous for the Centre for Progressive Capitalism in 2016 on the UK's economic system indicated three quarters of respondents said it was effective at providing opportunities for people from wealthy backgrounds compared with just 5 per cent who thought it effective at providing opportunities for those from poor backgrounds.

[2] Throughout the book I use Bell's distinction between classical and social liberalisms to describe the competing versions of liberalism that place their faith in either the market or the state respectively.

Chapter 2

[1] See UK Treasury Green Book 2020, New Zealand Treasury 2015 Guide to Social Cost Benefit Analysis, European Commission 2002 Guide to Cost Benefit Analysis.

[2] Examples include Dumenil & Levy 2011, Mirowski 2013, Cahill 2014, Davies 2017.

[3] Examples include Stiglitz 2015, Lindsey & Teles 2017, Tepper 2019.

[4] Examples include Luce 2017, Deneen 2018, Emmott 2017. See also *The Economist* bibliography for further reading: www.economist.com/essay/2018/09/13/liberalism-further-reading

[5] Speech to Policy Network AGM 2015.

[6] The drug Soma formed the basis of social cohesion in Aldous Huxley's *Brave New World*.

[7] Both terms were cited at the Walter Lippmann Colloquium in 1938

Chapter 3

[1] Hovenkamp (2019) notes that Bork defined consumer welfare as the sum of consumer and producer welfare, although under perfect competition these two concepts are the same.

[2] Kolev & Köhler (2021) explore the direct linkages between the early Chicago School and the German liberal tradition.

Chapter 5

[1] The natural rate of interest also had a theoretical role in Wicksell's system which was defined as the rate that maintains equilibrium with the money rate and which would subsequently maintain a constant price level as well as equalising ex ante saving and investment.

[2] Estimated from HBAI data by the author.

[3] The importance of Friedman's backing for flexible exchange rates was emphasized by Geoffrey Sachs with regards to the Asian Financial Crisis in a discussion with the author in Taipei 1998 which was published in *The China Post*.

[4] In 2017, the head of the SPD in Germany, Martin Schulz, proposed a United States of Europe. Opinion polls suggest that the peoples of Europe are against the idea with 30 per

cent in Germany in favour, 28 per cent in France and 25 per cent in the Netherlands. Despite the reluctance to back a European federal state there is broad support for continued membership of the EU with 61 per cent of respondents stating that membership is a good thing.

> www.politico.eu/article/spds-martin-schulz-wants-united-states-of-europe-by-2025/;
>
> https://yougov.de/news/2017/12/28/ein-drittel-der-deutschen-fur-vereinigte-staaten-v/;
>
> www.dutchnews.nl/news/2017/03/the-big-election-issues-europe-nexit-and-winning-back-support-for-the-eu/;
>
> www.europarl.europa.eu/news/en/press-room/20190417IPR41755/support-for-eu-remains-at-historically-high-level-despite-sceptics

5 https://infrastructure.planninginspectorate.gov.uk/application-process/

6 Hornsea Project One – an offshore windfarm located off the Yorkshire coast (power-technology.com).

7 Borio & Filardo (2007), Auer, Borio & Filardo (2017) and Forbes (2019) highlight the relationship between globalization and downward pressure on prices.

8 www.brookings.edu/events/whats-not-up-with-inflation/

Chapter 6

1 https://collections.ushmm.org/search/catalog/irn521586

2 Black (2001: 212) cites gross profits for IBM H1 1940 at US$6 m excluding $1 m profit blocked in Germany whereas 'reported' profits for full year were $9 m, and $10 m for 1941. The Collection of IBM Internal Post War Audit Reports (Edwin Black Collection) cites Dehomag Profit for full year 1941 RM34.8 million which is estimated at approximately US$7 m, although many transactions are unreported or blurred. Hence, more than half of profits is not an unreasonable estimate.

3 Geometric returns calculated by the author from the annual reports of the five largest Canadian funds. UK personal pension data derived from: www.ftadviser.com/pensions/2019/01/31/pension-funds-suffer-biggest-losses-since-2008/

4 The Dutch system of taxing residential property as a per cent of its capital value and commercial property minus plant and machinery largely prevents asset owners from benefitting from the hard work of others and should therefore be seen as best practice property taxation for liberal societies: www.centreforcities.org/wp-content/uploads/2020/10/Reforming_business_rates_technical_report.pdf

Chapter 7

1 While federalism and devolution are similar to the extent that powers are devolved to local areas, a federal system is a more permanent arrangement which is usually addressed constitutionally. Devolved governments in theory can lose their powers, reverting back to the unitary state.

2 The ECJ has taken a non-combative approach in the event of a conflict between EU and national laws. In the *Simmenthal* case (1978) the ECJ argued that national law should be seen as inapplicable (Aubrey, 1995). The *Bundesverfassungsgericht* in its ruling on the Lisbon Treaty re-emphasized that domestic law which contravenes EU law is merely inapplicable.

3 See Appendix for formula.

Chapter 8

[1] It has been argued that Germany's apprenticeship system would not exist without co-determination which prioritizes investment in the workforce (The Economist, 2020a).

[2] The analysis is based on log changes of unemployment and earnings. Trade openness is defined as (Imports + Exports)/GDP.

[3] For example, machines can be programmed to price financial assets by learning from a continuous cumulative analysis of the data using methodologies such as support vector machine learning. But a machine cannot respond to a customer querying the result, nor can a human understand why the machine has priced the asset in the way it has, to provide an explanation to the customer.

[4] See Appendix for formula.

Chapter 9

[1] www.statista.com/statistics/216573/worldwide-market-share-of-search-engines/

[2] Ranking useful pages is effectively achieved by popularity where Google looks 'for sites that many users seem to value for similar queries. If other prominent websites on the subject link to the page, that's a good sign that the information is of high quality.' www.google.com/intl/en_uk/search/howsearchworks/algorithms/

[3] https://ec.europa.eu/commission/presscorner/detail/en/IP_17_1784 https://ec.europa.eu/commission/presscorner/detail/en/IP_19_1770

[4] *United States v Google Complaint: US and Plaintiff States v Google LLC* (justice.gov).

[5] Analysis of UK wages data indicates a reasonably stable relationship between lower and median quintile wage growth.

[6] See Appendix for formula.

References

Abelshauser W. (2011) *Deutsche Wirtschaftsgeschichte*, Munich: Beck.

Acemoglu, D. and Autor, D. (2010) 'Skills, Tasks and Technologies: implications for employment and earnings', National Bureau of Economic Research.

Acemoglu, D. and Restrepo, P. (2018) 'Artificial Intelligence, Automation and Work', National Bureau of Economic Research.

Acemoglu, D. and Restrepo, P. (2019) 'Automation and New Tasks', *Journal of Economic Perspectives*, 33(2): 3–30.

Acemoglu, D., Autor, D., Dorn, D., Hanson, G. and Price B. (2014) 'Import Competition and the Great US Employment Sag of the 2000s', National Bureau of Economic Research.

Ahlener Programm (1947) *Zonenausschuß der CDU für die britische Zone*, Ahlen: KAS.

Akguc, S., Choi, J. and Kim, S. (2015) 'Do Private Firms Perform Better than Public Firms?', www.apjfs.org/resource/global/cafm/2015_3_1.pdf

Akman, P. (2012) *The Concept of Abuse in EU Competition Law*, Oxford: Hart.

Alchian, A. (1993) 'Property Rights', www.econlib.org/library/Enc1/PropertyRights.html

Alchian, A. and Demsetz, H. (1973) 'The Property Right Paradigm', *Journal of Economic History*, 33(1): 16–27.

Alt, P. and Schneider, M. (1962) 'West Germany's "Economic Miracle"', *Science Society*, 26(1): 46–57.

Amarnath, S. (2019) 'Floor It! Fixing the Fed's Framework With Paychecks, Not Prices', https://medium.com/@skanda_97974/floor-it-fixing-the-feds-framework-with-paychecks-not-prices-78171423e9c1

Andersen, A., Holmström, B., Honkapohja, S., Korkman, S., Söderström, H. and Vartiainen, J. (2007) 'The Nordic Model: Embracing Globalization and Sharing Risks', The Research Institute of the Finnish Economy.

Andersen, T., Bosch, N., Deelen, A. and Euwals, R. (2011) 'The Danish Flexicurity Model in the Great Recession', https://voxeu.org/article/flexicurity-danish-labour-market-model-great-recession

Antitrust Subcommittee (2020) 'Investigation of Competition in Digital Markets', https://judiciary.house.gov/uploadedfiles/competition_in_digital_markets.pdf?utm_campaign=4493-519

Arrow, K. (1971) *Essays in the Theory of Risk Bearing*, Amsterdam: North Holland Publishing Company.

Arrow, K. and Debreu, G. (1954) 'Existence of an Equilibrium for a Competitive Economy', *Econometrica*, 22(3): 265–90.

Atkinson, A. (2001) 'The Strange Disappearance of Welfare Economics', *Kyklos*, 54(2–3): 193–206.

Atkinson, A. and Stiglitz, J. (1980) *Lectures on Public Economics*, New York: McGraw Hill.

Aubrey, T. (1995) 'Continuing Relevance of Sovereignty Theory in Relation to European Integration', Cambridge University Seeley Library.

Aubrey, T. (2012) *Profiting from Monetary Policy*, Basingstoke: Palgrave.

Aubrey, T. (2013a) 'Are fund managers along with the North Koreans and Cubans alone in believing that markets don't work?', www.creditcapitaladvisory.com/2013/10/13/are-fund-managers-along-with-the-north-koreans-and-cubans-alone-in-believing-that-markets-dont-work/

Aubrey, T. (2013b) 'Making Markets Work', https://policynetwork.progressivebritain.org/publications/papers/making-markets-work/

Aubrey, T. (2014) 'A Swedish perspective on the equilibrium level of interest', www.creditcapitaladvisory.com/2014/09/04/swedish-perspective-equilibrium-level-interest/

Aubrey, T. (2015) 'Bigger is better for pension funds', https://centreforprogressivecapitalism-archive.net/bigger-is-better-for-pension-funds/

Aubrey, T. (2016a) 'Predistribution and Monetary Policy', https://centreforprogressivecapitalism-archive.net/pre-distribution-monetary-policy/

Aubrey, T. (2016b) 'Bridging the Infrastructure Gap', https://centreforprogressivecapitalism-archive.net/bridging-the-infrastructure-gap/

Aubrey, T. (ed) (2017) *Beyond Neoliberalism, Nationalism and Socialism*, London: Rowman Littlefield.

Aubrey, T. and Reed, A. (2016) 'Rebalancing the UK Economy', https://centreforprogressivecapitalism-archive.net/report-rebalancing-the-uk-economy/

Auer, R., Borio C. and Filardo, A. (2017) 'The globalisation of inflation: the growing importance of global value chains', Bank for International Settlements.

Autor, D. (2017) 'The China Shock IFS Lecture', www.youtube.com/watch?v=lUngEbyiaFs

Autor, D. and Salomons, A. (2018) 'Is Automation Labor-Displacing? Productivity Growth, Employment, and the Labor Share', National Bureau of Economic Research.

Autor, D., Dorn, D. and Hanson, G. (2013) 'The China Syndrome: Local Labor Market Effects of Import Competition in the United States', *American Economic Review*, 103(6): 2121–68.

Autor, D., Dorn, D. and Hanson, G. (2016) 'The China Shock: Learning from Labor-Market Adjustment to Large Changes in Trade', National Bureau of Economic Research.

Autor, D., Dorn, D., Katz, L., Patterson, C. and Van Reenen, J. (2019) 'The Fall of the Labor Share and the Rise of Superstar Firms', National Bureau of Economic Research.

Ayash, B. and Rastad, M. (2019) 'Leveraged Buyouts and Financial Distress', SSRN.

Baker, J. (2019) *The Antitrust Paradigm*, Cambridge, MA: Harvard University Press.

Barry, N. (1988) 'Classical Liberalism and Public Policy', *Il Politico*, 53(1): 17–33.

Baxter, S. (2018) 'How the Dutch disclosure regime reduced pension costs by a third', www.professionalpensions.com/analysis/3037130/exclusive-dutch-pension-costs-fall-mandatory-disclosure

Beckworth, D. (2010) 'Krugman, Mankiw, and the US as an OCA', http://macromarketmusings.blogspot.com/2010/05/krugman-mankiw-and-us-as-oca.html

Beckworth, D. (2019) 'Facts, Fears, and Functionality of NGDP Level Targeting: A Guide to a Popular Framework for Monetary Policy', Mercatus Center.

Beevor, A. (2018) *Arnhem*, Milton Keynes: Viking.

Behrens, P. (2014) 'The Consumer Choice Paradigm in German Ordoliberalism and its Impact upon EU Competition Law', Discussion Paper No 1/14, Europa-Kolleg Hamburg.

Behrens, P. (2015a) 'The Ordoliberal Concept of "Abuse" of a Dominant Position and its impact on Article 102 TFEU', SSRN.

Behrens, P. (2015b) '"Consumer choice" or "Consumer Welfare"? Ordoliberalism as the Normative Basis of EU Competition Law', www.uohs.cz/download/Konference_a_seminare/Svatomartinska_konf_2015/prednasejici/Behrens-Peter-Ordoliberalism-and-EU-Competition-Law.pdf

BEIS (2016) 'Corporate Governance Reform Green Paper', https://assets.publishing.service.gov.uk/government/uploads/system/uploads/attachment_data/file/584013/corporate-governance-reform-green-paper.pdf

Bell, D. (2014) 'What Is Liberalism?', *Political Theory*, 42(6): 682–715.

Bennett, J. (1950) 'The German Currency Reform', *Annals of the American Academy of Political and Social Science*, 267: 43–54.

Bentham, J. (1838–1843) *The Works of Jeremy Bentham 11 vols*, Edinburgh: William Tait.

Bergh, A. (2011) 'The Rise, Fall and Revival of the Swedish Welfare State: What are the Policy Lessons from Sweden?', Research Institute for Industrial Economics.

Berglöf, E. and Claessens, S. (2004) 'Corporate Governance and Enforcement', World Bank Policy Research Working Paper 3409.

Berlin I. (1953) *The Hedgehog and the Fox*, London: Weidenfeld Nicolson.

Berlin, I. (1972) 'The Roots of Romanticism', http://berlin.wolf.ox.ac.uk/lists/broadcasts/roots32.mp3

Berlin, I. (1993) *The Magnus of the North*, London: John Murray.

Berlin, I. (2006) *Political Ideas in the Romantic Age*, London: Chatto Windus.

Besley, T. (2002) 'Welfare Economics and Public Choice', https://econ.lse.ac.uk/staff/tbesley/papers/welfpub.pdf

Bessen, J. (2019) 'Automation and Jobs: When technology boosts employment', *Boston University School of Law, Law Economics Paper No 17-09*.

Bessen, J. and Meurer, M. (2008a) *Patent Failure: How Judges, Bureaucrats and Lawyers Put Innovators at Risk*, Princeton: Princeton University Press.

Bessen, J. and Meurer, M. (2008b) 'Do Patents Perform like Property?', *Academy of Management Perspectives*, 22(3): 8–20.

Bessen, J. and Meurer, M. (2008c) 'Of Patents and Property Regulation ', *Boston University School of Law*, 31(4): 9–18.

Bhagwati, J. (2002) *Free Trade Today*, Princeton: Princeton University Press.

Bhagwati, J. (2004) *In Defense of Globalization*, Oxford: Oxford University Press.

Bhatt, I. and MacKenzie, A. (2019) 'Just Google it! Digital Literacy and the Epistemology of Ignorance', *Teaching in Higher Education*, 24(3): 302–17.

Black, E. (2001) *IBM and the Holocaust*, London: Little Brown.

Blanchard, O. and Tirole, J. (2021) 'Major Future Economic Challenges' (Macron Commission), www.strategie.gouv.fr/english-articles/major-future-economic-challenges-olivier-blanchard-and-jean-tirole

Blaug, M. (1985) *Economic Theory in Retrospect*, Cambridge: Cambridge University Press.

Bloomberg (2019) 'Memorandum on ECB Monetary Policy by Issing, Stark, Schlesinger', www.bloomberg.com/news/articles/2019-10-04/memorandum-on-ecb-monetary-policy-by-issing-stark-schlesinger

Blumenthal, R. and Wu, T. (2019) 'What the Microsoft Antitrust Case Taught Us', www.nytimes.com/2018/05/18/opinion/microsoft-antitrust-case.html?searchResultPosition=1

Blustein, P. (2019) *Schism: China, America, and the Fracturing of the Global Trading System*, Waterloo: Centre for International Governance Innovation.

Blyth, M. (2002) *Great Transformations: Economic Ideas and Institutional Change in the 20th Century*, Cambridge: Cambridge University Press.

Blyth, M. (2013) *Austerity: The History of a Dangerous Idea*, Oxford: Oxford University Press.

Boadway, R. (1974) 'The Welfare Foundations of Cost-Benefit Analysis', *Economic Journal*, 84(336): 929–39.

Boese, F. (1932) *Deutschland und die Weltkrise*, Munich: Duncker Humblot.

Böhm, F. (1933) *Wettbewerb und Monopolkampf*, Berlin: Heymann.

Böhm, F. (1950) 'Die Idee des Ordo im Denken Walter Euckens', *ORDO: Jahrbuch für die Ordnung von Wirtschaft und Gesellschaft*, 3: XV–LXIV.

Böhm, F. (1958) 'Wettbewerbsfreiheit und Kartellfreiheit', *ORDO: Jahrbuch für die Ordnung von Wirtschaft und Gesellschaft*, 10: 167–203.

Boldrin, M. and Levine, D. (2005) 'Against Intellectual Monopoly', www.dklevine.com/general/intellectual/against.htm

Boneberg, F. (2010) 'The Economic Consequences of one-third Co-determination in German Supervisory Boards', University of Lüneburg Working Paper Series in Economics No 177.

Bonefeld, W. (2013a) 'Adam Smith and Ordoliberalism', *Review of International Studies*, 39(2): 233–50.

Bonefeld, W. (2013b) 'Human Economy and Social Policy', *History of the Human Sciences*, 26(2): 106–25.

Bonefeld, W. (2017) *The Strong State and the Free Economy*, London: Rowman Littlefield.

Borio, C. and Filardo, A. (2007) 'Globalisation and Inflation: New Cross-country Evidence on the Global Determinants on Domestic Inflation', Bank for International Settlements.

Borio, C., Erdem, M., Filardo, A. and Hofman, B. (2015) 'The Costs of Deflations: A Historical Perspective', Bank for International Settlements.

Bork R. (1993) *The Antitrust Paradox: A Policy at War with Itself*, New York: Free Press.

Boyle, D. (2016) 'Historical Drawbacks of Limited Liability', *Journal of Evolutionary Studies in Business*, 2(1): 276–302.

Brave New Europe (2019) 'The euro is a suicide pact', https://braveneweurope.com/steve-keen-the-euro-is-a-suicide-pact

Brende, B. (2020) 'The New Nordic Model: How to Reconcile Free Trade, Patriotism, and Inclusivity', www.foreignaffairs.com/articles/europe/2020-01-02/new-nordic-model

Bruegel Institute (2017) 'Flexicurity and Labour Market Reforms in Europe', www.bruegel.org/events/flexicurity-and-labour-market-reforms-in-europe/

Bry, G. (1960) *Wages in Germany 1871–1945*, Princeton: Princeton University Press.

Brycki, C. (2019) 'Fat Cat Funds Report Stockspot', https://blog.stockspot.com.au/fat-cat-funds-report-2019/

Buchanan, J. (1977) *Freedom in Constitutional Contract*, College Station, TX: Texas A&M University Press.

Buiter, W. (2014) 'The Simple Analytics of Helicopter Money: Why It Works – Always', *Open-Assessment E-Journal*, 8.

Bumke, C. and Voßkuhle, A. (2019) *German Constitutional Law Introduction, Cases, and Principles*, Oxford: Oxford University Press.

Bundesverfassungsgericht (1994) 'Manfred Brunner and Others v. The European Union Treaty', *Common Market Law Review*, 57(1).

Bundesverfassungsgericht (2009) 'Judgement Treaty of Lisbon', www. bundesverfassungsgericht.de/SharedDocs/Entscheidungen/EN/2009/06/ es20090630_2bve000208en.html

Bundesverfassungsgericht (2020) 'ECB Decisions on the Public Sector Purchase Programme exceed EU Competences', www. bundesverfassungsgericht.de/SharedDocs/Pressemitteilungen/EN/2020/ bvg20-032.html

Burda, M. and Hunt, J. (2011) 'What Explains the German Labor Market Miracle in the Great Recession?', Institute of Labour Economics.

Burgin, A. (2012) *The Great Persuasion Reinventing Free Markets since the Great Depression*, Cambridge, MA: Harvard University Press.

Busemeyer, M. and Trampusch, C. (2012) *Political Economy of Collective Skill Formation*, Oxford: Oxford University Press.

Cahill, D. (2014) *The End of Laissez Faire?*, Cheltenham: Edward Elgar.

Cantillon, R. (1932) 'Essay on the Nature of Commerce in General', http:// pdf.yt/d/MyCHcore9s5-YA66

Card, D., Kluve, J. and Weber, A. (2017) 'What Works? A Meta Analysis of Recent Active Labor Market Program Evaluations', National Bureau of Economic Research.

Carlin, W. (1994) 'West German Growth and Institutions, 1945–90', No 896, CEPR Discussion Papers.

Carnevale, A., Strohl, J. and Melton, M. (2015) *The Economic Value of College Majors*, Washington: Georgetown University.

Carpmaels Ransford (2019) 'Software and business method patents in Europe and the UK', www.carpmaels.com/software-and-business-method-patents-in-europe-and-the-uk-2/

Cass, O. (2018) *The Once and Future Worker*, New York: Encounter.

Chaloupek, G. (2015) 'The End of *Laissez-faire*: Keynes and the Freiburg School', Paper presented at the 19th Annual Conference of the European Society for the History of Economic Thought.

Clarida, R. and Gertler, M. (1997) 'How the Bundesbank Conducts Monetary Policy', National Bureau of Economic Research.

Clegg, S. and Haugaard M. (eds) (2009) *The SAGE Handbook of Power*, London: SAGE Publications.

Coase, R. (1960) 'The Problem of Social Cost', *Journal of Law Economics*, 3: 1–44.

Cole, A. (2006) 'Decentralization in France: Central Steering, Capacity Building and Identity Construction', *French Politics*, 4: 31–57.

Corden, M. (1997) *Trade Policy and Economic Welfare*, Oxford: Clarendon Press.

Court of Justice of the European Union (CJEU) (2020) 'Press Release No. 58/20', Luxembourg.

Coyle, D. (2014) *GDP: A Brief but Affectionate History*, Princeton: Princeton University Press.

Coyle, D. (2017) 'Universal basic services are more important than income', www.ft.com/content/734e8fe6-1880-11e7-9c35-0dd2cb31823a

Coyle, D. (2020) *Markets, State and People*, Princeton: Princeton University Press.

Crane, D. (2014) 'The Tempting of Antitrust: Robert Bork and the Goals of Antitrust Policy', *Antitrust Law Journal*, 79(3): 835–53.

Croly, H. (1912) *The Promise of American Life*, New York: Macmillan.

CWC (2018) 'Pension Fund Cost Transparency: A how-to guide for trade unions', Unison.

Dasgupta, P. (2021) 'The Economics of Biodiversity', www.gov.uk/government/publications/final-report-the-economics-of-biodiversity-the-dasgupta-review

Davies, W. (2017) *The Limits of Neo-liberalism*, London: SAGE Publications.

DeLong, B. (1990) 'In Defense of Henry Simons' Standing as a Classical Liberal', *Cato Journal*, 9(3): 601–18.

Deneen, P. (2018) *Why Liberalism Failed*, New Haven: Yale University Press.

Desai, M. (1981) *Testing Monetarism*, London: Frances Pinter.

Deutsche Bundesbank (1958) 'Report for 1957', Bundesbank.

Deutsche Bundesbank (2012) '55 Years Deutsche Bundesbank', Bundesbank.

Deutscher, E. and Makris, S. (2016) 'Exploring the Ordoliberal Paradigm: The Competition–Democracy Nexus', *Competition Law Review*, 11(2): 181–214.

Dicey, A.V. (2008) *Lectures on the Relation between Law and Public Opinion in England during the Nineteenth Century*, Indianapolis: Liberty Fund.

Directorate for Financial and Enterprise Affairs Competition Committee (DFEACC) (2016) 'Jurisdictional Nexus in Merger Control Regimes', DAF/COMP/WP3/WD16.

Dold, M. and Krieger, T. (2019) *Ordoliberalism and Economic Policy*, Abingdon: Routledge.

Dornbusch, R. (1993) 'The End of the German Miracle', *Journal of Economic Literature*, 31(2): 881–5.

Dornbusch, R. and Fischer, S. (1980) 'Exchange Rates and the Current Account', *American Economic Review*, 70(5): 960–71.

Drucker, P. (1946) *The Concept of the Corporation*, Boston: Beacon Press

Duan, D. (2018) *Liberty, Equality, and Humbug*, Oxford: Oxford University Press.

Duell, N., Tergeist, P., Bazant, U. and Cimper, S. (2010), 'Activation Policies in Switzerland', *OECD Social Employment and Migration Working Papers*, www.oecd.org

Duffie, D. and Sonnenschein, H. (1989), 'Arrow and General Equilibrium Theory', *Journal of Economic Literature*, 27(2): 565–98.

Dumenil, G. and Levy, D. (2011) *The Crisis of Neoliberalism*, Cambridge, MA: Harvard University Press.

Dunning, C. (2017) 'New Careers for the Poor: Human Services and the Post Industrial City', *Journal of Urban History*, 44: 669–90.

Dupuit, J. (1952) 'On the Measurement of the Utility of Public Works', *International Economic Papers*, 2: 83–110.

Duvall, Z. (2019) 'America has a Labor Farm Shortage', www.latimes.com/opinion/op-ed/la-oe-duvall-farm-labor-shortage-20190212-story.html

Dyson, K. (2021) *Conservative Liberalism, Ordo-liberalism and the State*, Oxford: Oxford University Press.

Economic and Social Research Aotearoa Report (2019) https://esra.nz/budget-2019-report/

The Economist (2003) 'A Place for Capital Controls', www.economist.com/leaders/2003/05/01/a-place-for-capital-controls

The Economist (2018a) 'A Manifesto for Renewing Liberalism', www.economist.com/leaders/2018/09/13/a-manifesto-for-renewing-liberalism

The Economist (2018b) 'Dynamism Has Declined across Western Economies', www.economist.com/special-report/2018/11/15/dynamism-has-declined-across-western-economies

The Economist (2019) 'Will a Robot Really Take your Job?', www.economist.com/business/2019/06/27/will-a-robot-really-take-your-job

The Economist (2020a) 'Deutschland AG Rethinks Workers Role in Management', www.economist.com/business/2020/02/01/deutschland-ag-rethinks-workers-role-in-management

The Economist (2020b) 'Covid 19 Blow to World Trade is a Heavy One', www.economist.com/briefing/2020/05/14/covid-19s-blow-to-world-trade-is-a-heavy-one

Eichengreen, B. (1991) 'Is Europe an Optimum Currency Area?', National Bureau of Economic Research.

Eichengreen, B. and Ritschl, A. (2008) 'Understanding West German Economic Growth in the 1950s', Working Papers No 113/08 LSE.

Elsby, M., Hobijn, B. and Sahin, A. (2013) 'The Decline of the US Labor Share', Federal Reserve Bank of San Francisco.

Emmett, R. (2009) *Frank Knight and the Chicago School in American Economics*, Abingdon: Routledge.

Emmott, B. (2017) *The Fate of the West*, London: Profile.

Erhard, L. (1958) *Prosperity through Competition*, New York: Praeger.

Eswaran, M. and Gallini, N. (2018) 'Can Competition Extend the Golden Age of Antibiotics?', Microeconomics working papers: Vancouver School of Economics.

Eucken, W. (1950) *The Foundations of Economics*, London: William Hodge.

Eucken, W. (1959) *Grundsätze der Wirtschaftspolitik*, Hamburg: Rowohlt.

European Commission (2004) 'Guidelines on the Application of Article 81(3) of the Treaty Official Journal of the European Union', C 101/97.

European Commission (2006) 'Annex to the Communication from the Commission to the Spring European Council: Time to move up a gear', European Union.

European Commission (2014) 'EU Employment and Social Situation: Recent trends in the geographical mobility of workers in the EU', European Union.

European Commission (2016a) 'EU Competition Policy in Action', European Union.

European Commission (2016b) 'Sick Pay and Sickness Benefit Schemes in the European Union', European Union.

European Commission (2017) 'European Semester Thematic Factsheet Unemployment Benefits', European Union.

European Commission (2020) 'Recovery plan for Europe', European Union.

European Economic and Social Committee (2002) 'On the Proposal for a Directive of the European Parliament and of the Council on the Patentability of Computer-implemented Inventions', European Union.

Federal Trade Commission (2003) 'To Promote Innovation: The Proper Balance of Competition and Patent Law', Federal Trade Commission.

The Federalist (2001) Indianapolis: Liberty Fund.

Feld, L., Köhler, E. and Nientiedt, D. (2018) 'The German Anti-Keynes? On Walter Eucken's Macroeconomics', *Freiburg Discussion Papers on Constitutional Economics*, 18(11).

Fergusson, A. (1975) *When Money Dies: The Nightmare of the Weimar Collapse*, London: William Kimber.

Financial Times (2017a) 'Water Privatisation Looks Little more than an Organised Rip-off', www.ft.com/content/2beee56a-9616-11e7-b83c-9588e51488a0

Financial Times (2017b) 'Macquarie "transferred £2bn of debt" on to Thames Water's Books', www.ft.com/content/61bd8f0a-9181-11e7-bdfa-eda243196c2c

Financial Times (2018) 'Investors Benefit from Water Groups' Borrowing at Expense of Customers', www.ft.com/content/b60e062e-9712-11e8-b67b-b8205561c3fe

Financial Times (2020a) 'UK companies are only "paying lip service" to Governance Reform', www.ft.com/content/b0c9684a-320a-11ea-9703-eea0cae3f0de

Financial Times (2020b) 'Dealmakers Warn of Chilling Effect on Buyouts from US Court Ruling', www.ft.com/content/01affe9d-89a7-4c0e-8a15-d6d544d4ce04

FitzRoy, F. and Kraft, K. (2004) 'Co-Determination, Efficiency, and Productivity', IZA DP No 1442.

Forbes, K. (2019) 'Has Globalization Changed the Inflation Process?', Bank for International Settlements.

Forcillo, D. (2017) 'Codetermination: the Presence of Workers on the Board. A depth analysis', SSRN.

Foucault, M. (2008) *The Birth of Biopolitics*, New York: Palgrave.

Freeden, M. (1978) *The New Liberalism: An Ideology of Social Reform*, Oxford: Clarendon Press.

Freeden, M. (2008) *Ideologies and Political Theory*, Oxford: Oxford University Press.

Fregert, K. (1993) 'Erik Lindahl's Norm for Monetary Policy', in L. Jonung (ed) *Swedish Economic Thought: Explorations and Advances*, London: Routledge.

Frey, C. and Osborne, M. (2013) 'The Future of Employment: How susceptible are jobs to computerisation?', www.oxfordmartin.ox.ac.uk/downloads/academic/The_Future_of_Employment.pdf

Friedman, M. (1962) *Capitalism and Freedom*, Chicago: Chicago University Press.

Friedman, M. (1968) 'The Role of Monetary Policy', *American Economic Review*, 58(1): 1–17.

Friedman, M. (1969) *The Optimum Quantity of Money and Other Essays*, Chicago: Aldine.

Friedman, M. (1970) 'The Social Responsibility of Business is to Increase its Profits', www.nytimes.com/1970/09/13/archives/a-friedman-doctrine-the-social-responsibility-of-business-is-to.html.

Friedman, M. (1997) 'The Euro: Monetary Unity to Political Disunity?', www.project-syndicate.org/commentary/the-euro-monetary-unity-to-political-disunity

Frost, J. (1984) *A Drop too Many*, Reading: Cox Wyman.

Fukumaya, F. (1992) *The End of History and the Last Man*, London: Penguin.

Genz, S., Bellmann, L. and Matthes, B. (2018) 'Do German Works Councils Counter or Foster the Implementation of Digital Technologies?', IZA DP No 11616.

Gerber, D. (1987) 'Law and the Abuse of Economic Power in Europe', *Tulane Law Review*, 62(1).

Gerner-Beuerle, C. and Schillig, M. (2019) *Comparative Company Law*, Oxford: Oxford University Press.

Getzler, J. (1996) 'Theories of Property and Economic Development', *Journal of Interdisciplinary History*, 26(4): 639–69.

Gierke, O. (1934) *Natural Law and the Theory of Society Volume I*, London: CUP.

Giersch, H., Paque, K. and Schmieding, H. (1992) *The Fading Miracle*, Cambridge: Cambridge University Press.

Gill, S. and Cutler, C. (2014) New Constitutionalism and World Order, Cambridge: Cambridge University Press.

Glaeser, E. (2009) 'Why Has Globalization Led to Bigger Cities?', https://economix.blogs.nytimes.com/2009/05/19/why-has-globalization-led-to-bigger-cities/

Glasner, D. (1989) *Free Banking and Monetary Reform*, Cambridge: Cambridge University Press.

Glasner, D. (2011) 'NGDP Targeting v Nominal Wage Targeting', https://uneasymoney.com/2011/12/09/ngdp-targeting-v-nominal-wage-targeting/

Glucksberg, L. (2016) 'A View from the Top', *City*, 20(2): 238–55.

Goldin, C. and Katz, L. (2009) *The Race between Education and Technology*, Cambridge, MA: Harvard University Press.

Goldschmidt, N. and Wohlgemuth, M. (2008) *Grundtexte zue Freiburger Tradition der Ordnungsökonomik*, Tübingen: Mohr Siebeck.

Gong, D., Jun, L. and Tsai, J. (2017) 'Trends in Medicare Service Volume for Cataract Surgery and the Impact of the Medicare Physician Fee Schedule', *Health Services Research*, 52(4): 1409–26.

Goodhart, C. and Lastra, R. (2019) 'Equity Finance: Matching liability to power', CEPR discussion papers (DP13494).

Goodhart, C., Baker M. and Ashworth, J. (2013) 'Monetary Targetry: Might Carney make a difference?', https://voxeu.org/article/monetary-targetry-might-carney-make-difference

Gorback, C. and Keys, B. (2020) 'Global Capital and Local Assets: House prices, quantities and elasticities', National Bureau of Economic Research.

Gormsen, L. (2007) 'The Conflict between Economic Freedom and Consumer Welfare in the Modernisation of Article 82', SSRN.

Gorton, G. and Schmid, F. (2002) 'Class Struggle inside the Firm: A Study of German codetermination', Working Paper 2000-025B, Federal Reserve Bank of St Louis.

Graaff J. (1975) *Theoretical Welfare Economics,* Cambridge: Cambridge University Press.

Gray, J. (2020) 'Roots of Identitarian Liberalism', https://unherd.com/2020/01/the-rise-of-identitarian-liberalism/

Green, A. and Pensiero, N. (2016) 'The Effects of Upper-secondary Education and Training Systems on Skills Inequality: A Quasi-cohort Analysis Using PISA 2000 and the OECD Survey of Adult Skills', *British Educational Research Journal*, 42(5): 756–79.

Guichardaz, R. and Pénin, J. (2019) 'Why was Schumpeter not more Concerned with Patents?', *Journal of Evolutionary Economics*, 29: 1361–9.

Gurri, M. (2018) *The Revolt of the Public*, San Francisco: Stripe.

Haagh, L. (2019) *The Case for Universal Basic Income*, Cambridge: Polity.

Hacker, J. and Loewentheil, N. (2012) 'Prosperity Economics: Building an economy for all', https://isps.yale.edu/research/publications/isps12-020

Haldane, A. (2015) 'Who Owns a Company?', Bank of England.

Hall, P. (2013) *Good Cities Better Lives: How Europe Discovered the Lost Art of Urbanism*, Abingdon: Routledge.

Halpern, P., Trebilcock, M. and Turnbull, S. (1980) 'An Economic Analysis of Limited Liability in Corporation Law', *University of Toronto Law Journal*, 30(2): 117–50.

Hamilton, J. (1989) 'A New Approach to the Economic Analysis of Nonstationary Time Series and the Business Cycle', *Econometrica*, 57(2): 357–84.

Hamilton, L. (2019) *Amartya Sen*, Cambridge: Polity.

Hart, H. (1994) *The Concept of Law*, Oxford: Clarendon Press.

Hartrich, E. (1980) *The Fourth and Richest Reich*, New York: Macmillan.

Hartwich, O. (2009) 'Neoliberalism: The genesis of a political swearword', CIS Occasional Paper 114.

Harvey, D. (2005) *A Brief History of Neoliberalism*, Oxford: Oxford University Press.

Haskel, J., Lawrence, R., Leamer, E., and Slaughter, M. (2012) 'Globalization and US Wages: Modifying Classic Theory to Explain Recent Facts', *Journal of Economic Perspectives*, 26(2): 119–40.

Hawtrey, R. (1925) *The Economic Problem*, London: Longmans

Hawtrey, R. (1930) 'Money and Index-Numbers', *Journal of the Royal Statistical Society*, 93(1): 64–103.

Hawtrey, R. (1967) *Incomes and Money*, London: Longmans.

Hayek, F.A. (1945) The Use of Knowledge in Society, *American Economic Review*, 35(4): 519–30.

Hayek, F.A. (1958) *Individualism and Economic Order*, Chicago: University of Chicago Press.

Hayek, F.A. (1960) *The Constitution of Liberty*, Chicago: Chicago University Press.

Hayek, F.A. (1994) *Road to Serfdom*, Chicago: University of Chicago.

Hayek, F.A. (2013) *Law Legislation and Liberty*, London: Routledge.

Heller, M. and Eisenberg, R. (1998) 'Can Patents Deter Innovation?', *Biomedical Research Science New Series*, 280(5364): 698–701.

Herder, J. (2016) *Outlines of a Philosophy of the History of Man*, Randomshack.

Hidalgo, C. (2015) *Why Information Grows*, London: Allen Lane.

Hien, J. and Joerges, C. (2017) *Ordoliberalism, Law and the Rule of Economics*, Oxford: Hart Publishing.

Hiilamo, H. (2019) 'Disappointing Results from the Finnish Basic Income Experiment', University of Helsinki.

Hillman, J. (2018) 'Testimony before the US China Economic and Review Security Commission Hearing on US Tools to Address Chinese Market Distortions', www.uscc.gov/sites/default/files/Hillman%20Testimony%20 US%20China%20Comm%20w%20Appendix%20A.pdf

Hilson, M. (2008) *The Nordic Model*, London: Reaktion.

HM Treasury (2015) 'Fixing the Foundations: Creating a more prosperous nation', www.gov.uk/government/publications/ fixing-the-foundations-creating-a-more-prosperous-nation

Hobbes, T. (1985) *Leviathan*, Harmondsworth: Penguin.

Hobson, J. (1974) *The Crisis of Liberalism*, Brighton: Harvester Press.

Hocking, W. (1926) *Man and the State*, New Haven: Yale University Press.

Hong, Y. and Needham, B. (eds) (2007) 'Analysing Land Readjustment', Lincoln Institute of Land Policy.

Hont, I. (2015) *Politics in Commercial society: Jean-Jacques Rousseau and Adam Smith*, Cambridge, MA: Harvard University Press.

Hort, S. (2014) *Social Policy, Welfare State, and Civil Society in Sweden*, Lund: Arkiv.

Hosman, M (2021) 'China's NME status at the WTO', *Journal of International Trade Law and Policy*, 20(1): 1–20.

House of Commons Library (2021) 'Food Banks in the UK', https:// commonslibrary.parliament.uk/research-briefings/cbp-8585/

Hovenkamp, H. (2019) 'Is Antitrust's Consumer Welfare Principle Imperiled?', SSRN.

Hume, D. (1988) *Enquiry Concerning Human Understanding*, Buffalo: Prometheus.

Hume, D. (1994) *Political Writings*, Indianapolis: Hackett.

Hunold, A. (ed) (1957) *Masse und Demokratie*, Zurich: Eugen Rentsch.

ILO OECD (2015) 'The Labour Share in G20 Economies Report prepared for the G20 Employment Working Group', Paris: OECD Publishing.

IMF (2011) 'Capital Flows, Exchange Rate Flexibility and the Real Exchange Rate', International Monetary Fund.

Institute for Fiscal Studies (2016) 'How English Domiciled Graduate Earnings Vary with Gender, Institution Attended, Subject and Socio-economic Background', Institute for Fiscal Studies.

International Water Association (2014) 'International Statistics for Water Services', www.iwa-network.org/wp-content/uploads/2016/06/ International-Statistics-for-Water-Services-2014.pdf

Issing, O. (2005) 'Why Did the Great Inflation Not Happen in Germany?', *Federal Reserve Bank of St. Louis Review*, 87(2): 329–35.

Jaffe, A. and Lerner, J. (2006) 'Innovation and Its Discontents in Innovation Policy and the Economy', National Bureau of Economic Research.

Jevons, W.S. (1888) *The Theory of Political Economy*, London: Macmillan.

Johnson, M. (2008) 'Wicksell's Unanimity Rule and Early Welfare Economics', Draft prepared for the History of Economics Society Meetings, Toronto.

Jones, C., Morgan, J. and Stephens, M. (2018) 'An Assessment of Historic Attempts to Capture Land Value Uplift in the UK', Scottish Land Commission.

Josten, P. (1949) *Entwurf zu einem Gesetz zur Sicherung des Lesitungswettbewerbs und zu einem Gesetz uber das Monopolamt*, Frankfurt: Bundesministers für Wirtschaft.

Jung, C. and Shiller, R. (2006) 'Samuelson's Dictum and the Stock Market', *Economic Inquiry*, 43: 221–8.

Kahneman, D. (2011) *Thinking Fast and Slow*, London: Penguin.

Kaldor, N. (1957) 'A Model of Economic Growth', *Economic Journal*, 67(268): 591–624.

Kant, I. (1992) *Political Writings*, Cambridge: Cambridge University Press.

Karabarbounis, L. and Neiman, B. (2013) 'The Global Decline of the Labor Share', National Bureau of Economic Research.

Karsten, S. (2005) 'Social Market Economics Revisited', *International Journal of Social Economics*, 32(7): 602–15.

Katz, B. and Nowak, J. (2017) *The New Localism*, Washington, DC: Brookings Institution Press.

Kay, J. (2012) 'The Kay Review of UK Equity Markets and Long-term Decision Making', https://assets.publishing.service.gov.uk/government/uploads/system/uploads/attachment_data/file/253454/bis-12-917-kay-review-of-equity-markets-final-report.pdf

Keay, A. (2014) 'The Public Enforcement of Directors' Duties: A Normative Inquiry', *Common Law World Review*, 43: 89–119.

Kempin, F. (1960) 'Limited Liability in Historical Perspective', *American Business Law Association Bulletin*, 4: 11–34.

Keune, M. and Jepsen, M. (2007) 'Not Balanced and Hardly New: the European Commission's quest', European Trade Union Institute.

Keynes, J.M. (1926) *The End of Laissez-faire*, www.hetwebsite.net/het/texts/keynes/keynes1926laissezfaire.htm

Khan, L. (2017) 'Amazon's Antitrust Paradox', *Yale Law Journal*, 126(3).

Khan, L. and Vaheesan, S. (2017) 'Market Power and Inequality: The Antitrust Counterrevolution and its Discontents', *Harvard Law Policy Review*, 11: 235–94.

Kindleberger, C. (1991) 'The Economic Crisis of 1619 to 1623', *Journal of Economic History*, 51(1): 149–75.

Kinsella, S. (2008) *Against Intellectual Property*, Auburn: Ludwig von Mises Institute.

Kishimoto, S., Lobina, E. and Petitjean O. (2015) 'Our Public Water Future: The global experience with remunicipalisation', Transnational Institute.

Kluve, J. (2006) 'The Effectiveness of European Active Labor Market Policy', IZA Discussion Paper No 2018.

Knight, F. (1923) 'The Ethics of Competition', *Quarterly Journal of Economics*, 37(4): 579–624.

Knight, F. (1929) 'Freedom as Fact and Criterion', *International Journal of Ethics*, 39(2): 129–47.

Knight, F. (1938) 'Lippmann's The Good Society', *Journal of Political Economy*, 46(6): 864–72.

Knight, F. (1967) 'Laissez Faire: Pro and Con', *Journal of Political Economy*, 75(6): 782–95.

Knight, F. (1982) *Freedom and Reform: Essays in Economics and Social Philosophy*, Indianapolis: Liberty Fund.

Knight, F. (2014) *The Ethics of Competition*, Mansfield Centre: Martino Publishing.

Köhler, E. and Kolev, S. (2011) 'The Conjoint Quest for a Liberal Positive Program: "Old Chicago", Freiburg and Hayek', Hamburgisches WeltWirtschaftsInstitut.

Köhler, E. and Kolev, S, (2021) 'Transatlantic Roads to Mont Pèlerin: "Old Chicago" and Freiburg in a world of disintegrating orders', Stigler Center New Working Paper Series No 309.

Kolev, S. (2009) 'Macht und soziale Kohäsion als Determinanten: Zur Rolle des Staates in der Wirtschaftspolitik bei Walter Eucken und Wilhelm Röpke', Hamburgisches WeltWirtschaftsInstitut.

Kolev, S. (2010) 'F.A. Hayek as an Ordo-Liberal', Hamburgisches WeltWirtschaftsInstitut.

Koslowski, P. (ed) (2000) *Theory of Capitalism in the German Economic Tradition*, Berlin: Springer.

Kovacic, W. (2007) 'The Intellectual DNA of Modern US Competition Law for Dominant Firm Conduct: The Chicago/Harvard Double Helix', *Columbia Business Law Review*, 1: 2–78.

Kraft, K., Stank, J. and Dewente, R. (2009) 'Co-determination and Innovation', IZA DP No 4487.

Krugman, P. (2019) 'Max Corden Lecture', www.youtube.com/watch?v=rWQ3jCURzy0

Kurachi, S. (2016) 'The Process of Universalism in the Danish Welfare System: The multi-tiered needs testing system in Denmark', Keio-IES Discussion Paper Series.

Labrousse, A. and Weisz J. (2001) *Institutional Economics in France and Germany: German Ordoliberalism versus the French Regulation School*, Berlin: Springer.

Laidler, D. (2004) 'Woodford and Wicksell on Interest and Prices: The place of the pure credit economy in the theory of monetary policy', EPRI Working Papers, University of Western Ontario.

Lampe, C. and Gabidullina, R. (2019) 'Is Russia Undermining Democracy in the West?', Conference Report Foreign Policy Research Institute, www.fpri.org/article/2019/03/is-russia-undermining-democracy-in-the-west-conference-report/

Larsen, C. (1999) 'States Federal, Financial, Sovereign and Social: A Critical Inquiry into an Alternative to American Financial Federalism', *American Journal of Comparative Law*, 47(3): 429–88.

Larsen, C. and Andersen, J. (2009) 'How New Economic Ideas Changed the Danish Welfare State', *Governance*, 22(2): 239–61.

Laxminarayan, R. (2001) 'Fighting Antibiotic Resistance: Can economic incentives play a role?', *Resources*, 143: 9–12.

Layard, R. (2005) *Happiness*, London: Allen Lane.

Leijonhufvud, A. (1997) 'The Wicksellian Heritage', www-ceel.economia.unitn.it/staff/leijonhufvud/files/wick.pdf

Lemley, M. (2004) 'Property, Intellectual Property, and Free Riding', SSRN.

Lindahl, E. (1970) *Studies in the Theory of Money and Capital*, New York: Augustus Kelley.

Lindsey, B. and Teles, S. (2017) *The Captured Economy*, Oxford: Oxford University Press.

Lippmann, W. (1938) *The Good Society*, Guildford: Billing & Sons.

Lipsey, R. (2007) 'Reflections on the General Theory of Second Best at Its Golden Jubilee', *International Tax and Public Finance*, 14: 349–64.

Lipsey, R. and Lancaster, K. (1956) 'The General Theory of Second Best', *Review of Economic Studies*, 24(1): 11–32.

Little, I. (1973) *A Critique of Welfare Economics*, Oxford: Oxford University Press.

Lobina, E. and Hall, D. (2001) 'UK Water Privatisation – a Briefing', www.psiru.org/reports/uk-water-privatisation-%E2%80%93-briefing.html

Locke, J. (1993) *Political Writings*, Harmondsworth: Penguin

Lonergan, E. (2016) 'Legal Helicopter Drops in the Eurozone', www.philosophyofmoney.net/legal-helicopter-drops-in-the-eurozone/

Lonergan, E. (2019) 'Dual Interest Rates Always Work', www.philosophyofmoney.net/dual-interest-rates-always-work/

Lord Acton, (1949) *Essays on Freedom and Power*, Boston: Beacon Press.

Lovelock, J. (1979) *Gaia*, Oxford: Oxford University Press.

Luce, E. (2017) *The Retreat of Western Liberalism*, London: Little Brown.

Mäding, H. (2017) 'Das SARO-Gutachten (1961): Beurteilung von Entstehung, Inhalt und Wirkung', *Raumforschung und Raumordnung*, 75: 371–87.

Madsen, J. (2010) 'Growth and Capital Deepening since 1870: Is it all Technological Progress?', *Journal of Macroeconomics*, 32(2): 641–56.

Madsen, P. (1999) 'Denmark: Flexibility, security and labour market success, Employment and Training Series', International Labour Organization.

Maier-Rigaud, F. and Maier-Rigaud, G. (eds) (2001) *Das Versagen der Wirtschaftliberalismus*, Marburg: Metropolis.

Mali, J. and Wokler, R. (eds) (2003) 'Isaiah Berlin's Counter-Enlightenment', *Transactions of the American Philosophical Society*, 93(5).

Mandel, M. (2017) 'The Creation of a New Middle Class?', www. progressivepolicy.org/wp-content/uploads/2017/03/Tech-middle-class-3-9-17b.pdf

Mandelbrot, B. and Taleb, N. (2010) 'Mild vs. Wild Randomness: Focusing on Those Risks that Matter', in F. Diebold, N. Doherty and R. Herring (eds) *The Known, the Unknown and the Unknowable in Financial Institutions*, Princeton: Princeton University Press.

Markert, K. (1975) 'Recent Developments in German Antitrust Law', *Fordham Law Review*, 43(5): 697–718.

Martin, J. (2015) 'Activation and Active Labour Market Policies in OECD Countries', IZA Policy Paper No 84.

Marx, K. (1976) *Capital Vol I*, London: Penguin

Mau, S. (2001) 'Patterns of Popular Support for the Welfare State: A comparison of the United Kingdom and Germany', WZB Discussion paper.

Mavroidis, P. and Sapir, A. (2021) *China and the WTO*, Princeton: Princeton University Press.

Mazzucato, M. (2013) *The Entrepreneurial State*, London: Anthem.

Mazzucato, M. (2018) *The Value of Everything*, London: Allen Lane.

McKinsey Global Institute (2011) 'Urban world: Mapping the economic power of cities', www.mckinsey.com/featured-insights/urbanization/urban-world-mapping-the-economic-power-of-cities

McKinsey Global Institute (2013) 'QE and Ultra-low Interest Rates: Distributional effects and risks', www.mckinsey.com/featured-insights/employment-and-growth/qe-and-ultra-low-interest-rates-distributional-effects-and-risks

McKinsey Global Institute (2017) 'A Future that Works: Automation, employment and productivity', www.mckinsey.com/featured-insights/digital-disruption/harnessing-automation-for-a-future-that-works/de-DE

Meade, J. (1966) *Trade and Welfare*, Oxford: Oxford University Press.

Meade, J. (1976) *Principles of Political Economy: Vol 4, The Just Economy*, London: Allen & Unwin.

Megay, E. (1970) 'Anti-Pluralist Liberalism: The German Neoliberals', *Political Science Quarterly*, 85(3): 422–42.

Melbourne Mercer Global Pension Index (2019), www.info.mercer.com/rs/521-DEV-513/images/MMGPI%202019%20Full%20Report.pdf

Merkel, W., Kollmorgen, R. and Wagener, H. (2019) *The Handbook of Political, Social and Economic Transformation*, Oxford: Oxford University Press.

Mersch, Y. (2011) 'Optimal Currency Area Revisited', Bank for International Settlements.

Mestmäcker, E.J. (1984) *Der Verwaltete Wettbwerb*, Tübingen: Mohr Siebeck.

Mestmäcker, E.J. (2003) *Wirtschaft und Verfassung in der Europaischen Union*, Baden-Baden: Nomos.

Michel, H. (2007) 'Co-determination in Germany: The Recent debate', Johann Wolfgang Goethe-Universität Frankfurt.

Micklethwaite, J. and Wooldridge, A. (2003) *The Company*, London: Weidenfeld Nicholson.

Mill, J.S. (1985) *On Liberty*, Harmondsworth: Penguin.

Mill, J.S. (1994) *Principles of Political Economy*, Oxford: Oxford University Press.

Miller, S. (2013) 'Where's the Innovation? An Analysis of the Quantity and Qualities of Anticipated and Obvious Patents', SSRN.

Millon, D. (2007) 'Piercing the Corporate Veil, Financial Responsibility and the Limits of Limited Liability', *Emory Law Journal*, 56(5): 1307–82.

Minda, G. (1978) 'The Lawyer – Economist at Chicago: Richard A. Posner and the Economic Analysis of Law', *Ohio State Law Journal*, 39: 339–475.

Minsky, H. (1965) 'The Role of Employment Policy', Levy Economics Institute of Bard College.

Mirowski, P. (2013) *How Neoliberalism Survived*, London: Verso.

Mirowski, P. and Plehwe, D. (2009) *The Road from Mont Pèlerin: The Making of the Neoliberal Thought Collective*, Cambridge, MA: Harvard University Press.

Moody's Investors Service (2020) 'US Speculative-grade Default rate Surges in Q2 2020 as Coronavirus Fallout Takes Toll', www.moodys.com/ research/Moodys-US-speculative-grade-default-rate-surges-in-Q2-2020- -PBC_1240217

Moretti, E. (2013) *The New Geography of Jobs*, Boston: Houghton Mifflin Harcourt.

Muellbauer, J. (2014) 'Combatting Eurozone Deflation: QE for the people', https://voxeu.org/article/combatting-eurozone-deflation-qe-people

Müller, C. (1961) *Kartelle und Monopole im Modernen Recht*, Karlsruhe: Institut für auslandisches und internationales Wirtschaftsrecht.

Müller-Armack, A. (1976) *Wirtschaftsordnung und Wirtschaftspolitik*, Bern: Paul Haupt.

Müller-Armack, A. (1978) 'The Social Market Economy as an Economic and Social Order', *Review of Social Economy*, 36(3): 325–31.

Müller-Armack, A. (1981) *Genealogie der Sozialen Marktwirtschaft*, Bern: Paul Haupt.

Müller-Armack, A. (1990) *Wirtschaftslenkung und Marktwirtschaft*, Munich: Kastell.

Mussa, M. (1984) 'The Theory of Exchange Rate Determination', National Bureau of Economic Research.

Myrdal, G. (1965) *Monetary Equilibrium*, New York: Augustus Kelley.

NAPF (2014) 'NAPF Engagement Survey: Pension funds' engagement with investee companies', www.plsa.co.uk/Policy-and-Research/Document-library/NAPF-Engagement-Survey

National Audit Office (2020) 'Investigation into Government Procurement During the COVID-19 Pandemic', www.nao.org.uk/report/government-procurement-during-the-covid-19-pandemic/

Nettlefold, C. (2017) *The Chamberlain Legacy*, Exeter: Imprint Acadamic.

Neufeind, M., O'Reilly, J. and Ranft, F. (2018) *Work in the Digital Age*, London: Rowman Littlefield.

New York Times (2008) 'Stopping a Financial Crisis, the Swedish Way', www.nytimes.com/2008/09/23/business/worldbusiness/23krona.html

New York Times (2015) 'The Typical American Only Lives 18 miles from Mom', www.nytimes.com/interactive/2015/12/24/upshot/24up-family.html

New York Times (2018) 'We all Have a Stake in the Stock Market, Right?', www.nytimes.com/2018/02/08/business/economy/stocks-economy.html

Nicholls, A. (1994) *Freedom with Responsibility*, Oxford: Clarendon Press.

Nicholls, D. (1975) *The Pluralist State*, London: Macmillan.

Nozick, R. (1974) *Anarchy, State and Utopia*, Oxford: Basil Blackwell.

Nutzinger, H. and Backhaus, J. (1989) *Codetermination: A Discussion of Different Approaches*, Berlin: Springer.

OECD (2004) 'Germany: The Role of Competition Policy in Regulatory Reform', Paris: OECD Publishing.

OECD (2010) 'Education Indicators at a Glance', Paris: OECD Publishing.

OECD (2012) 'OECD Employment Outlook', Paris: OECD Publishing.

OECD (2013) 'Education at a Glance', Paris: OECD Publishing.

OECD (2015a) 'G20/OECD Principles of Corporate Governance', Paris: OECD Publishing.

OECD (2015b) 'Education Policy Outlook Japan', Paris: OECD Publishing.

OECD (2017) 'Collective Bargaining in OECD and Accession Countries', Paris: OECD Publishing.

OECD (2019a) 'Under Pressure: The squeezed middle class', Paris: OECD Publishing.

OECD (2019b) 'Pensions at a Glance OECD and G20 Indicators', Paris: OECD Publishing.

OECD (2019c) 'Health at a Glance OECD Indicators', Paris: OECD Publishing.

OECD (2019d) 'Negotiating Our Way Up: Collective bargaining in a changing world of work', Paris: OECD Publishing.

OECD (2019e) 'Employment Outlook: The future of work', Paris: OECD Publishing.

Ohlhausen, M. (2016) 'US–EU Convergence: Can We Bridge the Atlantic?', www.ftc.gov/public-statements/2016/09/us-eu-convergence-can-we-bridge-atlantic

Olsson, S. (1990) *Social Policy and Welfare State in Sweden*, Lund: Arkiv.

O'Malley, E. (1981) 'The Decline of Irish Industry in the Nineteenth Century', *Economic and Social Review*, 13(1): 21–42.

O'Neill, J. (2016) 'Infections Globally: Final report and recommendations of the review on antimicrobial resistance', *AMR Review*.

Onaran, O. and Galanis, G. (2012) 'Is Aggregate Demand Wage-led or Profit-led? National and Global Effects', ILO Working Papers, International Labour Organization.

Ornhial, T. (ed) (1982) *Limited Liability and the Corporation*, London: Croom Helm.

Oswalt-Eucken, I. (1994) 'Freedom and Economic Power: Neglected Aspects of Walter Eucken's Work', *Journal of Economic Studies*, 21(4): 38–45.

Paine, T. (1894) *The Writings of Thomas Paine*, New York: G.P. Putnam's Sons.

Parkinson, J. (1993) *Corporate Power and Responsibility,* Oxford: Oxford University Press.

Parkinson, J., Gamble, A. and Kelly, G. (2000) *The Political Economy of the Company*, Oxford: Hart Publishing.

Paster, T. (2012) 'Do German Employers Support Board-level Codetermination? The Paradox of Individual Support and Collective Opposition', *Socio-Economic Review*, 10: 471–95.

Peacock, A. and Willgerodt, H. (1989a) *German Neo-liberals and the Social Market Economy*, London: Macmillan.

Peacock, A. and Willgerodt, H. (1989b) *Germany's Social Market Economy: Origins and Evolution*, London: Macmillan.

Pearce, D. (1985) *Cost Benefit Analysis*, London: Macmillan.

Phelps, E. (1968) 'Money-Wage Dynamics and Labor Market Equilibrium', *Journal of Political Economy*, 76(4): 678–711.

Philippon, T. (2019) *The Great Reversal*, Cambridge, MA: Harvard University Press.

Phillips, W. (1958) 'The Relation Between Unemployment and the Rate of Change of Wage Rates in the United Kingdom, 1861–1957', *Economica*, 25(100): 283–99.

Piketty, T. (2014) *Capital in the 21st Century*, Cambridge, MA: Harvard University Press.

Polanyi, K. (2001) *The Great Transformation*, Boston: Beacon Press.

Posen, A. (1997) 'Lessons from the Bundesbank on the Occasion of Its 40th (and Second to Last?) Birthday', Peterson Institute for International Economics Working Paper 97-4.

Posen, A. (2021) 'The Price of Nostalgia', www.foreignaffairs.com/articles/united-states/2021-04-20/america-price-nostalgia

Posner, R. (2006) 'Do We Have Too Many Intellectual Property Rights?', *Marquette Intellectual Property Law Review*, 9(2): 173–85.

Posner, R. (2012) 'Why there Are Too Many Patents in America', www.theatlantic.com/business/archive/2012/07/why-there-are-too-many-patents-in-america/259725/

Quinn, R. (2013) 'Rethinking Antibiotic Research and Development', *American Journal of Public Health*, 103(3): 426–34.

Rainmaker Information (2019) 'Superannuation Fees Fall for the First Time in Six Years', www.rainmaker.com.au/media-release/superannuation-fees-fall-for-first-time-in-six-years

Rajan, R. (2019) *The Third Pillar*, London: William Collins.

Rapp, M. and Wolff, M. (2019) 'Strong Codetermination – Stable Companies: An empirical analysis in lights of the recent financial crisis', Mitbestimmungsreport No 51, Hans Böckler Stiftung.

Rawls, J. (1973) *A Theory of Justice*, Oxford: Oxford University Press.

Reid, K. (2012) *A Practitioner's Guide to the European Convention on Human Rights*, London: Sweet & Maxwell.

Reinhoudt, J. and Audier, S. (2018) *The Walter Lippmann Colloquium: The Birth of Neoliberalism*, Cham: Palgrave Macmillan.

Renard, V. (2006) 'Rights for Reduction in Property Values Due to Planning Decisions: The Case of France', *Washington University Global Studies Law Review*, 5(3): 523–34.

Reuters (2019) 'Count Draghila is Sucking Our Accounts Dry', Says Germany's Bild', www.reuters.com/article/us-ecb-policy-germany-idUSKCN1VY0MN.

Rittershausen, J. (2007) 'The Post-war West German Economic Transition: From Ordoliberalism to Keynesianism', IWP Discussion Paper, No 2007/1.

Robbins, L. (1932) *An Essay on the Nature Significance of Economic Science*, London: Macmillan.

Robbins, L. (1938) 'Interpersonal Comparisons of Utility: A Comment', *Economic Journal*, 48(192): 635–41.

Rodrik, D. (2011) *The Globalization Paradox*, Oxford: Oxford University Press.

Röpke, W. (1946) *The German Question*, London: George Allen.

Röpke, W. (1950) *Social Crisis of our Time*, Chicago: University of Chicago Press.

Röpke, W. (1959) *International Order and Economic Integration*, Dordrecht: Reidel.

Röpke, W. (1960) *Humane Economy*, Chicago: Henry Regnery.

Röpke, W. (1963) *Economics of the Free Society*, Chicago: Henry Regnery.

Rosenhaft, E. (1983) *Beating the Fascists?: The German Communists and Political Violence 1929–1933*, Cambridge: Cambridge University Press.

Rothschild, E. (2002) *Economic Sentiments: Adam Smith, Condorcet, and the Enlightenment*, Cambridge, MA: Harvard University Press.

Rothstein, B. (1998) *Just Institutions Matter: The Moral and Political Logic of the Universal Welfare State*, Cambridge: Cambridge University Press.

Rothstein, B. (2004) 'Industrial Relations as a Social Trap', Paper to be presented at the European Consortium for Political Research Joint Session of Work Groups, Uppsala.

Rowley, C. and Peacock, A. (1975) *Welfare Economics: A Liberal Restatement*, London: Martin Robertson.

Royal Commission into Misconduct in the Banking, Superannuation and Financial Services Industry Final Report (2019) Commonwealth of Australia, https://treasury.gov.au/publication/p2019-fsrc-final-report

Ruggie, J. (1982) 'International Regimes, Transactions, and Change: Embedded Liberalism in the Post-war Economic Order', *International Organization*, 36(2): 379–415.

Rüstow, A. (1949) 'Zwischen Kapitalismus und Kommunismus', *ORDO: Jahrbuch für die Ordnung von Wirtschaft und Gesellschaft*, 2: 100–69.

Rüstow, A. (2009) *Die Religion der Marktwritschaft*, Berlin: Lit.

Ryan, A. (ed) (1979) *The Idea of Freedom: Essays in Honour of Isaiah Berlin*, Oxford: Oxford University Press.

Sainsbury, D. (2020) *Windows of Opportunity*, London: Profile Books.

Sampat, B. (2105) 'Intellectual Property Rights and Pharmaceuticals: The case of antibiotics', *Economic Research Working Paper No 26 WIPO*.

Samuelson, P. (1947) *Foundations of Economic Analysis*, Oxford: Oxford University Press.

Samuelson, P. (1998) 'Summing up on Business Cycles: Opening address', *Federal Reserve Bank of Boston*, 42: 33–6.

Sanandaji, N. (2015) 'Scandanavian Unexceptionalism: Culture, markets and the failure of third way socialism', Institute for Economic Affairs.

Sauermann, H. and Mestmäcker, E.J. (1975) *Wirtschaftsordnung und Staatsverfassung*, Tübingen: Mohr.

Saville, J. (1956) 'Sleeping Partnership and Limited Liability, 1850–1856', *Economic History Review*, 8(3): 418–33.

Schjoedt, R. (2016) 'India's Basic Income Experiment', *Pathways' Perspectives on Social Policy in International Development*, Issue No 1.

Schliesser, E. (2018) *Adam Smith Systematic Philosopher and Public Thinker*, Oxford: Oxford University Press.

Schmitt, C. (1996) *The Concept of the Political*, Chicago: University of Chicago Press.

Schwarz, H.P. (1995) *Konrad Adenauer*, Berghahn: Providence.

Selgin, G. (1995) 'The "Productivity Norm" versus Zero Inflation in the History of Economic Thought', *History of Political Economy*, 27(4): 705–35.

Selgin, G. (1997) *Less Than Zero*, London: Institute for Economic Affairs.

Selgin, G. (2015) 'A Rush to Judge Gold', www.cato.org/blog/rush-judge-gold

Sen, A. (1999) *Choice Welfare and Measurement*, Cambridge, MA: Harvard University Press.

Sen, A. (2014) *Commodities and Capabilities*, Oxford: Oxford University Press.

Sen, A. (2017) *Collective Choice and Social Welfare*, London: Penguin.

Shafik, M. (2021) *What We Owe Each Other*, London: The Bodley Head.

Shepley, C. (2017) 'Making the Duty to Cooperate Work? Good Luck with that, Mr Javid', www.theplanner.co.uk/opinion/making-the-duty-to-cooperate-work-good-luck-with-that-mr-javid

Siedentop, L. (2015) *Inventing the Individual: The Origins of Western Liberalism*, London: Penguin.

Siems, M. and Schnyder, G. (2013) 'Ordoliberal Lessons for Economic Stability: Different Kinds of Regulation, Not More Regulation', *Governance*, 27(3): 377–96.

Silverman, D. (1970) 'A Pledge Unredeemed: The Housing Crisis in Weimar Germany', *Central European History*, 3(1–2): 112–39.

Simons, H. (1934) *A Positive Programme for Laissez-faire*, Chicago: University of Chicago Press.

Simons, H. (1948) *Economic Policy for a Free Society*, Chicago: University of Chicago Press.

Slobodian, Q. (2018) *Globalists: The End of Empire and the Birth of Neoliberalism*, Cambridge, MA: Harvard University Press.

Smith, A. (1896) *Lectures on Jurisprudence*, Oxford: Clarendon.

Smith, A. (1904) *An Inquiry into the Nature and Causes of the Wealth of Nations*, Indianapolis: Liberty Fund.

Smith, A. (1982) *The Theory of Moral Sentiments*, Indianapolis: Liberty Fund.

Spencer, H. (1851) *Social Statics*, Indianapolis: Liberty Fund.

Stark, J. (2008) 'Monetary, Fiscal and Financial Stability in Europe', www.ecb.europa.eu/press/key/date/2008/html/sp081118_1.en.html

Stiglitz, J. (2015) *Rewriting the Rules of the American Economy: An Agenda for Growth and Shared Prosperity*, New York: Norton.

Stiglitz, J., Sen, A. and Fitoussi, J.-P. (2009) 'Report by the Commission on the Measurement of Economic Performance and Social Progress', https://ec.europa.eu/eurostat/documents/8131721/8131772/Stiglitz-Sen-Fitoussi-Commission-report.pdf

Stolper, F. and Roskamp, K. (1979) 'Planning a Free Economy: Germany 1945–1960', *Journal of Institutional and Theoretical Economics*, 135(3): 374–404.

Strubelt, W. (2009) *German Annual of Spatial Research and Policy Guiding Principles*, Heidelberg: Springer.

Summers, L. (2014) 'The Inequality Puzzle', *Democracy Journal* [online], 3.

Summers, L. (2018) 'A Jobs Guarantee: Progressives' Latest Big Idea', www.ft.com/content/8ee839aa-7dce-11e8-bc55-50daf11b720d

Sumner, S. (2012) 'The Case for Nominal GDP targeting', Mercatus Center.

Sumner, S. and Roberts, E. (2018) 'The Promise of Nominal GDP Targeting', Mercatus Center.

Svensson, L. (1996) 'Price level targeting vs, inflation targeting: A free lunch?', National Bureau of Economic Research.

Syrjämäki, S. (2012) 'The World of Ideologies: An interview with Michael Freeden', Academia.

Taleb, N. (2018) *Skin in the Game*, London: Allen Lane.

Teece, D. and Jorde, T. (1991) 'Antitrust Policy and Innovation: Taking Account of Performance Competition and Competitor Cooperation', *Journal of Institutional and Theoretical Economics*, 147(1): 118–44.

Tepper, J. and Hearn, D. (2019) *The Myth of Capitalism*, Hoboken: Wiley.

Thelen, K. (2004) *How Institutions Evolve: The Political Economy of Skills in Germany, Britain, the United States and Japan*, Cambridge: Cambridge University Press.

Thirlwall, A. (1974) *Inflation, Saving and Growth in Developing Economies*, London: Macmillan.

Thomas, B. (1935) 'The Monetary Doctrines of Professor Davidson', *Economic Journal*, 45(177): 36–50.

Thompson, E. (1982) 'Free Banking under a Labor Standard – The Perfect Monetary System', Academia.

Tocqueville, A. (2003) *Democracy in America*, London: Penguin.

Tönnies, F. (2002) *Community and Society*, Mineola: Dover Publications.

Tooze, A. (2017) 'Applying The Debt Brake – The Genealogy Of German Austerity Regime', https://adamtooze.com/2017/10/22/german-questions-3-applying-debt-brake-genealogy-german-austerity-regime/

Treasury Committee (2019) 'Economic Crime: Anti-money laundering supervision and sanctions implementation', https://publications.parliament.uk/pa/cm201719/cmselect/cmtreasy/2010/2010.pdf

TUC (2013) 'Workers on Board: The case for workers' voice in corporate governance', www.tuc.org.uk/publications/workers-boardthe-case-workers-voice-corporate-governance

Turecamo, D. (2010) 'Lessons from Germany's Banking Crisis: Taking a closer look at boardrooms', https://knowledge.insead.edu/economics/lessons-from-germanys-banking-crisis-647

Uhr, C. (1975) *Economic Doctrines of David Davidson*, Uppsala: Almqvist.

United Nations (2011) 'Illicit Money: How much is out there?', UNODC.

Vallee, S. (2021) 'A New Roadmap for the Euro Area', https://dgap.org/en/research/publications/new-roadmap-euro-area

Van der Zee, J. and Kroneman, M. (2007) 'Bismarck or Beveridge: A Beauty Contest between Dinosaurs', *BMC Health Services Research*, 7(1): 94.

Van Middelaar, L. (2014) *The Passage to Europe*, New Haven: Yale University Press.

Vanberg, V. (2004) 'The Freiburg School: Walter Eucken and Ordoliberalism', Freiburg discussion papers on constitutional economics, No 04/11.

Vanberg, V. (2005) 'Market and State: The Perspective of Constitutional Political Economy', *Journal of Institutional Economics*, 1(1): 23–49.

Vanberg, V. (ed) (2019) *Choice and Economic Welfare*, Cheltenham: Edward Elgar.

Varoufakis, Y. (2016) *And the Weak Suffer What They Must?*, London: Penguin.

Varoufakis, Y. (2018) 'Why Germany Neither Can nor Should Pay More to Save the Eurozone', www.youtube.com/watch?v=rFFx1uAAD1k

Veggeland, N. (2016) 'The Narrative of the Nordic Welfare State Model', Lillehammer University College.

Vergeer, R. and Kleinknecht, A. (2014) 'Do Labour Market Reforms Reduce Labour Productivity Growth?: A panel data analysis of 20 OECD countries (1960–2004)', *International Labour Review*, 153(3): 365–93.

Viner, J. (1923) *Dumping, a Problem in International Trade*, Chicago: University of Chicago Press.

Wade, A. (2019) 'How AI is Powering a Revolution in Medical Diagnostics', www.theengineer.co.uk/ai-medical-diagnostics/

Wall Street Journal (2019) 'Lenders Brace for Private Equity Loan Defaults', www.wsj.com/articles/lenders-brace-for-private-equity-loan-defaults-11574427600

Wandel, J. (2019) 'Prospects for an Ordoliberal Reform of the European Union', *Economic Affairs*, 39: 28–43.

Weale, A. (2016) 'Ordoliberalism Within and Outside Germany' s Co-ordinated Market Economy', prepared for the conference on Ordoliberalism as an Irritating German Idea, Hertie School of Governance, Berlin.

Weise, Z. (2019) 'Von der Leyen Rows Back on United States of Europe', www.politico.eu/article/ursula-von-der-leyen-rows-back-on-united-states-of-europe/

West, G. (2017) *Scale*, London: Weidenfeld Nicholson.

White, W. (2006) 'Is Price Stability Enough?', Bank for International Settlements.

Wicksell, K. (1936) *Interest and Prices*, London: Macmillan.

Wolf, M. (2020) 'The Dangerous War on Supply Chains', www.ft.com/content/e27b0c0c-1893-479b-9ea3-27a81c2506c9

World Bank (2017) 'The Evolution of the Canadian Pension Model', World Bank.

Wörsdörfer, M. (2012) 'Walter Eucken on Patent Laws: Are Patents just "Nonsense upon Stilts"?', *Economic Thought*, 1(2): 36–54.

Wu, M. (2016) 'The "China, Inc." Challenge to Global Trade Governance', *Harvard International Law Journal*, 57(2): 261–324.

Wu, T. (2018) *The Curse of Bigness*, New York: Columbia Global Reports.

Yearwood, K. (2018) 'The Privatised Water Industry in the UK. An ATM for investors', https://gala.gre.ac.uk/id/eprint/21097/20/21097%20YEARWOOD_The_Privatised_Water_Industry_in_the_UK_2018.pdf

Zamora, D. and Behrent, M. (2016) *Foucault and Neoliberalism*, Cambridge: Polity Press.

Zhou, W., Gao, H. and Bai, X. (2019) 'China's SOE Reform: Using WTO rules to build a market economy', *International and Comparative Law Quarterly*, 68(4): 977–1022.

Zimmer, D. (2012) *The Goals of Competition Law*, Cheltenham: Edward Elgar.

Zucman, G. (2015) *The Hidden Wealth of Nations*, Chicago: University of Chicago Press.

Zweynert, J. (2013) 'How German is German Neo-liberalism?', *Review of Austrian Economics*, 26: 109–25.

Index